797,885 Books
are available to read at

www.ForgottenBooks.com

Forgotten Books' App
Available for mobile, tablet & eReader

ISBN 978-0-282-62462-0
PIBN 10859288

This book is a reproduction of an important historical work. Forgotten Books uses
state-of-the-art technology to digitally reconstruct the work, preserving the original format
whilst repairing imperfections present in the aged copy. In rare cases, an imperfection in
the original, such as a blemish or missing page, may be replicated in our edition. We do,
however, repair the vast majority of imperfections successfully; any imperfections that
remain are intentionally left to preserve the state of such historical works.

Forgotten Books is a registered trademark of FB &c Ltd.
Copyright © 2017 FB &c Ltd.
FB &c Ltd, Dalton House, 60 Windsor Avenue, London, SW19 2RR.
Company number 08720141. Registered in England and Wales.

For support please visit www.forgottenbooks.com

1 MONTH OF FREE READING

at
www.ForgottenBooks.com

By purchasing this book you are eligible for one month membership to ForgottenBooks.com, giving you unlimited access to our entire collection of over 700,000 titles via our web site and mobile apps.

To claim your free month visit:
www.forgottenbooks.com/free859288

* Offer is valid for 45 days from date of purchase. Terms and conditions apply.

English
Français
Deutsche
Italiano
Español
Português

www.forgottenbooks.com

Mythology Photography **Fiction**
Fishing Christianity **Art** Cooking
Essays Buddhism Freemasonry
Medicine **Biology** Music **Ancient Egypt** Evolution Carpentry Physics
Dance Geology **Mathematics** Fitness
Shakespeare **Folklore** Yoga Marketing
Confidence Immortality Biographies
Poetry **Psychology** Witchcraft
Electronics Chemistry History **Law**
Accounting **Philosophy** Anthropology
Alchemy Drama Quantum Mechanics
Atheism Sexual Health **Ancient History**
Entrepreneurship Languages Sport
Paleontology Needlework Islam
Metaphysics Investment Archaeology
Parenting Statistics Criminology
Motivational

FROM GOTHAM TO JERUSALEM

BEING A CHRONICLE OF THREE OBSERVANT
PILGRIMS IN PALESTINE AND
ELSEWHERE.

BY

J. STAUNTON MOORE,

AUTHOR OF

"A TRANSATLANTIC ITINERARY," "REMINISCENCES,
LETTERS, ETC." AND "HISTORY OF
HENRICO PARISH AND OLD
ST. JOHN'S CHURCH."

RICHMOND, VA.:
WILLIAMS PRINTING COMPANY,
1906

CONTENTS.

CHAPTER I.

Pilgrims Sail Amidst Many Warnings—Pernicious Tipping System on the Ship—Seasickness Remedies—Party's Chief Amusement on the Ocean—The Sunday-School Class and Its Personnel—A Domino Expert Humiliated—The Judge and the Donkey—Some Queer Types in the Smoking Room—A "Blowhard" from New York—The Undertaker and the Liar—A Rheumatic Rip Van Winkle—Several Species of Cranks—A Superstitious Man and a Secret Order Fanatic—"The Young Voyager" Absent Minded—Study of Mankind on Shipboard—Petticoated Candidates for Matrimony—Widows and Spinsters—Masons Organize on the Ocean—Some Rusty Brethren—Ship's Larder.

CHAPTER II.

We Sight Madeira's Coast—Urchins Dive for Money—Beautiful Mountain Scenery—The City of Funchal—Primitive Methods of Locomotion—In a Land of Persistent Beggars—A Witty Little Girl Floors the Party's Historian—In the Footprints of Columbus—Ignorance of the People—Agriculture and Horticulture—Fair Cadiz and Her People—Where Murillo Perished—Chilly Days in a Southern Clime—Salt Pyramids and Much-Abused Donkeys—A Ride to Venerable Seville—Last Resting Place of America's Discoverer—Intense Farming—Absence of Song Birds—Memories of the Moors—The Cork Industry—Gibraltar and Its Monkeys—Heterogenous Population of the Town.

CHAPTER III.

Algiers and Her Former Slaves—In the Arab Quarter and Among Its Fakirs—Malta and Her Romantic History—Valetta and Its Sculptured Guardian—The Church of St. John—In the Chapel of Bones—Grecian Isles and the Temple of Athena—Policemen Attired Like Ballet Girls—The Acropolis and the Parthenon—Acres of Ruins—Mars Hill and Its Associations—Constantinople, the "Dogopolis" of the World—Mosque of Sancta Sophia and Other Points of Interest—Sights in the Grand Bazaar—Turkish Ladies—American Missionary Schools—"Smyrna the Lovely"—Along the Route to Ephesus—Tobacco "Octopus" Agent Corners Licorice Market—Glimpses of Troy, Rhodes and Cyprus—Carmel, the Dwelling Place of David's Nabal—In the Land of the Prophets.

CHAPTER IV.

Dr. S. D. Bartle's Description of the Holy Land—Two Days at Nazareth—Missionary Work Among Native Children—Weakness of the Turkish Government—Sea of Galilee—Scenes in the Home of Our Lord—Dr. John D. Jordan's Visit to Places Made Sacred and Historic by Christ—Nazareth of To-Day—Traditions Told the Traveler—Valley of Esdraelon—Mount of Transfiguration and Hills of Gilboa—Place of the Sacrifice—Jacob's Well and the Mount of Olives—Tomb of the Sons of Levi—Dr. F. D. Powers' Beautiful Rhapsody on Nazareth—Cradle of Religion—Pestiferous Children.

CHAPTER V.

Jaffa, the Joppa of Scripture—Queer Antics of Oarsmen in the Harbor—History of the Town—Our Author Speculates About Noah's Ark—The Orient the Cradle of Some of Civilization's Bad Features—An "Obiter Dictum" on Trusts—Rose-Bedecked Hills—Ekron—First Sight of Jerusalem—As to the Site of Calvary—Supposed Tomb of Jesus—Church of the Holy Sepulchre—Mount Olivet and Its Associations—Two Competing Churches.

CHAPTER VI.

Mosque of Omar Occupies Site of Solomon's Temple—"The New Calvary" and Its Authenticity—Persistent cry, "Backsheesh,' Heard Even in Sacred Places—Disputed Points About the Garden of Gethsemane—Jews Bewailing the Desolation of Israel—Via Dolorosa—John Doorsy and His Wee Son,"Jorge' —Semi-Domesticated Ravens—A City that was Accursed—River Jordan—Desolate Dead Sea Neighborhood—Bethany—A Glimpse of the Mount of Temptation—Birthplace of Jesus.

CHAPTER VII.

Alexandria and the Bay of Abukir—Rural Egypt a Land of Flies and Fertility—Irrigation Methods—Touching Scarab Beetles and Camels—Government Dispensary at Baliana—Ruins at Abydos—Egyptians of To-Day—Wished-for Crocodiles Never Appeared—Wonders at Karnack—Temple of Rameses—Thebes and Its Colossal Guards—Kings who Built Pyramids—The Ascent of Cheops—Facts About the Inscrutable Sphynx—Sights in Cairo—An Ostrich Farm.

CHAPTER VIII.

Mount Ætna, Naples and Vesuvius—Excavations at Pompeii—Among the Gamblers at Monte Carlo—Up the Rhine to Cologne—The Bishop and the Mice—Pilgrims See the Skulls of 11,000 at the Church of St. Ursula—Foul Canals at Amsterdam—Sights in Holland—The Hague and Antwerp—Perley Seeks the "Circus" in London—Adventures in Ireland—Shandon Bells and Comments on Old St. John's Church—Blarney Castle and the Irish Girls—Westward, Ho!—Betting on Shipboard—A Prince of Liars—Old Virginia the Best of All.

PREFACE.

In submitting this hastily-prepared little volume to the critical public, the writer distinctly disavows any intention of obtruding himself into the ranks of the "authors," or of seeking, at his time of life, to snatch literary laurels. "You know me all, a plain, blunt man," and in this knowledge of yours lies my salvation.

The major portion of this chronicler's life has been spent in the mercantile world and not until the years had crept well up on him did he close his ledger to turn to pleasanter things. Then it was that he sought a well-earned recreaton in travel; and this book is one of the results of his peregrinations. Its leaves quiver like the foliage of a wind-racked aspen at the mere suggestion "critics," and the very printer's ink between its covers becomes tearfully blurred at the thought of close scrutiny by those who go through libraries with Addisonian standards.

The writer claims only one accomplishment, which, in its peculiar line, he reckons second not even to those of the greatest rhetoricians—the ability to use his eyes. When he crossed the ocean and journeyed into foreign lands he *saw,* and when not seeing, he listened. In a way his "optics" were a camera obscura and his ears the sensitive cylinders of a phonograph, so that what is submitted in these pages may be likened unto undeveloped photographic films or the strident representations of a graphophone. In short, this chronicler would fain think that some of his defects are the reflected defects of other persons and other things.

And be it said that if ever he had any conceit, those

who read his manuscript in the rough have bludgeoned it out of him. In this respect, at least, he is like immortal John Bunyan, for it was that author who said:

> "Well, when I had put my ends together,
> I showed them others that I might see whether
> They would condemn them, or justify;
> And some said: Let them live; some, Let them die;
> Some said, John, print it; others said, Not so;
> Some said, It might do good; others said, No."

Apropos of the foregoing lines, I recall that one cynical reader, scoffing at the vein of sentiment which underlies my whole nature, and noting the frequency with which I quote the poets and other literary exemplars, scornfully said: "Bosh, it's nothing but pedantry!" To him this chronicler answered meekly: "Not pedantry, but its very antithesis, Modesty—an admission that others can say certain things a thousand times better I."

Another "arbiter elegantiarum" has assailed what he calls the "spirit of iconoclasm" that pervades the writer's references to objects of interest in the Holy Land. "You tear down every idol," complained he. And so the writer hopes he does, for who would not have the idols go? Wherever he has seen fraud or selfishness or greed or blind adherence to prejudice, he has sought, in his fashion, to expose them—yea, even at the Gates of Jerusalem. Christianity needs no accessories in the way of guide books, fanaticism, traditions or folklore. Far firmer are the foundations on which It stands. Sweep away all the Palestine the traveler sees to-day, and Christianity's pure, illumining ray will still shine as brightly and as serenely o'er the world as though the winds had overturned but an anthill.

In this connection, too, the writer would say that his book equals any he has ever seen in the force of its references to the Holy Land, for not trusting his own ability to describe so important a subject, he called for aid from the pens of certain preacher friends—the Rev. S. D. Bartle, of Mechanicsville, Iowa; the Rev. Dr. John D. Jordan, of Savannah, Ga., and the Rev. Dr. F. D. Power, of Washington, D. C. The result has been three contributions which could not be surpassed in beauty and grace of diction or in their dignified spirit of reverence. Unquestionably these constitute the most pleasing feature of this volume.

Last of all, the author begs to say that he will feel deeply flattered by the attention of all probable or prospective readers, but he beseeches no one to read his volume. His family and a dear little circle of friends, as well as some of his companions in distant fields, have pledged the book their moral support. And this will suffice even though vanity crave more.

J. S. M.

CHAPTER I.

Pilgrims Sail Amidst Many Warnings—Pernicious Tipping System on the Ship—Seasickness Remedies—Party's Chief Amusement on the Ocean—The Sunday-School Class and its Personnel—A Domino Expert Humiliated—The Judge and the Donkey—Some Queer Types in the Smoking-Room—A "Blowhard" from New York—The Undertaker and the Liar—A Rheumatic Rip Van Winkle—Several Species of Cranks—A Superstitious Man and a Secret Order Fanatic—"The Young Voyager" Absent Minded—Study of Mankind on Shipboard—Petticoated Candidates for Matrimony—Widows and Spinsters—Masons Organize on the Ocean—Some Rusty Brethren—Ship's Larder.

After I had made my arrangements to take the Mediterranean and Orient trip in February, 1906, under the auspices of Mr. Frank C. Clark in the specially chartered White Star Line steamer Arabic, and again to cross the briny deep, I received a letter from one of my friends saying it was possible he might never see me alive again, but hoped to meet me in "a land that is fairer than this." A gentleman with whom I was negotiating a land transaction demurred to my suggestion about putting it off until my return, and insisted upon a consummation of the deal before my departure. He, too, alluded to the uncertainty of life, etc., while still another friend, on the eve of my departure, inquired if I had made my will. These Job's comforters gave me pause and quite naturally made me ask myself the question: Have I developed symptoms of senility, or reached the sixth or seventh ages, so graphically described by the immortal bard?

I parted with several of my teeth years ago, and have been compelled to use glasses for some time, but I did not think my "natural force abated" to such an extent as to warrant the interest and concern manifested by my friends, or the seeming inference that I had at last attained the "sere and yellow leaf" of old age and decrepitude. Under the combined pressure above alluded to I could but ask myself if I had overestimated my vigor and powers of endurance; but I am happy to state that I not only survived the trip, but returned physically improved and in a better state of health than when I left. I trust also that I am yet in possession of *mens sana in corpore sano*.

To sum things up, I did not miss a meal, nor was I sick a day either going or coming. Our immediate party consisted of my son, Harry T. Moore, whom we dubbed "The Young Voyager," as this was his first trip abroad; J. Vincent Perley, of Charlottesville, Va., and the writer.

We who came from the cities found it very delightful once more to breathe the pure, salt-laden atmosphere and to feel our lungs expanding under its stimulating and exhilarating influence. The weather was quite cold; in fact, uncomfortably cold during the entire trip, except on the Nile, as the boat was insufficiently heated—a piece of negligence which caused many passengers to contract colds. Whilst there was a feeling of expectancy and anticipation before us—

> "I can't but say it is an awkward sight
> To see one's native land receding through
> The growing waters; it unmans one quite."

The Arabic is a magnificent ship, 600 feet long, and large in proportion. It is fitted up with libraries, smoking-rooms, barber-shops, etc., and its elegance justifies me in describing it as a floating hotel.

It took us a day or two to get our sea legs, obtain our bearings and make acquaintances. The sea for the first day or two was smooth and quiet and we held our course—

> "As idle as a painted ship
> Upon a painted ocean,"

for Neptune and his trident amiably remained quiet in the depths below in his emerald caves.

The Arabic being an English ship, we were struck with some of the singularities of her people: For instance, we wanted some water without going to our staterooms for it, and naturally expected to find it in the library or smoking-room. But to quote the "Ancient Mariner" again there was—

> "Water, water everywhere,
> Nor any drop to drink."

This incident reminded us of the old Mother Goose melody which runs "houseful, yardful, but can't get a spoonful."

Another curious thing struck us—we could not understand why the White Star Line should pay its servants insufficient wages and thus make them dependent upon "tips," in other words, encourage them to blackmail the passengers. Let me say here that this practice creates dissatisfaction both among servants and passengers.

Some Americans, having more money than judgment, would give their steward an unreasonable sum for his services, which were understood to be included in the cruise; others were not financially able to give the same amount and thus discontent was caused.

I will relate my own experience with my saloon steward: The second day out I offered him a dollar and told him that if he showed me proper attention I would give him a dollar a week during the trip. He remarked that he did not think this was enough, to which I made no reply. The next day he came to me with an insolent air and stated he wanted two dollars a week; that he needed money for his family.

I replied that I had nothing to do with his family; that I had paid my passage money as a first-class passenger, which embraced his services, and that if he mentioned the matter to me again during the trip I would not give him a cent. As I was very positive, and he saw I could not be bulldozed, further annoyance was spared me; but when on quitting the ship I placed a sovereign in his hand he took it with a most ungracious air.

We paid our bedroom steward a sovereign and a half. He demanded more. We declined to give more, whereupon he said he would not attend to the delivery of our luggage to the baggagemaster when the ship arrived at Liverpool, we leaving the ship at Nice and our baggage going on to Liverpool. In addition to this it was expected that each passenger would give a fee to the baggagemaster, the deck steward, the bath steward, the chief steward, the smoking-room steward and the stewardess, as well as contribute to the band for the very poor music furnished on the trip.

Towards the end of the journey some enthusiastic American actually proposed making up a purse of $1,000 for the captain of the ship. An amendment was suggested that we also be permitted to pay for the fuel used so sparingly on the vessel, since we had all suffered from colds. The proposition to give the captain a thousand dollars was tabled.

In concluding my comments along this line, let me say the whole system is a disgrace to the service. Any first-class passenger would prefer paying $50 more for his ticket rather than be annoyed in this way.

"The Young Voyager" for the first day or two, having, we suppose, left his heart in the keeping of some fair damsel at home, went around softly humming in accents sweet and low a melancholy air, the words of which I could not catch. And occasionally, too, a gentle sigh would escape him, while a tinge of seriousness rested on his comely features, and a moisture bedewed his vision, causing "a feeling of sadness to come o'er him which his spirit could not resist." But in a few days he was making "goo-goo" eyes at some of the ship's beauties, to whom he devoted himself assiduously, with the result that he became more cheerful.

Perley, in remembrance of his trip with us to Cuba the year before, when he thought he would die of *mal de mer* on the Gulf of Mexico, provided himself in New York with "a sovereign remedy" for seasickness. This remedy, for which he paid 75 cents, was warranted never to fail, but on investigation it proved to be an ordinary Seidlitz powder, worth just 5 cents. When the day came for him to "cast his bread upon the waters" we had a good laugh at him.

On the Arabic we had about 650 passengers, classified as follows: Thirty-four preachers, seven "honorables," one general, two colonels, one major, ten physicians, about four hundred women and children and the rest men of various professions and vocations. Among the "honorables" were included two or three judges. The paucity of jurists and colonels was probably due to the fact that there were comparatively few Southerners aboard.

Our passengers hailed from nearly every State in the Union. There were in our ship's company many pleasant, sociable ladies and gentlemen, some wise and some otherwise; some polite and some courteous, and alas, also a few with vinegar-visaged countenances and sour-faced features, who had a supply of rudeness constantly on tap, from which they drew at random. One remembering the famous epigram applied to Charles the Second might have been justified in supposing that these disagreeable folk

> Never said a polite thing
> And never did a wise one.

But the majority of our companions were pleasant and agreeable, and we soon found that "a life on the ocean wave" was associated with most pleasing environments.

In a few days "affinities" were formed upon the basis of natural attractions and the congenialities of kindred spirits, thus demonstratng the old adage that "birds of a feather flock together." A coterie of congenial souls gradually gathered in the smaller smoking-room, the recognized leader being a minister, and we organized what was called "the Sunday School Class."

The chief occupation of this organization was playing cards and dominoes, relating anecdotes, experiences, etc., and taking now and then a glass of Bass's ale, ginger ale, or an occasional "Scotch." But I never saw a man in this party under the influence of liquor and never any actual gambling. All the games were played purely for amusement and to kill time.

So far as my knowledge and observation went, there was less drinking and gambling on this ship during the entire cruise than on any other I ever sailed in.

As it might be unpleasant to call the names of the gentlemen constituting "the Sunday School Class," I will designate them by States or cities, as I attempt in a facetious vein to present a pen picture of some of them. The idiosyncracies of one individual may appear under different heads, too, thus showing several characteristics in the same person. These pictures may be recognized by the members of the "class," and if the invocation of Bobby Burns—

> "O wad some power the giftie gie us,
> To see ourselves as others see us"—

is realized, each may pick out his own portrait.

In the game of dominoes "The Young Voyager" and the gentleman from Charlottesville were generally pitted against the gentleman from Philadelphia and the writer. Early in the voyage the gentleman from Charlottesville, with a self-sufficient air and vaunting manner, said: "If there is one game I can play it is dominoes." We played day after day and night after night and at first with varying fortunes. But after a while the gentleman from Philadelphia and the writer got the whip hand of their opponents and beat the gentleman from Charlottesville and "The Young Voyager" so badly that we demonstrated beyond a doubt that there was no game so little understood by them as dominoes.

Their defeat became a standing joke, and when the "class" assembled, or when any of its members met the gentleman from Charlottesville he was regaled with the mockery, "if there is any one game I can play it is dominoes." Finally he wished he had never seen a domino.

On one occasion later on when we were visiting a certain cathedral in Europe, the priest began repeating from the Litany the words, *"Agnus dei, qui tollis peccata mundi, exaudi nos Domine,"* whereupon the Charlottesville representative turned to us and said, "I wonder how *he* found out I said I could play *dominoes!* The last game of note we played before the gentleman from Charlottesville surrendered and revoked his assertion, the score was 64 to 32—this was his Waterloo!

This worthy from the Albemarle capital, be it understood, was conceded to be the best natured man on board. No amount of badinage, no joke or pranks could ruffle his temper or cause him to show anger or resentment. He labored under a complaint, diagnosed *cacoethes loquendi,* and owing to this fact, he was known as the "Rattler."

He also deluded himself with the belief that he was a chronic sufferer from insomnia, whereas the fact was that if his tongue was not wagging he was not only somnolent but sound asleep. He might be snoring vociferously, but if aroused would declare that he had not been asleep—simply resting his eyes. And in this assertion he really seemed to be entirely sincere.

The gentleman from Philadelphia was a clergyman, not overburdened with religion, but full of pleasant anecdotes, "wise saws and modern instances." And like Goldsmith's Schoolmaster—

"E'en though vanquished, he could argue still."

In truth he was a jolly companion.

Then we had the Judge from far-away Wisconsin—a quiet, sedate gentleman, having the courage of his convictions, but conservative and deliberate in the expression of them, as becomes the mind judicial. The Judge was not without a sense of humor, however, as was evidenced by the fact that he was the only man known to have gotten ahead of a donkey. This incident occured in the desert near Luxor. He and this chronicler were riding at a canter, our animals under the lash of the driver, or donkey boy, when my stirrup leather broke and off I went sideways into the sand. The Judge's boy, expecting largess in the way of increased "backsheesh," said to the Judge: "Your donkey, good donkey—his donkey (pointing to mine) bad donkey." Pleased with this information our friend, the jurist—

"Had just been proclaiming his donkey's renown
For vigor, for spirit, for one thing or other—
When lo! 'mid his praises, the donkey came down'—

and the Judge went over his head in the most graceful

fashion. The rider stood poised on his head in as dignified a manner as the circumstances would admit of for a second or two, and then measured his full length on the desert. The Judge to this day avers he will never forget how long that donkey's ears appeared as he passed between them in his descent.

This good jurist was also a little testy on occasions, and when inordinately importuned for "backsheesh" would lose his temper. At Jerusalem, having found this weak spot in his generally well-regulated and equable poise, we set the beggars on him, particularly the women with babies in their arms. If the truth must be told, we informed these pests that he was a widower, carried the purse and was the moneyed man of the crowd.

The Judge would hastily beat a retreat from his tormentors. On one occasion he had gotten some distance from his persecutors, when he turned and saw his own shadow. This he mistook for an applicant for "backsheesh," so he waved his hand with an impatient gesture and bade the shadow begone. But it still pursued him until he got out of the sunlight.

On another occasion, at the Pyramids, he was surrounded and set upon by a gang of Arabs, and had to threaten to strike with his cane before he could get clear of them. His determined and resolute manner prevented his tormentors from again annoying him. We are satisfied that the Judge's ermine was as spotless when he retired from the bench as when he assumed it, for his character was stainless and all his actions above reproach.

In our party we had a pilgrim from "bleeding Kansas," a pleasant gentleman who liked his joke as well as the rest of us, and occasionally got off one on the gentleman from Charlottesville. This jocund Kansan had his wife with him and consequently was not with the "class" as frequently as he otherwise might have been.

There was also the gentleman from Rochester with his congested liver and enlarged spleen—the cynic of the crowd—whose *naw* had a peculiar snarl that grated on one's nerves like the rasping of a file. At first, he seemed a regular Ishmaelite and his ill temper stuck out "like quills upon the fretful porcupine." Indeed, he was heard to express the wish that the ship would sink with every one on board, his wife included. He was bilious, very bilious, this gentleman, but after he had associated with the "class" for some days, he mellowed under the genial influence of the gentleman from St. Louis, and became quite congenial. Once in a while he actually smiled. This cynic was in the insurance business, and perhaps his condition was occasioned by the investigations and revelations then going on in New York.

One of the most congenial of all the "class" was the gentleman from St. Louis, who, by the quality of his anecdotes, easily won the distinction of being "The Decameron" of the smoking-room. He was an Englishman by birth—but only by birth, for he was thoroughly Americanized, and could give, take and appreciate a joke, a faculty not generally possessed by the people of his native land.

The chaffing and rasping he gave the gentleman from New York city was truly amusing; when the two began to spar, and in a good-natured way abuse each other, the rest looked to see the wool fly with smiling faces. It was a case of Greek meeting Greek. The gentleman from St. Louis, like Fitz James when he met Rhoderick Dhu, would face the gentleman from New York with a "come-one-come-all! this-rock-shall-fly-from-its-firm-base-as-soon-as-I" expression, and the wordy contest would begin. The intellectual sparks of humor emitted in these combats were exhilarating and entertaining. As a rule, the gentleman from New York at first had the best of these pleasant contests. He would compare the great metropolis with St. Louis, belittle the Missouri town and ask where it was, whether it was on the map, etc., etc. He would likewise compare the wealth, commerce and importance of Greater New York, the great clearing-house of America, with that of St. Louis. All of this the gentleman from St. Louis would take with his usual good nature, but on one occasion he remarked to the New Yorker: "You remind me of the city you hail from; you are a fair type of your people; you are as pompous and as much of an air-bag as the average Gothamite; you think the sun rises and sets for New York alone; you would have the entire nation pay tribute by making everything exported from or imported into the country pass through her gates. But," added he with a kindling eye, "we of the West have begun to shake off the shackles of slavery that once bound us to the octopus of greed, and by the heavens, we will be free of her!"

This speech floored the New Yorker for a while, but he came back with statistics, and the usual arguments in favor of New York as the great metropolitan center of the nation, until his opponent was silenced. But when we reached Naples the gentleman from St. Louis scored a victory over the New Yorker. In that city, the Gothamite purchased, at a great bargain, six Italian silk umbrellas, and in triumph brought one of them to the smoking-room to show the gentleman from St. Louis, who is a dry goods merchant, and asked him what he thought of the purchase.

The umbrella was carefully examined, and without cracking a smile, the gentleman from St. Louis remarked that it was worth about one dollar, and that he would give $5 for the half dozen. "Why, you old humbug," replied the New Yorker, "they cost me $4 each; the regular price was $5."

The purchaser was assured that he was badly stuck. Such umbrellas, said the Missouri man, might be worth $5 in Naples or New York, but he sold better in St. Louis for one dollar. This took the wind out of the New Yorker, and he was the most crestfallen individual I ever saw. When the "class" would ask him "how about those umbrellas?" he would become discreetly silent.

The gentleman from New York may not be a good judge of umbrellas, but as an interpreter of German and Italian, it would afford me great pleasure to recommend him to the government as ambassador or plenipotentiary extraordinary to either of the above mentioned countries. What he could not say to them by word of mouth, he could certainly convey by mysterious and occult signs. He and his daughter were two of the most agreeable persons on board the ship.

There was a member of the "class," an undertaker, who believed in combining business with pleasure, and by way of advertisement he stated that in his establishment he had a most elegant "royal purple coffin" in which he laid out the remains of those entrusted to his care, preliminary to their encasement in their final resting places. He also stated that he had a fine "rubber-neck hearse" with a modern invention for silently lowering the coffin into the tomb. In fact, he pictured this grave subject in such glowing colors that he figuratively strewed the pathway to the cemetery with flowers. Moreover, he intimated that if any of the party could make it convenient "to shuffle off this mortal coil" at his place he would see him decently and properly planted at popular and reasonable rates. This gentleman actually invited a young lady to his city, assuring her that if she should die it would afford him pleasure to see her obsequies beautifully performed. She sweetly declined his generous hospitality, and begged to be excused.

But the funereal gentleman occasionally indulged in hyperbole, too. He told of a town he once visited that had eighty-six manufacturing establishments, despite a population of only twenty-five hundred. Some of the mathematicians present got to work on this, and demonstrated, after deducting the women and children, those engaged in other occupations, negroes, etc., that it left but ten employees to each factory, including the boss, clerk, porter and stenographer. But the undertaker stuck to his tale.

This gentleman was not only a "romancer," but, like Joseph of old, "a dreamer of dreams." He would tell of the most extraordinary compliments some one had paid him, and as they were all drawn from his imagination, he was dubbed the "unconscious liar." The word, be it understood, is used in no offensive sense, for he appeared to be entirely unconscious of the absurdity of his statements. He imagined things and really believed them. Ah! he was a genial, good-natured fellow, and his society was far from boring.

We also had another gentleman who lived in the mountains and who was pronounced "the amiable liar" (likewise not offensively used), because he could tell yarns in the most innocent manner. He would, with his dark-brown eyes, look into yours, and tell, without batting a lid or cracking a smile, the most plausible of tales. He possessed, he said, a wonderful grapevine with which he had had remarkable adventures, and told other extraordinary rustic tales. His adventures at Monte Carlo, where he "dropped" exactly $326, were deeply interesting. This hyperbolical soul would suck his pipe, which he smoked almost incessantly, and spin out yarns in a gentle monotone, characteristic of his Southern idiom, and local vernacular. He was one of the most companionable fellows of the "class."

The next character of interest in our organizaton was a gentleman from New Jersey, long past his prime, who in his youth was "one of the boys," but who, with the firmness of a rock, has for years ignored the follies of his earlier days, and could not now be tempted into danger. His lambent fires could only be aroused by a mesmeric incantaton of cabalastic words, accompanied by certain movements of the hands and fingers, known only to those initiated in the occult science of signs.

When he made these signs and said "shish, shish," his eyes would temporarily light up with their wonted fires and his features would assume the hue of youth, as the flood tides of memory passed before his mental vision, as you have seen the glow return to the cheek of the old warrior when fighting o'er his battles again, or when the strain of some old martial air smites upon the ear of the scarred veteran of a hundred battles.

This gentleman demonstrated to my mind the fact that great battles are fought and won within the arena of the human breast as well as upon the field of arms. He conquered self. But whatever self-restraint he practiced he played his game of euchre with the zest of youth. The fires of his once ardent manhood, however, have been cooled by years of experience, and are now in a state of repression. Firmness and decision of character are stamped upon his features, and no temptation could induce him to plunge into his quondam excesses.

We also had aboard a genial physician from the Old Dominion who was sick on every occasion when the sea was a little rough or the weather stormy. When he was prescribing for others, as he frequently did gratuitously, I several times called his attention to the injunction, "Physician, heal thyself," but it had no effect. And when he would caution his patient about eating, I reminded him of what St. Paul said, "When I have preached to others I keep my body in subjection lest that by any means, I myself should be a castaway." Yet, notwithstanding all this, he continued to preach to others and to cast away his own food upon the waters!

The Doctor discussed long and learnedly the skill of Galen, once the supreme authority in medical science, and the treatises of the "Hippocratic collection." He believed in Sangrado's theory of the drinking of hot water, but did not have much confidence in his other pet scehme of profuse blood-letting. Our medical friend was inclined to ridicule the "pellet" system of the homeopathist, and occasionally referred to the subjectivity of heteropathy, but was a firm advocate of allopathy in everything, and more particularly as it applies to the use of tobacco. This theory he exemplified in his own habits. He claimed with Bulwer, that smoking makes a man think like a sage and act like a Samaritan. The Doctor contended that the more a man smoked the greater his fecundity of generous and ennobling thoughts, and as a consequence, he was generally under the benign influence of the weed. He applied Pope's lines to this habit and acted accordingly:

> "A little learning is a dangerous thing;
> Drink deep, or taste not the Pierian spring;
> The shallow draughts intoxicate the brain,
> And drinking largely sobers us again."

These influences made him very susceptible, and he fell in love with all the pretty women he saw—the liquid-eyed senorita of Spain, the raven-tressed beauties of Greece, the olive-tinted Turk, the cosmopolitan ladies of Cairo, and the fickle maids of la belle Paris. When he became weak or indifferent, all his companion, the gentleman from New Jersey, had to do was to utter that mysterious "shish, shish" with the usual sign and the Doctor was himself again.

Some time after the "class" had been organized, there came into the smoking-room a gentleman of quiet and sedate manners, whose soft and gentle voice and courteous address proclaimed him a Southerner. There was a world of pathos and suppressed emotion in his sad brown eyes, and a touching and appealing smile on his gentle and earnest, but careworn, face.. He was suffering from nervous prostration and was taking the trip for recuperation and relaxation from the cares of business. His digestion was bad; he could not sleep and had but a poor appetite. This chronicler warmed to him, and the Southerner proved himself to have a most lovable nature. He had beeen a great smoker, but now, by order of his doctor, eschewed tobacco in every shape.

In the language of Macbeth, I bade him "throw physic to the dogs" and have "none of it," but join me in a smoke, which he did nearly every day to his relief and enjoyment. The sad-eyed voyager had left the Sunny South expecting warm and balmy breezes in Spain and on the Mediterranean, but so far had met with nothing but cold and discomfort on board ship. He was chilled and uncomfortable. I induced him to join in our games, gave him a book to read and tried to get him to forget himself—and his troubles. Finally we got him to laughing and joking, and he became both mentally and physically improved.

When he arrived at Malta it was cool, and when we reached other points it was still colder; but he fully expected to find warm and balmy weather under the sunny

Italian skies at Naples. Alas! the only warm object he saw there was the lava flowing from the creater of Mount Vesuvius. We parted at Naples. He said he was going to find a nice warm place for a month or two in or near Rome. When a few days later I went to the Eternal City, and en route, saw the snow-capped hills and felt a breeze seemingly from "Greenland's icy mountains," I could but fancy how disapponted my friend would be. As I journeyed along the thought of him suggested these lines:

> "Gaily bedight
> A gallant knight
> In sunshine and shadow,
> Had journeyed long,
> Singing a song
> In search of warm *weather.*
>
> "But he grew *cold*,
> This knight so bold;
> O'er his heart a shadow
> Fell as he found
> No spot of ground
> That felt like warm *weather.*"

The wife of this gentleman is one of the most charming of women, whose amiable disposition and pleasant manners make her a delightful friend.

Another "classman" was the gentleman from Ohio— our oldest member, and so venerable in appearance that we called him "Rip Van Winkle." But notwithstanding his age, he played his rubber at cards with the skill and enthusiasm of youth, and not infrequently was the victor.

This representative of the Buckeye State, calm and quiet in manner, was at one period of his life so afflicted with rheumatism that he could neither walk nor use his hands. His physicians gave him up, as they could do nothing for him, but he had grit, and by sheer will power continued to work out his own salvation. He began by moving his limbs a fraction at a time. Day by day, and week after week, he kept this up until locomotion and the use of his hands were restored. He would have himself placed in a chair every day, and then would operate, as it were, on himself, until he unhinged his locked joints from the clasp of his dread enemy and finally got upon his feet. And now he walks, if not with the vigor of youth, certainly without any evidence of descrepitude. His is an heroic nature. To know such manly characters is a genuine pleasure. It is such men—men like Paul Jones, who "never give up the ship"—that ennoble humanity.

The men described in the foregoing paragraphs constituted our "Sunday School Class." Of course, we had other habitutes of the smoking-room—many genial gentlemen who joined in games and conversation, but the characters already sketched, though imperfectly drawn, were the most prominent features.

I was told we had a gentleman on board who got "seasick" and lost his teeth. They said he was so unconventional as to dine the balance of the trip without a *plate*.

Then there was a citizen who partook of all treats but was never known to *re*-treat. Like Marshal Ney, he was the bravest of the brave.

We had a minister so very abstemious that he asked the steward if he could not take the brandy out of the mince pie and the plum pudding.

Then, too, we had another crank who complained of his poor appetite, saying the food did not agree with him, but at every meal he ate heartily. On being asked why he ate when he neither liked nor relished his food, he replied that he was afraid lest provisions might run short, and as he might be put on limited rations, he thought it best to eat as long as the food held out.

Then there was still another individual, who occasionally visited the smoking-room—one who was with us, but not of us. This person indulged in his favorite game of solitaire, a characteristic of selfishness. He appeared to find all the pleasure essential to his enjoyment in trying to make his left hand beat his right. This individual showed his rudeness and his boorish character on one occasion by crowding into a carriage that had been taken by three other gentlemen. He rushed in unbidden without even saying "By your leave."

We had a dude, of course, and he affected the dress of the different countries he visited, reminding one of Æsop's fable about the ass in the lion's skin. This chap imagined himself the Beau Brummel of the cruise, when in fact he was being laughed at continually behind his back.

An individual, whose rough aspirates and idiomatic expressions betrayed his Northern origin, sometimes dropped in. This gentleman rolled his r's with a remarkable continuity and a tiresome redundancy and superfluity, frequently supplementing his "r" with many er er-rars as well as errors.

Most people aspirate the letter "h," but this particular mortal dwelt persistently on "r," which he rolled on his tongue as if it were a rich and delectable morsel of intellectual pabulum too precious to dispense with. He was one of those who "know it all," or at least thought he was. There was no subject "in the heavens above, the earth beneath or the waters below" that he would not tackle and argue on, if not to the entertainment and enlightenment of others, at least, to his own gratification and profound satisfaction. What he lacked in ratiocination and consistency he made up in gesticulation, boisterous talk and offers "to bet" he was right.

He presented a conspicuous and illustrious example of that class who

"—convinced against their will
Are of the same opinion still."

And we should not forget the superstitious crank who, before sitting down to table, always counted the guests to see if there were thirteen. This number he regarded as an unlucky one and nothing could induce him to be the thirteenth person or one of thirteen. He was fully persuaded that some occult influence was associated with these mystic figures. Religiously he believed in omens, signs, portents and charms. The spilling of salt was an evil omen to him and to meet a funeral possession was bad luck. In other respects, however, this individual was reasonable and sensible, but along the lines indicated he was altogether illogical and unreasonable. He believed in the potency of the horse chestnut or buckeye as a sovereign remedy against rheumatism and invariably carried one in his left trousers' pocket. Irish potatoes he regarded as equally efficacious for some other ill that flesh is heir to, and he carried one in his right trousers' pocket. When these talismen became shriveled and dried from age or contact with the heat of the human body they were replaced by new specimens. And when the full moon first showed herself in the heavens he always propitiated her good graces by exhibiting to the shining orb a bright silver quarter exhibited over the left shoulder. This, in his opinion, was a harbinger of good luck. Of course, there is a modicum of superstition in all of us, but it was most ridicuously developed and emphasized in the individual referred to.

Then we had a free and easy gentleman who emphasized the fact that he was a secret order man by wearing on the lapel of his coat a badge about two inches long and of nearly the same width. This insignia was further set off by a large ring on his left little finger with the device of another order, while just below the sign manual of large dimensions above referred to was a smaller token of still another secret society.

His cuff buttons had the insignia of yet another order, and on his card, which he most amiably presented as a means of introduction, was a roster containing a list of forty-two secret organizations to which he belonged. This amiable character rarely approached a stranger without first scanning his person to see if he could discover an emblem of any kind. If he recognized the charm or badge a conversation something like this would ensue:

"You're a Mason? So am I." "Yes, I am a Mason." "I thought so. Where are you from?" "New York. I suppose you have been there." "Oh, my, yes indeed. Why, I know New York like a book—have been there several times. Do you belong to any other society besides the Masons?" "No."

"Oh, my, I belong to forty-two—am treasurer of fourteen, high-muck-a-muck of seven, grand sachem of one, past grand high-cock-a-lorum of eight and traveling delegate for five."

"How do you find time to attend so many?" "Oh, my! I just run in, give the signs and spend a few minutes in each when they meet—kinder make the grand rounds, as it were. Do you know Mr. Blank, of New York?" "I have met him once or twice."

"Oh, my, I have known him all my life and am well acquainted with him." "Is that so?" "Oh, yes. Have you made many acquaintances on the ship yet?" "Only a few at the table, and my next stateroom."

"Oh, my; in a day or two I will know everybody on the

boat. I travel for the accommodation of others and make acquaintances to be of service, you know." "Indeed?"

"Yes; as soon as I find out a man belongs to the same order as I do, I feel like a brother to him, and go right up and slap him on the back. I believe in making myself agreeable to every one." "That is very nice in you."

"Well, I see right now a gentleman with a badge on; I will go over and shake hands with him. I am glad to have met you; so long." And off he goes.

The next gentleman he accosts offers no visible sign of being a secret order man, so the following queries and

"You are not a member of any secret order, are you?" "No, I don't believe in them." "Oh, my; I belong to forty-two—am treasurer of fourteen, high muck-a-muck of seven, grand sachem of one, past grand high cock-a-lorum of eight and traveling delegate of five."

"It must cost you a considerable sum to keep up your dues?" "Well, you see I'm treasurer of fourteen and traveling delegate for five. Where are you from?" "England."

"England is all right. America and England can whip the world. I was in England some years ago—— was much impressed with her. She's all right!"

"England and America should be friends." "Yes, indeed. Is this your first trip?" "No, I have been to the Orient several times."

"This is my second trip. I was in London in 1900 and was impressed with London, but did not like Paris. You are not a Mason, are you? Oh, I beg pardon, I asked that before—well, so long. I am glad to see you; will be delighted to continue our acquaintance."

But our busybody does not permit his acquaintance to end with the gentlemen. Seeing a lady and little girl on deck, he approaches them with these words:

"Is this your little girl?" "No, sir," comes the reply; "I am not married."

"She is so much like you—a dear, charming little lady—I thought she was your daughter. Where are you from?" "California."

"Oh, my! I have been there twice—fine country. I was very much impressed. California is all right." "Yes, we have a fine country."

"Is your husband a Mason? Oh, I beg pardon, you told me you were not married! Is your father a Mason?"

"Yes; where do you live?" "I am from Masonville, the finest place in the world." "Where did you say you were from? California."

"Oh, my; I asked you that before. Do you know anybody from Masonville?" "No, but I have heard my father speak of a Mr. Smith of that town. Do you know him?"

"Do I know him? I should say I did. I have known him over a week; am well acquainted with him. He is a gentleman of character and integrity." "How long did you say you had known him?" "Oh, my! I have known him over a week."

"Do you like to make acquaintances?" "Sometimes." "Well, you see I travel for the convenience and accommodation of others; I like to know everybody. Won't you accept my card?" "Thank you."

"Well, I am glad to have met you; you're all right, California is all right, and I am all right." And off he goes.

The Young Voyager insisted on taking the trip not only for his health and pleasure, but in order to take care of *pater familias* and Perley, who came to grief on their first foreign tour by losing some money through robbery. Now, the funny part about it all is that The Young Voyager lost his letter of credit at Grenada, and did not recover it until he got to Cairo. Then also on two different occasions he left his pocket-book under his pillow at hotels. Next he lost his gloves and subsequently his umbrella, while morning, noon and night he lost his heart to every pretty woman he saw. I can see him now as he sweetly smiles at the girls of Andelusia, the women of Madeira, the maids of Athens and the dusky damsels of Egypt. To tell the truth, he had an eye or eyes for them all. And this young man was the self-constituted guardian and protector of father and Perley!

We all grew much attached to our good ship Arabic. She was our city of refuge, our haven of quiet and rest after many a weary trip on land, and we invariably climbed her sides with feelings of relief that seemed like homecoming. And not only did we learn to love the ship, for many of us were drawn to one another by the strong cords of real affection. After our party had broken up at Naples I returned to the old smoking-room before debarking at Nice and there I could but exclaim—

> "I feel like one
> Who treads alone
> Some banquet hall deserted,
> Whose lights are fled,
> Whose garlands dead
> And all but he departed!"

Take it all in all we had a very quiet passage to Madeira, our first stopping place. But two or three times the ship rocked considerably and the wind was quite high. On these occasions we had quite a number of absentees from the dining-rooms. Many of the ladies would appear, and then, as the motion increased, they would disappear, like the Arab who folds his tent and silently steals away. These sufferers had no fancy for "swell" dinners or swell seas; they did not stand upon the order of their going, making no excuse and offering no apology, but their pallor told the tale more sadly, more forcibly and more eloquently than words.

For amusement we had euchre parties and we heard interesting lectures on the lands we were about to visit by several clergymen and professors. On Sundays we had services by different ministers, with music and song. A lady from "Bosting" usually led the improvised choir and her singing was very fine.

One of the jolliest persons on board—he once in a while honored the smoking-room with his persence—was a gentleman then in his eighty-sixth year. We dubbed him "the Patriarch of Jerusalem." He was the oldest person on the ship, but lively and active, and his conversation was exceedingly interesting.

The invincible and irrepressible Perley, with his usual propensity to discover badges and charms indicating secret orders—gracious! I shouldn't have called his name—on one occasion espied a pair of cuff buttons on a member of the "Sunday School Class" and at once asked if he were a Mason. The gentleman replied, "I am," and exhibited his cuff buttons in evidence as an outward sign.

Perley, being an expert, examined them and said, "This is not a Masonic emblem." "Yes it is," replied the gentleman; "don't you observe the square and compass and the letter 'G'?"

"But," replied Perley, who, as I have said, belongs to nearly every order under the sun, "don't you see 'Jr. O. U. A. M.,' which stands for a different organization?"

"Yes," says the gentleman, "but what does the 'G' stand for?"

"Why," replied Perley, " 'Gimlet,' of course."

The gentleman was an Englishman by birth, and, therefore, could not belong to the Junior Order of United American Mechanics. He took the buttons out of his cuffs, and with an air of disgust declared he would throw them overboard. But Perley said he would like to have them, so they passed into his possession.

The Rev. David G. Wylie related to me the following amusing incident: There was a clergyman on board from Oklahoma who had never been on an ocean steamship before. The first night out he awakened and heard the noise of running water. It was only a leaking pipe, but he thought it more serious, and called to his companions in the stateroom: "Get up boys, quick, the old ship is going down." We got a good deal of fun out of this incident, as the timorous parson was a serious sort of fellow and made much of little things.

February 12th, being the anniversary of the birth of Abraham Lincoln, the day was observed by a lecture or eulogy by a reverend gentleman from the State of Michigan, who lauded Mr. Lincoln to the skies. In fact, he went so far as to compare his death to the martyrdom and sacrifice of our Lord. I have always felt kindly towards Mr. Lincoln and concede to him many attributes of greatness and kind heartedness, but there are certain comparisons that sound sacrilegious and greatly out of place. This was one of them.

It is Pope, I think, who says "the proper study of mankind is man," but I very much doubt if the knowledge acquired in this process has a tendency to promote one's happiness or is calculated to increase one's admiration for humanity, unless he looks upon the subject with the eyes of a philosopher and makes due allowance for the frailties, frivolities and follies of human nature. There are to be met with on a cruise such as ours many curious types, who strikingly illustrate the idiosyncracies, peculiarities and singularities of the *genus homo*.

Many bear their characters written on their features. These are generally the simple, kindly, lovable kind—as easy to read as the face of a clock. Then we have the masked face, as impenetrable as the veiled features of the Prophet of Khorasan; the dough-faced, with their boundless stupidity, and the lively, nervous, cheerful countenance indicative of good nature and hopefulness——as optimistic in its nature as the dough-faced is pessimistic. Perhaps worst of all, we have the snob, who apes gentility, has acquired wealth by inheritance or in a questionable way, and imagines he is better than any of his fellow creatures—the newly rich, the contemptible rich.

The evil effects resulting from the acquisition of sudden wealth are, I regret to say, more conspicuously shown by women than by men. We had, for instance, a widowed lady on board who came regularly to the table with her fingers so laden with diamonds that she could scarcely manipulate her knife and fork. The discomforts she had to undergo to gratify her vanity must have been extreme. At any rate, the glittering gewgaws on her person were quite enough to excite the cupidity of those inclined to a breach of the tenth commandment.

Then, too, we had a type of the imaginary, or would-be rich, who at the table would remark to her companion, "I wonder if I put my diamonds in my trunk, I am so afraid they may be stolen." If this apprehensive person owned a diamond no one ever knew it. All she said was for effect.

Among the ladies were two old maids from the Bay State. We presumed they were candidates for matrimony. One of them smiled sweetly and frequently at the Judge and gave unmistakable hints that his company was agreeable, but the Judge was not easily taken in the net of the fowler.

And yet a man on matrimony bent could between the two spinsters have had an antipodal choice. In Mother Goose melodies there is a rhyme that runs—

>Jack Spratt could eat no fat,
>   His wife could eat no lean,
>And so between the two
>   They licked the platter clean."

Now, apropos of this, one of these ladies was over five feet high and weighed about two hundred, while she had dark eyes and a florid complexion. The other was about four feet in height and tipped the scales at about seventy-five pounds. She had blue eyes, a fair face and sorrel-top hair—or Cleopatra auburn, I suppose I should call it. So you see the Judge had two opposites to choose from, and yet the insatiate man was not satisfied.

We had a consequential lady, too. On a certain occasion she approached one of the "class," who wore a cap very much like that ornamenting the captain of the ship, which gave the landlubber a nautical appearance. This individual she mistook for the captain, and as such addressed him. The landlubber, feeling flattered at being taken for the captain, at first did not undeceive her. Said the fair one: "Captain, I wish you to understand I am a lady, accustomed to all the comforts and luxuries of life. I have not had proper consideration shown me. I demand proper respect and attention, sir." Our classmate, then scenting danger, tried to convince her he was not the captain, but all in vain. She left him very indignant.

One of our lady passengers was known as the "Hummingbird," not that she was a 'hummer,' as used in the slang sense, nor because her attire was as brilliant as the plumage of the bird that bears this name, but because of a peculiar habit. The appellation was conferred on the fair one because when the spirit moved her she emitted a humming sound, and the spirit, be it said, always inspired her when the band struck up. As soon as the music started, she would hum a bar or two in a gentle monotone—a kind of gurgling, rippling, purling sound, in accents sweet and low, as though she saw, in her mind's eye, "some sunny hope, some day dream bright" of memories long ago, touched into life as gently as an Æolian harp breathed upon by kindly zephyrs.

This humming or music of the throat was generally accompanied by time beating with the hands in a rapturous state of exaltation—eyes cast heavenward in such ecstatic delight that one would have fancied their owner entranced, enthralled or captivated by the seraphic melody of her own music.

No amount of insistance could induce this lady to burst forth into full song. Her declination was a head shake, but of that character that left the impression, "I could if I would." A gentle warbling, a slight motion of the throat was all.

No matter what the tune played by the band, her hum was always the same—like Poe's Raven, she sang only one melody "as if her soul in that one sound she did outpour." We became so accustomed to this sound that whenever the band played and we did not hear the usual refrain, some one was sure to ask, "Where's the 'Hummingbird?'"

On the ship were several wealthy widows and a number of spinsters, who, I am told, were decidedly averse to celibacy. One widow made it generally known that the man who married her need never do another day's work. Notwithstanding the great inducements of this offer, it had not been taken when I left the ship. But Cupid did get in some work, for there were one or two marriages during the trip, and several couples entered into "engagements."

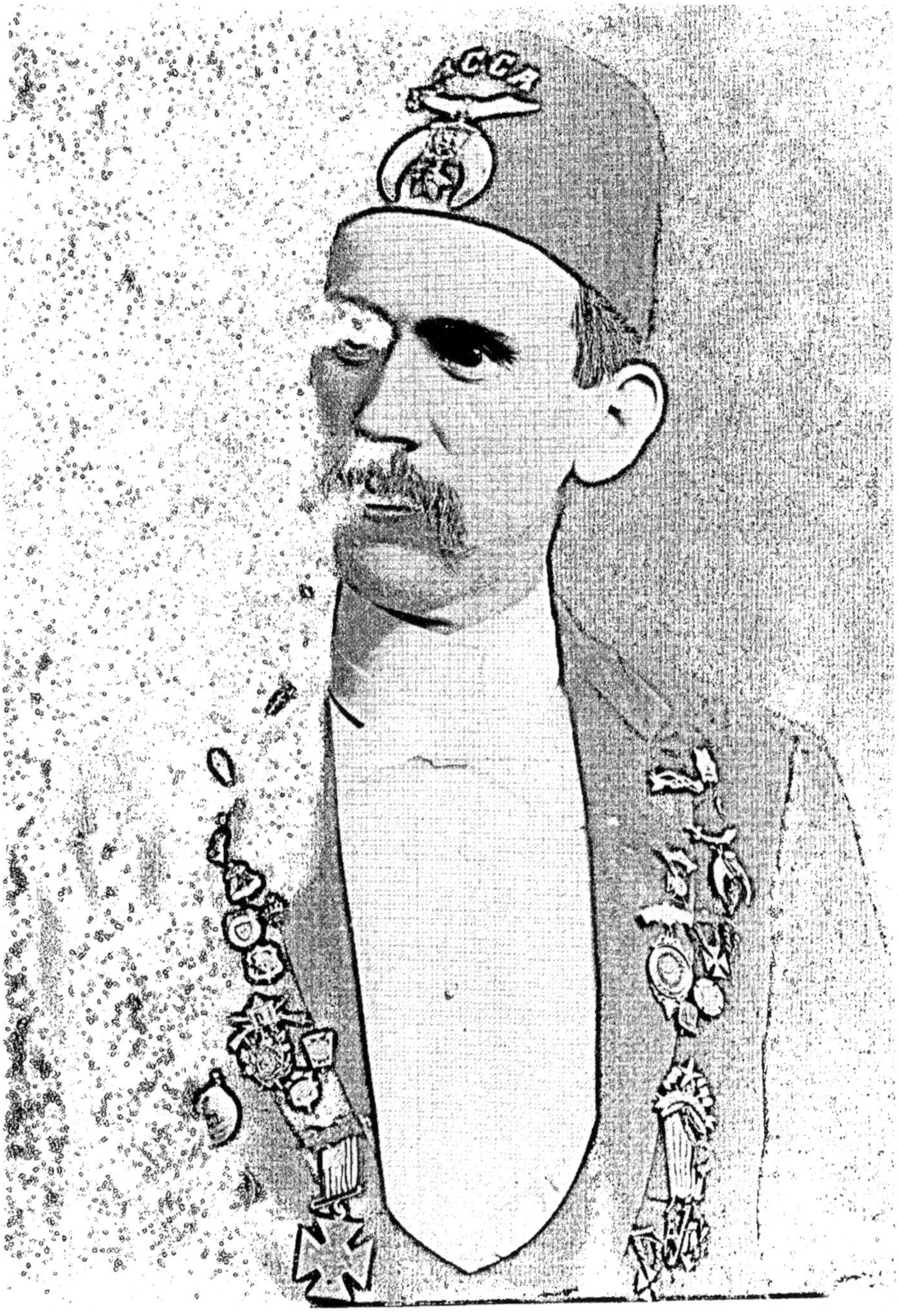
CCA

It is said—I know not with what degree of malice—that many women take these trips alone on husband hunting bent. Having exhausted themselves in vain on the home market, they try new fields and pastures green. I hope I am not writing ungallantly, but only truthfully, when I state this.

One of the most pleasant of all our ladies, a widow of means, was my right-hand companion in the dining-room. She was intelligent and thoroughly agreeable in every respect.

We also had a tired lady, who sat down if the crowd halted for a second, and on some occasions, we are satisfied, she was more fatigued by her constant sittings and quick risings than she would have been had she remained standing.

And there was still another lady, who, when on shore, invariably took a position at one shoulder of the guide. No matter how quick any one else was, she "got there all the same." She could ask more questions than any person I ever met. For this reason she was known as the "Interrogation Point." With note book and pencil in hand she asked a multiplicity of questions, designed not so much to gain information for herself as to show how little the rest of us knew. She even asked what material the row of wooden buildings on the Bosphorus was made of, and received the prompt answer "Of wood, madam." Her persistent queries in regard to some Athenian statuary at the Stadium actually brought a blush to the Grecian guide, to say nothing of the embarrassment it occasioned among the passengers.

One woman in our company invariably made it a rule to be the last of the party. She took her own time and would not be hurried. When the guide had gotten through with his explanations she would cry out in a loud, harsh voice, "Now hold on, guide; stop right here. I have not heard all you said." Then she would insist on his repeating his tale over again. Finally she became such a nuisance that the guide declined to pay any attention to her, and, to the satisfaction and relief of all, she dropped out of our party.

The self-conceited lady, who "knew it all," or at least thought she did, was likewise in our company. She, as well as a few of her satellites, regarded herself as a walking encyclopedia—the apotheosis of history, particularly of her own country—when, as a matter of fact, she knew very little about it. On one occasion, when she was expatiating upon the eloquence of Patrick Henry's famous "Give-me-Liberty-or-Give-me-Death speech," she said it was made in Philadelphia. "I beg your pardon, madam," said I, "the speech you refer to was made in old St. John's church, Richmond, Va." I doubt to this day whether she believed my statement.

On another occasion she remarked in my presence—she was a Western lady—that she had to be very cautious in talking about Southern people, their customs, and the "rebellion," as persons from that section were very sensitive. But for *her part,* said this dame, she thought the war had settled the whole matter and convinced every one that the South was in the wrong. As I inferred that this remark was made for my benefit, I told her in a gentlemanly way that knock-down arguments were never convincing; that we of the South had accepted the results of the war, were loyal to the government and reverenced the flag; but we had no apologies to make or excuses to offer for our course. Indeed, I added, that we were now more strongly convinced than ever that our fight for constitutional liberty was the proper thing. This silenced her, and ever afterwards she treated me with pleasant consideration. The fact that I had the courage of my convictions inspired her with respect.

It took several days on shipboard before we could get our bearings. On one occasion I started to my stateroom and got lost. I walked down the companion way—the route I usually walked—but could not find my room. I came out on deck, looked around, and went down again with the same result. I then tried the other end of the ship, but finally had to go to one of the stewards and get him to conduct me to my room. The fact was, the door, which previously had been open, was closed and shut off my compartment. Perley and The Young Voyager had a good laugh at my expense, when I told them of my adventure.

We had on the Arabic sixty-seven Masons hailing from twenty-eight different States. An association was formed by them for the purpose of visiting foreign lodges and Solomon's quarries near Jerusalem. I had the honor to be elected president of this organization, which bore the name

"Masonic Association
of
Clarke's Oriental Cruise
on S. S. Arabic."

Brother John D. Jordon, of Savannah, Ga., was elected secretary, and Brother J. Vincent Perley, of Charlottesville, Va., treasurer. The latter and Brothers J. Q. McAtee, of Philadelphia, Pa., and S. D. Bartle, of Mechanicsville, Iowa, constituted a committee to get up a proper souvenir, with pictures of Jerusalem, which duty they faithfully discharged. We cherish this souvenir as a delightful memento of our trip.

As president of the association it was encumbent upon me to examine and vouch for the brethren. I found among the members three past masters besides myself. Holding, as I did, a certificate from the Grand Master of Virginia, I was accepted as being all right. I examined the other three and we formed a committee to examine the rest, whom we found to be the rustiest lot we ever encountered. Some did not know a sign, word or grip of the order; we had to take them upon faith and other slight indications. But what will seem strange to the Craft in America is the fact that when we visited an English lodge at Constantinople and a Greek lodge at Cairo, they admitted me without any examination and accepted my avouchment for the entire party.

As a matter of curiosity I submit the contents of the ship's larder for our party on the cruise described. It follows:

Beef	88,000	pounds
Poultry	28,000	"
Potatoes	144,000	"
Coffee	7,500	
Butter	32,000	"
Flour	95,000	"
Eggs	60,000	dozen
Sugar	25 000	pounds
Tea	750	"
Milk	10,000	gallons
Coal	5,800	tons

Fresh fish, oysters, vegetables and fruits are not included in the above. While this statement may seem startling, it is entirely correct. The fare on the ship was fairly good, except the pigeon pie, which was so tough that we suspected the birds of having been some that old Noah had in his ark. Possibly they were relatives of the dove that was released to find the olive leaf which indicated that the waters were subsiding. The geese also were pretty tough, and may have been of Roman origin. Doubtless they were of the breed that made themselves famous when the Eternal City would have been captured but for anserine vigilance.

CHAPTER II.

We Sight Madeira's Coast—Urchins Dive for Money—Beautiful Mountain Scenery—The City of Funchal—Primitive Methods of Locomotion—In a Land of Persistent Beggars—A Witty Little Girl Floors the Party's Historian—In the Footprints of Columbus—Ignorance of the People—Agriculture and Horticulture—Fair Cadiz and Her People—Where Murillo Perished—Chilly Days in a Southern Clime—Salt Pyramids and Much-Abused Donkeys—A Ride to Venerable Seville—Last Resting Place of America's Discoverer—Intense Farming—Absence of Song Birds—Memories of the Moors—The Cork Industry—Gibraltar and Its Monkeys—Heterogeneous Population of the Town.

On the morning of February 16th—our eighth day out—upon going on deck, we perceived on the distant horizon a dark and heavy cloud; but on our nearer approach there loomed up a massive rock, rising from the very depths of old ocean's bed and projecting boldly into the circumambient waters.

At a distance it looked like a rugged, barren waste, but closer inspection proved it to be the beautiful Island of Madeira, which has been described as "the verdant mountain isle, towering in a glistening haze like some realm of enchantment." Our ship, on approaching still nearer, was surrounded by native boats laden with willow chairs, baskets and a variety of fruits, or filled with diving boys, stripped to the waist, who amused the passengers on deck by leaping from their little craft as soon as a coin was cast into the water.

Previous to the invasion of this island by the American tourist a penny was sufficient inducement to make the divers go overboard, but now it requires the shimmer of silver or the glint of gold to persuade them to leap into the chilling waters of the ocean. Little fellows not more than ten or twelve years old are experts in these diving feats and they rarely fail to get the money before it goes out of sight. As soon as they grasp the coin in their hands they clap it into their mouths, climb back into the boat and sit there shivering with cold until another piece of money is thrown, when over they go again. Some full-grown men were also in the boats but most of the passengers preferred patronizing the boys.

There is a tradition that the ancients regarded this shadowy mass of rocks in the west as the "mouth of hell" and avoided it accordingly, hence it was uninhabited for many years after the other lands adjacent had been occupied. The Madeiras, it is certain, were known to the Romans. Pliny refers to them as "the purple islands." The main island was settled by Portugal in 1418, and still remains under that government. Madeira has very truthfully been described as a "neglected paradise,' for its climatic conditions, its rich soil, and balmy breezes render it capable of being converted into a second Garden of Eden.

In fauna, fruits, flowers and cane it is unsurpassed. Plants and vegetation flourish in Oriental luxurance and abundance.

We sailed along the coast of the island for a distance of about twenty-five miles, and never witnessed a more lovely panorama than its gradually unfolding beauties. The distant hills seemed dotted with sheep, but upon our getting nearer the white objects proved to be houses perched upon the cliffs or sleeping in the valleys and hollows of the mountains. Lofty peaks towered upwards in the background—magnificent precipices overlooking the sea and in some instances two thousand feet high. The tallest peak on the island is over six thousand feet in height. The brilliant verdure on every rock and hillside gives Madeira a most inviting appearance.

Funchal, the chief city, was our landing place. It has a population of about 50,000, but strange to say, besides the consul there are only two American residents in the town. We were met at the landing by bullock sleds (or "caros," as they are called by the natives) which carry four persons, and go at a speed of about three miles an hour. The teamster moves on foot and prods his patient oxen with a sharp stick, while his assistant occasionally places a cloth, saturated with oil, under the runners in order to make them run smoothly. This renders the rocks so sleek that walking is not only difficult, but in some places dangerous. After the teamster handles the cloth, as above indicated, he uses the bullock's tail as a towel.

A ride in this unique vehicle is both pleasant and picturesque, and I venture to say that a drive down the principal streets of an American city in a "caro" would create quite a sensation. A "caro" assuredly would stand no show beside an automobile.

Another medium of locomotion is the "rede," or hammock, a sort of palanquin carried by two men on their shoulders. Very few horses or carriages are seen, for the ascents and declivities are so acute it is dangerous to use them. How the natives manage when a fire breaks out is a problem I cannot solve.

A ride on the inclined railway to the top of the mountain to the Church of Our Lady opens a beautiful view of the ocean, which lies before you like a sheet of molten silver shimmering in the sunshine, and dotted with many sails. As you ascend you pass orange and lemon groves, sugar cane and banana plantations, vineyards and ripening figs, peach and almond trees in full bloom, gardens laden with lovely and fragrant flowers, roses in rich and luxuriant profusion, honeysuckles perfuming the air, heliotropes, fuchsias and geraniums—and all this in midwinter.

The climate varies here only about 12 degrees the year around, registering between 60 and 70. Madeira is a winter resort patronized largely by the English. The road up the mountain continues to wind through a most picturesque landscape of variegated scenery, past deep gorges, yawning precipices, gaping ravines, terraced mountain sides and cultivated slopes. There is scarcely enough soil on the rocks to sustain the vegetable growth, but all is bathed in balmy sunshine. Here on one of these lofty peaks or in lonely mountain glens, "far from the madding crowd's ignoble strife" one could find "silence coeval with eternity"—that repose and rest from trouble and care that might be sought in vain elsewhere.

We descended the mountain, a distance of two miles, on a toboggan, and made the trip in about ten minutes—a thrilling experience. It is easy going down, but when one sees the poor, sweating devils toiling up again with their tobaggans on their backs, panting for breath and with their faces livid from heat, one is reminded of those famous lines from Virgil which begin *"Facilis descensus Arerno"* and end with the words, *"Sed revocare gradum, superas evadere ad auras, hoc opus, hic labor est."*

Notwithstanding its beauty and fertility Madeira is a land of beggars. The native children can speak but little English, yet their shibboleth is "give me a penny." This sentence is plainly and naturally spoken—"merely this and nothing more." I fancy it is taught the children by their mothers in place of the "Now I lay me down to sleep" taught by American mothers. They are a most insistent and persistent set—worse than flies and more annoying than fleas.

After the children attain some bigness they add to their appeal, "You vera rich, we vera poor; give me a penny please." They bothered us so much that even "The Young

Voyager," who is a mild-tempered youth, actually shook his fist at them, while Perley, the best natured of men, threatened to draw his "gun." Finally, I suggested for our own protection that we turn the tables, take the initiative and give the youngsters a dose of their own medicine; so every time we met an urchin we held out our hands and said, "Give me a penny, give me a penny." This novel proceeding so nonplussed them they began to shun us. Some of the children seemed to enjoy the joke and went off laughing.

But begging, let me say, was not entirely confined to the children. When we came out of any public building there stood lined up before us, in appealing array, quite a concourse of vagrants—men and women, the halt, lame and blind. Many of them so appealed to our sympathy it was not long before our pockets were depleted of small change.

At the doors of the shops we noticed certain small statues, something like the wooden Indians that once ornamented our cigar stores, and held in their hands a bunch of cigars. These statues represented their subjects with an empty hand extended and in the attitude of begging. We supposed these were designed to perfect the children in the art of mendicancy or to remind them to keep it up. At any rate, the effigies apparently worked like a charm on the pestiferous youngsters.

The children at Madeira, however, are exceedingly bright and many of them are comely and pretty.

One day we were walking along a beautiful road winding around the mountain, followed as usual by a gang of child-beggars asking for pennies. I stopped to make an entry in our note book, whereupon a little girl stepped up and remarked, "Me read English." Our note book was handed to her and she was requested to read what I had written. She looked askant at it and smilingly replied, "You no write good English." Those acquainted with my chirography will immediately recognize the truthfulness of the remark. We at once gave her two pennies for her most truthful witticism.

Through the center of the town runs an immense ravine, which is a public lavatory and laundry, upon whose rugged sides, held down by small stones, the washed linen of the inhabitants appears. Each resident is thus enabled to make a complete inventory of his friend's garments and to see the number of holes in his neighbor's stockings and other habiliments.

This chasm divides the city, but it is spanned by several bridges, which afford easy access to each side.

All articles, such as food, furniture and fuel, owing to the steep declivities, are conveyed on sleds or toboggans. Sugar cane and wood are also moved in the same way. There is now very little timber on the island, but the public laundry referred to above, is embellished by a long row of gigantic sycamores, probably hundreds of years old.

We know of no more pleasant winter resort than Madeira. We tried a bottle of the native wine and found it fine. About fifty years ago the wine from this island was quite extensively used, but in 1852 a disease almost destroyed the vines. Other wines were substituted, and although vine culture has somewhat recovered, the wine, so famous years ago, has not regained its former prestige.

The name Madeira signifies wood, and the island was so named on account of the luxuriant forests which covered the place when it was first settled. The woods subsequently were destroyed by fire, it taking but seven years to obliterate the growth of centuries. This was the primitive method of preparing the land for cultivation.

Columbus, the great discoverer, is identified with the

early history of Madeira. He followed his sweetheart to this island, rediscovered her and married her here in 1473. His father-in-law was a seafaring man, it is said, and Columbus got his taste for the sea from this connection. There is a tablet on a house bearing his name and built on the site of the structure in which he lived. It will be remembered that Napoleon was brought to Madeira in 1815, before being exiled to St. Helena.

The people of this island are very ignorant. Dr. Lorenz states that in 1881 the son of a wealthy merchant wished to know if our civil war was over. Another fairly intelligent person expressed regret at just hearing the news of the death of the popular President, George Washington. A large number of slaves at one time were held in bondage in Madeira, but about two hundred years ago they were freed. Their descendants have intermarried with the natives, which accounts for the dark complexion of the inhabitants.

There are a few public schools, but the children do not attend regularly or in large numbers. The land is cultivated by irrigation and so sparse is the soil on the mountain sides that earth is carried there on the backs of donkeys. We even saw earth being carried by the children in baskets poised on their heads. Women also carry stones in the same way. Wheelbarrows seem to be unknown to the inhabitants. The wages are about 25 cents a day, and the laboring classes are, of course, very poor, but industrions. The women make beautiful embroideries and the men fine basketwork, which they sell. The houses outside the cities are mere hovels, with neither floors nor windows, and though the island is small, there are many who have never been out of sight of their homes. Though these people possess but little they are strongly attached to their little plot of Mother Earh.

Madeira is an island of flowers. Geraniums grow to a height of twenty feet in a few months. There are 363 genera of native wild flowers and 717 species. Some of the houses are fairly hidden under brilliant blossoms. Palms five feet across the stump are the growth of fifteen years. This is the home of the so-called English walnut, which is carried to England and from thence exported. We were regaled at the hotels (in February) with strawberries, lettuce, new potatoes, snaps and other fresh vegetables.

A short horse-car line leads to the inclined railway. We were struck with the original, if not primitive, method of punching the car tickets. (They don't know about Mark Twain.) The ticket is a thin piece of paper, which the conductor folds across the middle—"folds with care in presence of passenjare." He then tears out a part of the fold, thus saving the trouble of using the ordinary punch.

The boundaries of each person's little garden or tract of land are separated by stone fences. We took a tour of the town in a bullock sled—oh! such a ride. We never before had one we enjoyed more. Not only did we drive through the business and fashionable sections of the city, but through the old streets and closes, so narrow in some places, and with walls so high on each side that the sun rarely shone in them. One could sit in this novel vehicle and touch the walls on each side. The charge is only 25 cents an hour and the enjoyment great.

We witnessed a funeral procession while in Madeira. The corpse was borne on a frame on the shoulders of four men and was followed by twelve little boys with lighted candles. A priest brought up the rear.

We left Madeira deeply impressed with its beauty, its delightful climate and its salubrious atmosphere.

Our next stopping place was "fair Cadiz, rising o'er the

dark blue sea." This was once a magnificent city of over 200,000 inhabitants. Before the decadence of Spain set in it exceeded even London in wealth. The present population, however, is only about 70,000. Once the largest town in Spain it is now the eleventh. Still it is a charming city.

As you approach Cadiz the town gives you the impression of a magic city rising out of the sea. It is surrounded with massive stone walls from thirty to fifty feet high and about twenty feet in width. The streets are narrow, but clean, and are lined with bright colored houses, most of them ornamented with balconies. There is a great abundance of marble both without and within.

The dark-skinned senoritas have large, liquid, black eyes, raven tresses, shapely feet and delicate hands. Many of them are exceedingly beautiful, and on them "The Young Voyager" beamed his most enticing smiles.

The Alemeda, or public garden, is the fashionable resort of the town. The city is a very ancient one, having been founded by the Phœnicians, who regarded it as the limit of the world—the *ultima thule* of the globe.

But it was captured by the Romans, whose handiwork and landmarks were left in almost every European country, their eagles having been borne before their solid phalanxes over the whole of the Old World. Cæsar gave Cadiz the name "Augusta Urbs." Juvenal speaks of it as "the City of Venus," on account of its pretty women and fine wines.

In the Church of Los Capuchinos are some celebrated paintings, chiefly by Murillo, who met his tragic end in this building, falling from a scaffold in the midst of his work, and expiring soon after.

We also visited the art gallery, which contains many fine pictures, chiefly drawn from Bible history.

We were not annoyed by beggars in Spain. The Dons, as a rule, are too proud to beg, and when it was attempted the police at once took charge of the mendicants. The houses generally have no chimneys. Fuel is so scarce in Spain that the inhabitants cannot afford fires; and the weather for the greater part of the year does not require it. When the people have fires they use charcoal in brasiers.

The bull ring of the town is capable of holding 11,000 spectators, but there was "nothing doing" in that line while we were there, so we did not witness the national sport.

My friend, the Rev. John D. Jordon, gives in one of his letters the following experience: "My guide and driver could speak no English. With a few Latin words and signs, I made him understand pretty well. On hearing him say 'parkie' I understood him to mean park. I cried *'bono parkie'* and he at once drove into a beautiful park or botanic garden. They have a famous tree there called the 'dragon tree.' I called out *'dragoona,'* pointed to a tree and he drove us to the very spot. It was amusing to see and hear the various Americans trying to make themselves understood. People with all kinds of things to sell accosted us. I put them to flight by yelling at them *'no bono,'* which I meant for them to interpret as 'no good.' It worked like a charm, and soon others were freeing themselves from undesirable solicitors by quoting my magic words."

En route to Seville, which is ninety miles from Cadiz, we passed many salt pyramids. Seeing these, we at first thought the Dons were attempting to copy after the ancient Egyptians, but on inquiry we were informed that these mounds were salt cones, the source from which Spain draws her salt for preserving her olives and for domestic purposes.

The water from the ocean is let into ponds or reservoirs, and as, in the summer the weather is very hot and dry, it soon evaporates and leaves a deposit of salt, which is heaped up until the mound is fifteen or twenty feet high. Then it is given a conical shape and covered with a composition of sand to keep it from being damaged by the weather.

We lunched on the train on squab and toast and hard boiled eggs, which we washed down with a bottle of wine. Along the railroad we observed extensive hedges of cacti, but occasionally we noticed that this ancient method of enclosure was being supplanted by American barbed-wire.

At the railroad stations the flagging is done by women instead of men. The poor, oppressed donkeys which one sees in Seville excite the compassion of all beholders. These unhappy brutes are monuments of patience and endurance. The donkey is the chief medium of transportation. He is hitched to a cart large enough to carry a dozen of the tiny creatures, and yet he does not cry out or protest, as did Balaam's long-eared beast, though he doubtless has greater reason to complain. We saw boards sixteen feet long strapped to their backs and also panniers containing wood, coal and all kinds of goods, wares and merchandise.

En route we noticed that the olive trees are cut back or pruned so closely as to leave the trunk, though probably a hundred years old, but a gnarled stump, covered only with the foliage and branches of one or two years' growth. In fact, all trees are trimmed frequently in order to procure timber, which is converted into charcoal or sold as fagots for cooking purposes. Cadiz has no chimneys; Seville has chimneys, but no fires.

The Spanish people think Seville an earthly paradise, and there is a saying among them "God gives His favorites a house in Seville."

The ride from Cadiz to Seville is less than a hundred miles, and yet it took us, by *special train,* five hours to make the journey. They are a slow people, these Spaniards. We go through a beautiful, fertile country. The principal crops are wheat, beans and barley. Herds of cattle and flocks of sheep and goats dot the landscape. Thousands of acres are planted in olives and oranges, which form lovely groves.

Here, as elsewhere, are found evidences of Roman occupation—the remains of the characteristic aqueduct can be traced for miles. The ancient Roman believed in a bountiful supply of pure water, and the Rome of to-day is noted for it as of old.

We were not shaved by the famous "Barber of Seville," immortalized by Rossini, but were shorn by the guides and fakirs.

At Seville we visited the cathedral, considered by many the finest in Christendom. In area is exceeded only by St. Peter's at Rome. The architecture is a massive Gothic, but the interior is so cold and cheerless that one's religion, I imagine, would ooze out like Bob Acres' courage. No man could possibly be made enthusiastic or ardent while worshiping under such circumstances. The edifice is without heating apparatus of any sort. Yet it contains many splendid paintings and works of art. Its stained glass windows are magnificent, while its rich silver and wood carvings are invaluable and unsurpassed. If one could visit this superb structure in warm weather and pure sunlight he could not fail to be profoundly impressed. Some of the magnificent windows are five hundred years old and the most beautiful in existence.

The town contains nearly five hundred streets and lanes, and they are so narrow and tortuous (many of them) that one easily gets lost. Seville, like Cadiz, was founded by the Phœnicians, but was conquered by the Romans. Later it became the stronghold of the Moors, from whom it was taken by the Spanish. Its hotel accommodations are poor, and it offers no hope of the fulfillment of the Scriptural text "The last shall be first and the first last," for the reason that dinner is served in courses, and the "next course" is not brought until each individual has gotten through with the previous course. Thus it will be seen that there is no advantage to be gained by the fast eater.

We visited the King's palace, or as it is called, the Aleazer. The gardens belonging to the palace are very elaborate and beautiful.

One of the curiosities of Seville is the counterpart or duplication of the house of Pontius Pilate. It was built several hundred years ago by some wealthy Don, who went to Jerusalem and there had the plans drawn. The measurements were taken from the original some fifty years before it was destroyed. This is the only duplicate or fac simile of the kind in existence. The building shows the Judgment Hall in which Christ was tried, the pillar to which He was bound before being scourged and the room in which Peter stood when he denied his Lord.

In the cathedral at Seville is the sarcophagus containing the ashes of the great discoverer, Columbus. It is a curious circumstance or coincidence that this wanderer should continue to travel even after death. He was first buried in San Domingo. When this island passed into the hands of the French the remains of Columbus were carried to Cuba. When the Americans drove the Spaniards from Cuba the ashes were removed to Seville. We trust they have made their last journey and may now be permitted to remain in Seville until the resurrection morn. The reason of their removal is carved in bold letters on the foundation on which stands the bronze allegorical figures. The legend alludes to "ungrateful America," doubtless referring to the historical fact that Spain was our friend in the dark days of the Revolution.

Trains travel very slowly in Spain. The conductor locks the doors of the compartments, presumably to prevent the passengers from jumping off to gather fruit as they go along. A cow catcher would be more serviceable in the rear than in the front of the locomotive. Wood is so scarce in Spain that the disused and rejected ties are used for fences.

The land between Seville and Granada is rich and well cultivated. Vast fields of wheat and barley and thousands of acres of olive, cork and almond trees are to be seen. I have never beheld more intense farming. No weeds are seen and every foot of arable ground is made to yield, but the absence of farm houses and barns strikes one as peculiar. The farmers, after the old feudal system, live in villages just as they did when the custom was for the lord of the manor to gather his retainers and vassals around him for common protection and defense. The great scarcity of timber prevents the building of barns, and granaries are established, like warehouses, in the towns. Many persons even rent a portion of their dwellings for this purpose until the grain is marketed.

On our trip to Granada we had in our compartment two priests, five other gentlemen and four ladies. The manager of the tour served each person a bottle of Spanish wine with the luncheon.

After the imbibition of this wine it was curious to note its effects. One gentleman called attention to the supposition on his part that the train was going backward; another—an Irishman—maintained that it was *still* going forward. One of the priests was of the opinion that it was going around, while the other contended it was "going every way." Two of the gentlemen went to sleep and the ladies talked so fast and furiously it was impossible to gather their opinions on the matter. Verily we had a regular picnic.

While on this journey we passed many quaint old walled towns and cities, dating back to the times of the Romans and Moors. These have their ancient watch towers, perched like sentinels upon the nearest hill tops.

As we get nearer Granada the country becomes mountainous; first the land is rolling, then appear the foothills, soon to be succeeded in the distance by lofty, towering peaks and next snow-capped ridges unfold themselves in panoramic view, extending along the horizon as far as the eye can reach. The mountains being denuded of timber, are barren and unattractive.

We found it disagreeably cold at Granada, our heavy overcoats being necessary for comfort. The hotels were not heated, and one night we went to bed quite early in order to keep warm. The only way to get a fire is to order a charcoal brasier. These are had on special application and at extra charge. A lady of our party remarked at the hotel table that she had seen the magnificent buildings and lovely scenery of Spain, but had looked upon nothing so pleasant and cheering as the steam emanating from a friendly looking musical tea kettle.

We saw the Spanish mail express, an old-fashioned, "ante-bellum" stage-coach, looking very much like the one in Buffalo Bill's show, and so high that a ladder had to be used to enable the driver to get his bags on top.

At night we took a ride over the city on the poorly patronized street cars. The conductors are very accommodating, stopping occasionally to let the passengers get a drink or buy cigarettes. Spaniards smoke all the time and allow the passengers the same privilege. The ladies of Spain do not object to tobacco and many of them use cigarettes.

The Dons of Granada look very picturesque in their long cloaks lined with green, red or purple velvet and having a cape attachment. They wear the cloak with peculiar grace. It is thrown over the left shoulder and envelopes the lower part of the face. The men also wear slouch hats and almost invariably when on the street they are seen smoking.,

We put up at the Hotel Victoria, and on the morning after our arrival were aroused quite early by the noises and cries incident to the awakening of a large city. On looking out from our balcony we could see droves of goats and cows being driven by their keepers down the public streets and pausing in front of the doors of their patrons. The animals are milked "on the spot" and the lacteal fluid drawn warm and fresh from the fountains of life.

We were induced to believe we would find genial, balmy weather in Andelusia and would hear the nightingales caroling by moonlight amidst the ruins of the Alhambra. We were inclined, too, to think—before experience taught us the contrary—that Spain was a soft southern region, like sunny Italy, but it struck us as being a cold, melancholy country.

This impression was intensified by the absence of trees and increased by the lack of song birds, which are so numerous in England and America. The absence of woods and hedges, of course, makes the country inhospitable to the feathered songsters.

The way to the Alhambra is up a deep, narrow road, and the hills on each side are covered with beautiful trees, which in February are just beginning to sprout their leaves. Along the road on both sides is a lovely stream of limpid water, glistening and sparklng in the sunlight, while above us are the Alhambra and the Vermillion towers. It is supposed the latter were built by the Romans, but their origin is unknown.

The Alhambra itself is an ancient fortress and castle of the Moorish kings of Granada—the place where they made their last stand for liberty against Spanish invasion. It was erected upon a spur of the Sierra Nevada or Snowy Mountain and has been so frequently described that any words from me would be superflous. I refer all interested in this magnificent view to Washington Irving.

The cisterns and reservoirs cut in the living rock go to prove that the Moors valued a good supply of pure water. In front of the Esplanade is the splendid pile commenced by Charles V., but never completed, and intended, it is said, to eclipse the original of the Moslem kings.

The Moorish palace is the most magnificent of its kind in existence. One indeed feels when he visits it that he is treading the places depicted in the Arabian Nights stories. The arcades of elegant filigree work, the splendor of the architecture, the delicate fluted columns and the graceful tracery of fretwork on the walls and in the dome suggest the touch of a magician's wand or the agency of something superhuman. The honey-combed stalactite vaulting in the Room of the Two Sisters, the largest of all Arab ceilings, has no less than 5,000 pieces in its construction. Each differs from all the others, and yet all blend together in wonderful order and symmetry. In the center stands the famous fountain with its alabaster basin just as it did in the days of the unfortunate Boabdil.

We also visited the Court of Lions and the Hall of the Abencerrages, who were treacherously murdered here. The lovely filigree work, the unique ornamentations and the beautiful decorations reminded us of the descriptions of Fairyland. We have been told that they are unsurpassed, and that frequent attempts have been made, without success, to imitate them. It is said that the peculiar art they represent perished with the overthrow of the Moors. As we surveyed these splendid remains of a once powerful fortress and grand palace and looked out over the surrounding country, we did not wonder that Boabdil, the last of the Moorish kings, shed tears when he took a last view of his domains. The reproach of his stouthearted mother—"You do well to weep as a woman over what you could not defend as a man"—must have added inexpressibly to his grief.

> "For brightly fall the morning rays
>   Upon a conquer'd king;
> The breeze that with his banner plays,
>   Plays with an abject thing.
> Banner and king no more will know
>   Their rightful place 'mid friend and foe;
> Proud clarion, cease thy blast!
>   Or, changing to the wail of woe,
> Breathe dirges for the past.'

The site once occupied by the Moorish aristocracy is now the dwelling place of gypsies, who have burrowed into the sides of the hill like ancient cliff dwellers. Such are the atmospheric conditions that I thought it only a few hours' journey to the snow-capped mountains before us, but was told it would take three days to reach them.

The cathedral at Granada is, externally, rough and uninviting, but inside it is strikingly beautiful. The columns are of massive Corinthian marble, decorated in white and gold. The remains of Ferdinand and Isabella repose beneath a splendid monument in this edifice.

The people of Granada are suppled with pure, fresh water from the mountains. It is brought in daily in tin cans and skins on the back of the genial factotum, the donkey. Faggots are brought from the hills in the same manner for fire wood. We saw car loads of faggots that we would burn as useless brush.

Perley, in his peregrinations, always carries a thousand or two of his visiting cards. This card is as unique as its owner is peculiar. To be appreciated, it has to be seen. On the front side is his picture, astride a donkey or camel—I do not now recall which. On the back is a partial list of the secret orders to which he belongs—in all fifty-one—and he is still a joiner or rejoiner.

This card is scattered from the St. Lawrence to the Rio Grande in America, and from Venice and Paris on the Continent; also throughout England, Scotland, Holland and Belgium—in fact, wherever he has been.

At Granada, with his usual courtesy, he presented one of the natives with his picture, but the recipient mistook it for the portrait of some distinguished American traveling incognito. The Spaniard exhibited it with great enthusiasm as the picture of the man in whose honor the trip was gotten up, and did his best to sell it to his fellow-countrymen.

We left the Alhambra and Granada with feelings of regret and took the train of the Bobadilla and Algeciras Railroad for Algiers, en route to Gibraltar, a distance of about two hundred miles—the grade one in fifty and for a short distance one in seventy.

At one of the stations at which we stopped a bright wood fire was burning and it was soon surrounded by an appreciative crowd, as its genial warmth was much enjoyed.

About one hundred and ten miles of the B. and A. is owned by an English company, and is in excellent condition. The general manager, who is a fine fellow, put at the disposal of Mr. Clark his private observation car, and Mr. Clark in turn was kind enough to invite our party of three to take seats in it.

At Aronda we saw another old Roman aqueduct. We passed large groves of cork trees, as Spain is the largest producer of cork in the world. The bark that constitutes the cork of commerce is cut into sections; one-half is taken from the trees every five years. The trees look somewhat like our oaks. When their trunks and some portions of their limbs are denuded of their natural covering they present a spectral appearance and lose much of their beauty.

The cars in this country are lighted from the top; one of the trainmen climbs to the roof of the coaches for that purpose. Ralroad ties cost one dollar each in Spain. In less than fifteen miles we passed through fourteen tunnels one-half a mile long and so straight you could see through them from one end to the other. The road cost $150,000 a mile.

The scenery in this section is grand; magnificent gorges, immense precipices, beautiful valleys and lofty mountains, tiny rills and lovely cascades of sparkling waters—the whole well timbered and watered.

A most delightful feature of this journey was the constant attendance for miles of a perfect rainbow that seemingly followed the train, encircling the cars with a halo of colors brilliant and pleasing.

> "Far up the blue sky a fair rainbow unroll'd
> Its soft-tinted pinions of purple and gold."

The general manager of the road informed us that the Spanish government taxed the road twenty per cent. of the receipts from passenger fares and five per cent. on all freights.

The next point in our itinerary was Gibraltar, which rises up from the sea in grand and massive form, like a mighty lion in stone, crouching to spring upon an invading host. These are historic waters; between this point and Cadiz Nelson made his last signal to his fleet—"England expects every man to do his duty"—and sailed to meet his foe. The result was one of the greatest naval battles ever fought, but England paid dearly for it in the death of the brave and intrepid Nelson.

Opposite Gibraltar, on the African side, is Apes Hill, quite a high mountain, from which at certain seasons of the year the monkeys go over to Gibraltar, but how they get there is a mystery. Some suppose there is a cave extending from the rock to Apes Hill under the Strait and that the simians go through this pass.

On our arrival in the Straits on February 22nd, we found several American warshps decorated in honor of Washington's birthday. Cheers were given and returned.

The famous Rock of Gibraltar has been owned by many nations. It was first in the hands of the Phœnicians and then the Romans. Afterwards it passed into the possession of the Goths and Vandals, who were succeeded by the Moors. Next it was owned by Spain, and now the flag of England flies over the place. It has been truly described as "unique in position, in picturesqueness and in history." The rock fairly bristles with cannon, and should any nation punch the sleeping lion or pull his whiskers they would roar with a mighty detonation. The town is built upon the slopes of the rocks and the Titanic boulders are honey-combed with tunnels and galleries for port holes.

We climbed for about a mile through one of these immense galleries and enjoyed the first perspiration we had experienced since we left America. It was indeed tedious, uphill work and many fell by the wayside, but our party of three, believing in the sentiment, "old Virginia never tires," kept up and went to the end.

The streets are very irregular and are just as they were

when the place was a Moorish possession. It is said the Moors built them crooked, so that at any hour of the day shade might be found on one side or the other. The shrubbery, vines and flowers are quite luxuriant and attractive. This is one of England's strongholds and is her key to the Mediterranean. She has spent many millions in its defences and has just completed at a cost of $20,000,000 a new harbor which can receive the largest ships.

The population of the town is about 25,000. One sees all nations in its streets—Arabs, Africans, Spaniards, Turks, Jews and the sad-faced Moors, who look as if they never smiled. Martial law prevails here. No foreigner can reside on the island without his consul or householder becoming responsible for him. There is a large sprinkling of Red Coats——Tommy Adkins is always in evidence. A strip of neutral ground lies between the fortifications and the Spanish guns at Linea.

A magnificent view can be obtained from the rock. You can see the waters of the Mediterranean and the Atlantic Ocean, in addition to the Bay and the Straits of Gibraltar. The continents of Europe and Africa are also visible.

CAPTER III.

Algers and Her Former Slaves—In the Arab Quarter and Among its Fakirs—Malta and Her Romantic History—Valetta and its Sculptured Guardian—The Church of St. John—In the Chapel of Bones—Grecian Isles and the Temple of Athena—Policemen Attired Like Ballet Girls—The Acropolis and the Parthenon—Acres of Ruins—Mars Hill and its Associations—Constantinople, the "Dogopolis" of the World—Mosque at Sancta Sophia and Other Points of Interest—Sights in the Grand Bazaar—Turkish Ladies—American Missionary Schools—"Smyrna, the Lovely"—Along the Route to Ephesus—Tobacco "Octopus" Agent Corners Licorice Market—Glimpses of Troy, Rhodes and Cyprus—Carmel, the Dwelling Place of David's Nabal—In the Land of the Prophets.

Algiers is "a city set upon a hill, whose light cannot be hid." As one enters the harbor one's attention is called to the moles and breakwaters built many years ago by Christian slaves held in bondage when Algiers was dominated by pirates.

These buccaneers captured certain American citizens and demanded a big ransom for their release. In reply, Uncle Sam, in 1815, sent Commodore Decatur to demand the immediate release of all Americans held in slavery.

The crafty Dey acceded to the demand, but asked that in order that he might not lose prestige among other nations, the United States would, as tribute, make him a nominal annual gift of some powder. The sturdy Commodore grimly declared that "if the Dey took the powder he must take the balls, too," so the unwilling Dey, fully understanding the implied suggestion, yielded up his prisoners. It is said that 30,000 of these Christian slaves were employed in this work for many years.

From the bay the view of the city is very beautiful, with its terraces of dazzling white and its background of emerald green, blending with the purple sea and azure skies.

We drove over the entire city in hacks. The terraced gardens and parks were planted with palms, orange, lemon and pepper trees—all in full foliage.

The Arab quarter, exemplifying, as it does, the extreme primitiveness of five hundred years ago, was unique and presented a curious picture with its strangely costumed people and its narrow streets and alleys. We saw the inhabitants buying, eating and sleeping in full view of the public; we smelt strange and unsavory odors; we heard the intonations of prayers, yet saw gambling going on almost under the very noses of the religious zealots.

Whilst the ancient piratical government has been succeeded by French rule, the descendants of the former Corsairs are strongly in evidence to-day among the sellers of curios and antiques, all warranted genuine, but doubtless made in Germany or Paris. I saw articles which were priced at $2 but sold for 25 cents. The streets were filled with many people in curious costumes and almost all known tongues could be heard.

The bazaars, which are the most wonderful in the world, are filled with all kinds of goods—brilliant and dazzling wares—but no one is expected to pay the prices first asked. If you do the seller gets his neighbor to kick him as soon as you leave because he did not ask more.

The contrast between the inhabitants of Algiers and Madeira is quite pleasant. We saw no beggars at the first-mentioned place, but many villanous-looking Arabs and Turks.

The bay was filled with flags of many nations. Among other vessels we noticed two Russian warships that had escaped Togo and had been in these waters ever since. The ships are coaled by natives, who carry the fuel in baskets on their shoulders.

This must be a great wine-producing country, as the wharves, when we saw them, were full of immense casks of this liquid.

Perley drifted off here in his usual aimless way from my son, Harry, and myself, and when he got back to the ship had many wonderful yarns to tell. He must have gotten hold of some of his favorite Parisian "cafe au lait," as he mistook a long section of fire hose for a sea serpent and started to jump overboard, but "The Young Voyager" and I managed to control him. He brought on board a fat, stuffed lizard, which he intended as a companion for the alligators he had purchased the year before in Florida. Perhaps he wished to crossbreed the saurians.

Malta is another British stronghold in the Mediterranean chain of defenses which Great Britain regards as essential to guard her interests in this great sea. The Maltese call the island, in their poetic language,

"The flower of the world,"

probably because they do not know other flowers. It is closely identified with Biblical history, romance and war, and has been controlled by Phœnicians, Romans and Vandals and later occupied by Germans, Spanish, French and English.

One of the little group was called Hyperia by Homer. It was the supposed residence of Calypso, the nymph, whose siren songs brought grief to Ulysses when that unfortunate hero was on his way from Troy.

Malta, in the year 1530, was granted to the Knights of St. John, better known as the Knights of Malta, by Charles V. The renown which the order acquired on the fields of Palestine is well established by history. Originally the members were keepers of a hospital for pilgrims at Jerusalem. They eventually became a military order, and under the banner of the White Cross showed their valor during the crusades on many a hotly-contested field. After being driven from Palestine with the Christian armies that engaged in the crusades, they settled on the Island of Cyprus, whence they were expelled by the Turks. Then they went to the Island of Rhodes and thence to Malta.

Under the leadership of La Valetta, the most famous of the Grand Masters of their order, the Knights founded the city of Valetta and began a series of fortifications that have been without a parallel.

The Knights also became masters of the sea, and by maintaining constant piratical expeditions, turned the tables on the Turks. But alas! this grand order, founded on vows of temperance and chastity, with the growth of wealth and power lost its virtue and its moral and religious standards, while its members degenerated into adventurers and libertines.

The Island of Malta, independent of its several smaller groups, is only seventeen miles long and eight miles broad, but it is the most densely populated place on earth. The island is nothing more than a huge rock covered with scanty soil. On account of the frequency of hurricanes there are but few trees. The climate is so mild, however, that two or three crops are produced every year. While the highest point of the island is less than a thousand feet, the shores are very steep, giving rise to Byron's "Farewell to Malta"—

"Adieu, ye cursed streets of Stairs,
How surely he who mounts you swears."

Valetta, at which we landed, owing to its towers and fortifications, presents quite a formidable appearance. As one enters the harbor one sees sculptured in the living rock a mounted knight, who guards the entrance and stands as a symbol of the ancient order, which so long held the island. In fact, the "Knights" are very much in evidence. The museum contains many relics and antiques pertaining to them. There are parchments bearing the orders and signatures of many of the Grand Masters, some, not being able to sign their names, affixed their marks to these documents.

The Church of St. John is remarkable for its historic associations, and its rich internal decorations, monuments, tapestries, pictures and relics. The facade is surmounted by an octagon cross, the symbol of the Knights. Below is a bronze figure of Our Lord. Over the entrance are the coats of arms of the Grand Master, La Cassiere, during whose rule the church was built. The pavement contains about four hundred sepulchral slabs, made of marbles of many colors and placed there in memory of the Grand Masters and Knights. These memorials are richly adorned with coats of arms and heraldic emblazonments.

The altar of the church is carved with gold and silver. The railing in front of the altar is made entirely of virgin silver and would have been appropriated by Napoleon when he captured the island in 1800, had not the priests painted it black. It is said that the tapestries in this church cost over $30,000, while there are many rare and costly paintings.

The chapel of San Carlo contains many reputed relics, among others a thorn from the Saviour's crown, the stones with which Stephen was beaten to death and bones of some of the apostles. The alleged right hand of John the Baptist, encased in a glove of gold and with a large diamond on the finger, was here when Napoleon took the island. History or tradition says he slipped the ring on his own finger, but thrust the hand aside with the sneering remark, "Keep the carrion."

In the Church of the Monks lie the unburied remains of the monks, whose skeletons still wear the cloaks used in life—a ghastly array that smells like a charnel house. In the chapel of Bones are arrayed in symmetrical order, tier upon tier, the skulls of over two thousand Knights. Their thigh bones are also laid out in regular order, like billets of wood, while the arm and smaller bones are fixed to form curious designs. The display is nothing if not strange and gruesome.

The Maltese women go enveloped in a curious hooded garment, called a "faldette"—a kind of sunbonnet shaped like a coal scuttle. This is attached to their black cloaks. Over the faldette is a veil, which the women close or open as fancy or curiosity dictates, but the only features usually discernable are their large, liquid black eyes, in which slumber the passions of their Oriental natures. The fair ones marry at twelve and age very rapidly.

"The Young Voyager" sprouted a mustache on this trip, and a lass from New York generously supplied cold cream to nourish and cherish it. Another lady suggested that he ought to have waited until he got to Belgium before letting it grow, as he could then have called it "Brussels sprouts." This was the first "hirsute effort" he had ever made, and he was very proud of it.

We happened to be in Malta during the carnival. The streets were filled wth people. It looked as if all the inhabitants of the island had turned out, so great was the crowd. Scores of masqueraders appeared in grotesque costumes, and there was a perfect saturnalia of fun and frolic, battles of candy, flowers, paper and confetti. We were bombarded on all sides. Paper streamers were thrown from the streets over the heads of people in carriages, and those in the vehicles retaliated by pelting others on the side walks with bouquets and confections. The boys, beating drums and blowing horns, reminded us of our Christmas; every one was jolly, full of merriment and laughter. It was a noisy, but good-natured and well-behaved crowd, and we enjoyed their frivolities immensely.

The Cathedral Church of St. Paul is built upon the supposed site of the house in which the great Apostle is said to have preached when on this island. It contains what is believed by many to be a perfect picture of the old saint. St. Paul's Bay is identified as the place "where two seas met," and a statue of the Apostle stands there.

It is related in Acts that "When Paul had gathered a bundle of sticks and laid them on the fire, there came a viper out of the heat and fastened on his hand." This would lead to the inference that in those days there were serpents at Malta, but none can be found there now. A popular tradition says that Paul put a curse upon them and they all died.

At the point at which St. Paul is supposed to have landed is built St. Paul's Tower and nearby stands a chapel, with paintings representing the shipwreck of that inspired man.

The island is dominated by priests, there being two thousand, or one to every twenty families, and yet the people are very ignorant, as only one-tenth of them are able to read and write.

We drove to the Garden of St. Sebastian, a lovely place, where we bought and ate most luscious oranges fresh from the trees.

And now again we take ship and plough our way through the waters of the Mediterranean. We before had no conception it was such an extensive body of water; its appearance on the map and its stated length and width afford no idea of its size. The Mediterranean has to be seen and traversed in order for one to realize its vast dimensions.

For two days after leaving Malta we continue our course until we find ourselves in the blue waters of the Ægean Sea, catching an occasional glimpse of some Greek island, with its sloping sides, or some green valley dotted with the white houses of a fishing village. As we draw nearer, we discern the ruins of the Temple of Athena, which for so many centuries has crowned the rocky promontory of the Acropolis. These are—

> "The Isles of Greece, the Isles of Greece!
> Where burning Sappho loved and sung,
> Where grew the arts of war and peace,
> Where Delos rose and Phœbus sprung!"

Now we are in the Saronic Gulf and soon we see the shores of Salamis on one side, while on the other the eye distinctly beholds the Acropolis. Ahead of us before we turn to enter the harbor is the Strait of Salamis, and beyond are the Bay of Eleusis and the "City of the Mysteries." In the little bay on the left, nearly 500 years B. C., the Greek fleet under Themistocles and Eurybiades, gained a great victory over the Persian armada. We enter Phalerum Bay, land and proceed four miles in carriages and—

> "Athens, the eye of Greece, mother of arts
> And of eloquence

lies before us. The mountain to the east is Hymettus, called the Mountain of the Bees, on account of the large quantity of honey produced there by these busy little insects. We are now on classic ground, which appeals profoundly to every one at all imbued with love and admiration for the ancient in art, literature and sculpture. Nor do we forget that the germ of democracy planted by the Athenians, and watered with their blood, has been a potent force in the freedom of the human race. This is indeed the—

> "Clime of the unforgotten brave!
> Whose land from plain to mountain cave
> Was Freedom's home or Glory's grave!"

Not far distant lies Marathon, where 10,000 Athenians defeated Darius with his 100,000 Persians. No occasion in the world's history was fraught with more far-reaching consequences than the day on which this great battle was fought and won. The barbarians of the East were driven back, and the civilization of the Western world was saved.

Before landing we are transferred from our ship to tugs, and from tugs to small boats. The country, as outlined from the steamer, is barren of timber and uninviting in appearance; but after the traveler touches the soil this impression is soon dispelled by the verdant green of the hills, for is not this the place—

> "Where the virgins are as soft as the roses they twine
> And all, save the spirit of man, is divine?"

The singular costumes of the country, the curious signs—all in Greek letters—over the stores and the incomprehensible jargon produce strange impressions and remind one of the confusion of tongues at the Tower of Babel. The police appear dressed like ballet girls, with a blue petticoat coming down to their knees, white tights and shoes that turn up at the toes and have a fringe at the end. Each "cop" wears a red fez and a belt with a holster containing an ancient and cumbersome-looking pistol, while a cheese-knife sword dangles about his knees. They are unique—these Grecian policemen—but not very formidable in appearance.

The carts used in transporting goods are singular-looking contrivances, and it must have taken a good deal of time, thought and ingenuity to have contrived anything so uncomfortable and inconvenient both for man and beast.

The population is cosmopolitan in character, all nations being represented, with even a sprinkling of the ubiquitous American.

A short distance from our landing stands the Theseum, the best preserved edifice in ancient Greece. A good deal of the frieze over the pilasters and columns is well-nigh gone, yet the massive solidity of its construction, the golden yellow of the weather-beaten Pentelic marble and the grace of the Doric columns are very impressive.

But the chief glory of Athens is the Acropolis and the Parthenon, rising over the city like a crown of glory, from the summits of which a magnificent view of the city and the bay is obtained. The Acropolis is a precipitous rock which towers 260 feet above the city and extends about 1,000 feet east and west and 400 in its greatest width. It was the site of the earliest Athens known to history and was a strong fortification. For a long period the palace of the King stood on it.

Among the other monuments of the Acropolis are the Temple of Athena and the Temple of Wingless Victory. The slopes of the Acropolis once were occupied by the Dionystic Theatre and other buildings. The Parthenon was a cathedral and afterwards a mosque, while the Proplyaea was a government building. It was nearly destroyed by an explosion of gunpowder induced by lightning. The Parthenon also was partially ruined by gunpowder during the Venetian siege.

On the north side of the Acropolis is the beautiful Erechtheum, with its famous porch of the Maidens—the Caryatids—and remarkable for its complex and architectural variety, as well as for its technical perfection. It originally included a shrine to Athena Polias (as guardian to the city), altars to several other deities and the tomb of Erechtheus (whence its name).

The rich entabulature of the famous Porch of Caryatids rests—or formerly rested—on the heads of six female figures, ranking among the world's finest works of art. One of these figures, as were other marbles, was taken to England by Lord Elgin. The missing statue is now represented by one in terra cotta. In architecture the Erechtheum was Ionic.

The climb to the Acropolis is no easy task, and many of our party give out, while some have to rest and take it in easy stages. We go up the sloping west side of the rock, mounting great steps, such as have doubtless existed for thousands of years. To the left once stood the colossal statue of Athena Promachus, wrought by Phidias and composed of the spoils of the Persians captured at Marathon. It was sixty-six feet in height and the figure was clad in full armor. Her lance-head served as a landmark to approaching mariners. This statue has long since disappeared.

As we stand on the plateau we are in the midst of magnificent ruins—marble columns, fallen pillars, elegant frieze work, entabulatures of graceful columns, architraves, fractured pilasters, crumbling cornices and beautiful ornamentations—yea, acres of ruins, grand and glorious even in their overthrow. What must the place have been in its pristine grandeur and glory! It must have taken centuries of time and millions of money to rear these splendid structures. And a superb genius such as modern art has not evolved, must have conceived, planned and erected the buildings. Think of it—this hill was a fortified stronghold 1,000 years before the birth of Christ.

We next turn to the right and visit the little Temple of Athena Nike, the "Wingless Victory," a most perfect and fascinating Ionic structure, which was restored some seventy years.

Opposite us across the road by which we came, is the lower hill of the Areopagus, separated by a considerable depression of ground. The rock is rugged and bare; but a few steps are cut in the stone to assist in the ascent. Upon this hill sat the famous court of the same name, which exercised a general censorship over the affairs of the city and had jurisdiction in cases of life and death.

From the slope of the Areopagus, or Hill of Mars, St. Paul is said to have delivered his address (Acts XVII). As we stood upon the spot where it is supposed the great apostle stood when he spoke to the Athenians about "the unknown God," the significance of the place and its environments profoundly impressed me. I fancied Paul with his eyes resting on the Acropolis itself and with the Parthenon in full view—that Parthenon in which the religion of the Greeks was taught. Near by was the Temple of Olympian Zeus and close at hand was the Theseum erected to Vulcan, or the God of Fire. And doubtless on his way to Mars Hill the Apostle saw on the roadside the altar to the unknown God.

A little to the left we see the Hill of the Pnyx, a great artificial area about 400 by 200 feet, on whose slopes is the large terrace which formed the forum or place of assembly of the Athenians, as well as the rock "bema," from which the orators addressed them.

From this forum Demosthenes uttered his famous

"Philippics," and his great orations. Here, too, doubtless the virtuous Socrates, in vain, pleaded for his life. From this rock the people were aroused by the demagogue to deeds of infamy and injustice, as well as to acts of exalted patriotism, and true bravery.

Within sight of the Pnyx we behold on the slopes of the Museum Hill the doors that lead into the chambers cut in the living rock, in which Socrates was imprisoned, and where he drank, with the stoicism of the philosopher and the resignation of a believer in the true God, the fatal hemlock.

My friend, Dr. John D. Jordon, in one of his letters kindly placed at my disposal, says:

"Just beyond the Temple of Theseus is the cemetery in which many of the ancients are buried. Twenty-five hundred years some of them have slept here. The ancient tombs are very peculiar. On one monument I saw a huge bull, on another a lion, on another a bear, and on another a hound, standing guard over the grave. On some of the tombs may be seen husband and wife, standing with hands clasped in lingering farewell. There is no looking up looking up or pointing heavenward, as is so often seen in American cemeteries. Alas, for all their art, learning and oratory when the Greeks had such poor theology!"

The ancient Stadium, where the Olympic games were played, was entirely destroyed by modern vandalism, but through the noble generosity of a Greek gentleman of wealth living at Alexandria, it has recently been restored, and is now one of the most magnificent structures of its kind in existence. It was laid out in a natural hollow between two hills, the complete length of the course being 670 feet. The restoration of the Stadium cost half a million dollars. It is semi-amphitheatrical in shape, tier above tier of solid white marble seats, with steps at regular intervals for egress and ingress. The seating capacity is over 50,000. We also visit the Art Museum, which contains the most valuable collection of art treasures in the way of statues, marbles and paintings in all Greece.

Our first night in Athens is lovely, for the weather is warm and pleasant and the stars shine brightly, while

> "Towering above
> In her lightest noon,
> The emerald moon
> Blushes with love."

Byron, in one of his poetical rhapsodies, says of Greece:

> "Know ye the land where the cypress and myrtle,
> Are emblems of deeds that are done in their clime;
> Where the rage of the vulture, the love of the turtle,
> Now melt into sorrow, now madden to crime?"

The same poet also pays a glowing tribute to the Grecian beauties in his famous "Maid of Athens." I have looked in vain for her counterpart, but without success. In sooth, I am tempted to think that while swayed by the Muse, Byron used that license peculiar to his tribe, or that the lovely maid was a figment of his fancy—a creature of his fervid imagination.

Byron—if I may quote him still another time—also wrote that the Greece of his day was

> "Greece, but living Greece no more."

And whilst it is true she has at present no Sappho, Anacreon or Pindar in poetry; no warriors such as Leonidas, Themistocles, Aristides and Cimon; no such lawmakers as Lycurgus, Draco and Solon; no philosophers of the Anaxagorian or Socratian order; no statesman like Pericles and Demosthenes, and no Phidias in art, she can still point to Marathon, Thermoplylae, Salamis and Plataea for inspiration, embalming as they do a most glorious past. We can but believe that there still burns in the hearts of her people a fire of liberty, that may yet be kindled into a flame that will arouse them from their humiliation and make their altars blaze again with their wonted fires of freedom.

Modern Athens is forging to the front. In 1870 it had a population of 45,000. To-day it has a population of 150,000. The city has an electric road, fine public buildings and good hotels. There are also many manufactories in the city. I suspect that these are chiefly occupied in the making of antiques for American and other tourists.

The bread for sale on the streets here is patterned after the ancient discus and is carried around strung on sticks. We noticed shoemakers and blacksmiths plying their vocations on the public thoroughfares and without shelter in the way of a house.

We visited the King's Palace. The throne is a gorgeous affair and the ball-room, with its splendid chandeliers, paintings and antiques, is very beautiful; at night when lighted up it presents a most magnificent appearance. One of the ladies of our party, we regret to say, attempted to seat herself upon the throne of His Majesty, George, but she was quickly told by the guide that this was not permitted. There are always those in every party who, like "fools, rush in where angels fear to tread."

In Athens we witnessed another funeral. The decedent was a woman, whose body, exposed in a coffin lying on a litter, was followed by two mourners.

Perley, on this trip, developed a mania for postal cards that seemed insatiable. He bought them at every place he stopped, after having previously acquired nearly all the ship's barber possessed. He counted them twenty times a day and then recounted them at night. When not rattling or sleeping he could always be found going over his cards. He should have conferred on him the title, "Count Perley."

Leaving Athens we steamed through the Dardanelles, or Hellespont, and through the Sea of Marmora, into the Bosphorus and anchored opposite the Golden Horn and Constantinople.

"The Thirteenth Century Chronicle" describes Constantinople as being "The eye of the world, the ornament of nations, the fairest sight on earth." Well, externally this is true. From a distance its graceful minarets, magnificent domes, beautiful white palaces and quaint buildings are very attractive; but closer inspection proves that it is like unto "whited sepulchres, which, indeed, appear beautiful outward, but are within full of dead men's bones and of all uncleanliness."

On the shores of the Hellespont was situated the tower in which dwelt Hero. Here she nightly displayed from the casement as a beacon "her bright and ruddy torch" by which Leander steered his course—

> "For that was love's own sign and beacon guide
> Across the Hellespont's wide weary space,
> Wherein he nightly struggled with the tide;
> Look, what a red it forges on her face,
> As if she blushed at holding such a light,
> Even in the presence of the night."

Byron says Leander went "To woo, and, Lord knows what besides." In one of these expeditions he lost his life. Byron, for "glory," performed the same feat.

The shores along the Bosphorus are very beautiful—a panorama of palaces, mosques and private dwellings, interspersed with verdant pastures and gently sloping hillsides clothed with flowers or shrubbery.

Many of the hills fairly bristle with artillery, and are crowned with heavy fortifications, this being the stronghold of His Majesty, the Sultan. The widest point is about two miles and the narrowest eight hundred yards, so it is, of course, easily defended.

Constantinople has a population of 1,125,000, not including the dogs. It is the Dogopolis of the world. I would designate it as the city of the three D's, signifying dirt, dogs and darkness. The streets are the filthiest I have ever seen, as the town has no sewerage system. Everything is dumped into the public highways, and the garbage lies in monumental piles, which are seldom removed. The dogs are kept as public scavengers. There are 100,000 in the city, of all ages, sizes and sexes—

"Both mongrel, puppy, whelp and hound,
And curs of low degree."

These pests sleep all day and howl and bark all night. They are not canines of the famous "old dog Tray" order, "ever faithful and kind, whom grief could not drive away," nor do they belong to the same courageous stock as the celebrated Sancho, the Bagman's dog, who "would carry and fetch and run after a stick." It is written of Sancho—

"He could well understand
The word of command,
And appear to doze
With a crust on his nose."

The dogs of Constantinople are a stupid looking set, with wolfish faces, something like those of the coyotes of our prairies. They evidently descended from the wolves that anciently wandered over Turkey before civilization. These animals answer to no name; they recognize no owner or master; they wag no tail in friendly recognition.

No one pats their heads in kindly greeting. They belong to the public—they are tolerated, but not loved, and are recognized as city scavengers. They lie on the sidewalks (differing from men, who lie anywhere), on the door steps, in the windows and on the curbstones; yet no one dares harm them, it being against the law to do so. The killing of a man is punishable with three years' imprisonment; the slaughter of a dog with seven years. So the killing of a dog in Constantinople is a *dog*-matic proposition and terribly illogical. One certainly does not wish to discuss it with the legal authorities.

Constantinople is surely the *doggonest* city in the world—a canine paradise—where the "purps" can lie down under any one's vine, fig tree, veranda or fence without molestation or disturbance, and "none shall make them afraid." The very air is impregnated with the odor of dogs, the streets saturated with their effluvia, the eye offended with their unsightly appearance and the ear shocked with their howls and barks. All days here are dog days.

On the arrival of our ship at Constantinople we were met by the only Shriner in the city, and by the Junior Warden of the only Masonic Lodge, who came aboard, presented us (the Masons) with a beautiful Masonic emblem and invited us to visit their lodge that night and see "the work."

As president of the Masonic Association of the Arabic I accepted the invitation. Some forty of us from the different State jurisdictions left the vessel about 8:30 o'clock and were soon carried to the city, where we were met by guides. The distance was probably half a mile, but as the streets are very dark, there being no electric lights, lamps very far apart, the way dirty, the rocks slippery and the declivities on an angle of about forty-five degrees, it was, both literally and figuratively, an uphill business. When we finally reached the lodge room we were panting like lizards and covered with perspiration.

The lodge is English and the only one in the Turkish Empire. It may sound curious to the Masons of this country when I state that as president of the association I was accepted without examination as to signs, grips or words, and upon my vouching for the entire party, all my companions were admitted. We had the pleasure of seeing the work done in one of the degrees.

After the lodge closed we were conducted to the finest hotel in the city where a nice lunch was served, with beer, wine, champagne, highballs and cocktails. We had many toasts, the first, of course, to His Majesty, the Sultan, the next to King Edward and the third to Roosevelt. Our entertainers were a jolly set of Johnnies, and expressed great affection and good will for Brother Jonathan.

We were, to our profound gratification, provided with hacks on our return trip. I do not know whether our fraters feared we might be unable to navigate, and might "fall by the wayside" after our libations, or whether they feared we might be devoured by the dogs; but suffice it to say, we drove through dark and filthy thoroughfares, followed by a yelping pack, whose barks were echoed and answered from every street, byway and alley, by every kennel in Constantinople. We reached our ship in the small hours of the morning.

One would naturally suppose that when a bone was thrown into the streets or a waiter emptied in front of the house, there would be a mad rush of dogs—a charge equal to that at Balakava—but notwithstanding the fact that the tail-waggers of Constantinople are a stupid looking set, they are said to be very intelligent, which brings forcibly to my mind the old Roman saying, *ne crede colori*.

Whether these dogs are governed by a "boss," as most of our American municipalities are, or by a king or president, I do not know, but it is said that there is no bone of contention between them—no graft and no struggle for spoils. As individuals, these dogs, of course, have troubles of their own—their personal loves, quarrels, barks, snarls and fights. I saw many battle-scarred veterans, earless, tailless and partly blind; also mathematical curs, many navigating by the rule of three.

Whatever may be the character of the dogocracy of Constantinople, it is perfect and complete. The city is divided into wards or sections by some king dog, or by some unwritten but recognized law, and no dog of one section is allowed to trespass upon the preserves of another.

The first invasion of another's territory is punished by having the ears gnawed off and the second offense by death. This is *dog*-matism with a vengeance, but it is effective.

I was told that this rule or dog law has been in existence for centuries. An English gentleman, who has lived in Constantinople for many years, informed me that there is a pack that regularly meets an express train daily to get the fragments from the dining cars. No other pack but this meets the train, and it never fails to show up, summer or winter, rain or shine. If these dogs should contract hydrophobia I fancy the people would have an awful time.

The city of Constantinople was founded in the seventh century B. C. by the Greeks. It was on the Asiatic side of the Bosphorus and was known for more than a thousand years as Chalcedon. A new settlement was made later on the triangle which the Golden Horn forms at its junction with the Bosphorus, and was called Byzantium. The name remained Byzantium until changed to Constantinople in honor of Constantine.

These shores have many legends attached to them—

legends that antedate the dawn of authentic history. The Bosphorus derived its name from the divine (bos) bull, which carried Europa across in safety. There are also fables about the Golden Fleece, the Harpies, Apollo, Pan and Aphrodite.

Darius, on his expedition against Greece, captured the city, and Xerxes built the first pontoon or bridge of boats across the Hellespont in order that his vast army might cross over.

The Macedonians, under Philip, attempted to capture the city by night, but the moon appearing through the clouds, revealed the enemy to the defenders, hence the adoption of the crescent by the Turks. This emblem was afterwards adopted by the followers of the prophet.

The city has suffered many sieges and assaults from Goth, German and Moslem. To-day in Stamboul may be seen a nameless grave, secretly revered by the Greeks, because it contains the remains of the last Constantine, who threw himself in the breach made in the walls by Moslem cannon when the final assault occurred, and there perished. Riding in triumph through the Hippodrome Mohammed, with his mace, struck off the head of one of the brazen serpents that the first Constantine had taken from Delphi, commemorative of the defeat of Xerxes.

The most attractive building in the city is the mosque of Sancta Sophia, the great cathedral of Constantine and Justinian. It is a magnificent pile, and its marble floor is covered with thousands of dollars' worth of rich rugs. No one is allowed to enter its sacred precincts unless barefooted or slipper-shod. On the occasion of our visit I happened to get a pair of slippers that were too large for me. The struggles I made to shuffle along and keep them on were amusing to others, but quite embarrassing to me. One old fellow, in spite of his efforts, got one slipper off at nearly every step, and was finally ordered out for profaning the temple.

This superb building cost $64,000,000, and was completed in the year 537. It is said that when Mohammed entered the city in triupmh he rode his horse into Sancta Sophia. The print of his bloody hand is shown high up on the wall, but no explanation is given as to how a man, even on horseback, could reach that elevation.

This beautiful edifice is the abode of thousands of pigeons, which are allowed free access to all parts of the interior, and, consequently create a good deal of filth. The pigeon is sacred with the followers of the prophet, owing to the tradition that Mohammed, when in great distress, was fed by these birds, just as Elijah is said to have been fed by the ravens.

Near Seraglio Point Constantine erected his Cathedral Church (326) and consecrated it, not to an inferior saint, but to the Lord Himself, the Divine "Wisdom" of Proverbs viii.—the Hagia Sophia. The church was destroyed by fire in 404. It was rebuilt with such magnificence by Justinian, that when it was finished he entered the completed edifice exclaiming, "Solomon, I have conquered thee." The great dome rises 180 feet from the floor and presents a most impressive and imposing appearance. Some of the splendid columns used in this building came from the Temple of Diana at Ephesus.

It is indeed sad to think that this splendid structure, erected originally by Constantine, the first Christian Roman Emperor, should have become a Turkish mosque.

There are many other mosques in the city. The Mosque of Ahmed I. is very fine with its six graceful, towering minarets. Next comes the Mosque of Mohammed, the Conqueror, and then the Mosaic Mosque, though there are still others of less import.

In the Treasury building is the celebrated Persian throne made of beaten gold and ornamented with rubies and emeralds. This was captured in 1514 by Selim I. In this building is also the emerald referred to by Lew Wallace in his "Prince of India."

The Imperial Museum contains many archæological treasures, notably the Sidon Sarcophagi, from the city of that name, the oldest town of Phoenicia. It also contains colections from Greece, Rome and Jerusalem. Another sarcophagus, called "The Weepers," shows eighteen women, each in a different attitude of grief. The Alexander Sarcophagus of Pentelic marble is regarded as the finest sample of Greek art in existence, and is in a fine state of preservation. It has carved upon it battle and hunting scenes of exquisite design and workmanship. The Tabnith Sarcophagus, which was found to contain the withered body of Tabnith, a Sidonian King, is supposed to have been made in Memphis the fourth century before Christ and sent to Sidon.

Notwithstanding the following inscription it was moved: "If you raise the cover, may you have no posterity among the living nor any bed among the dead." But the warning served no purpose and has not been respected, as has the imprecation written by Shakespeare on his tomb.

Many remains of the old walls are to be seen, as well as some of the great subterranean cisterns that supplied Constantinople with water when besieged.

The Grand Bazaar is a town in itself and contains, it is said, 700 stores, all under one roof or numerous cupolas, through which the sun never penetrates. The veiled women, attended by eunuchs, the vast crowds of people from different countries, the great variety of Oriental wares and the incomprehensible jargon all serve to make an engrossing and bewildering scene. Perley and "The Young Voyager" could not resist the temptation to buy some of the curiously shaped Turkish swords.

Among the novelties extensively purchased here, particularly by the ladies, is that delicious confection known as "Turkish delight," the choicest of the sweets of the Orient. The men also buy largely of Turkish cigarettes.

Many curious sights strike one's eye in this city. The invariable headgear of the Turk is the fez, a most uncomfortable covering for the cranium, as it is no protection against either sun or rain. The religion of the prophet requires that the Turk shall wear it, and after death the fez rests in stone over the slab that stands at the head of his grave. Every Turk wears a fez, but every one who wears a fez is not a Turk.

Another religious law requires that Turkish ladies shall cover their faces in the street, but from the glimpses I got I think it quite unnecessary, as they are not very attractive. Turks are not allowed by their religion to marry one of another religion. It sometimes happens, however, that a man of another creed falls so much in love with a Turkish beauty that he even turns Turk to get her. This is a simple process. A small vein is opened or a cut made in the flesh and a little blood allowed to flow, but woe to the fellow if he recants. The Sultan asks for his head, and as the Sultan's will is law he gets what he calls for.

The head cover of the Turkish ladies is called, in the Turkish language, "yoshmok." Theological students are designated by a white band or turban around the fez. The priests who wear green turbans have made the pilgrimage to Mecca and are regarded with more reverence than the ordinary priest.

Turkish women dress chiefly in black, but colors are

permissible. The bright red head dress of the Turk, mingling with the peculiar clothes of the Armenian, the quaint costumes of the Greek and of other nations, make the streets quite lievly and the scene an animated one.

In Spain and Italy the miserable little donkey is the beast of burden, but here it is man himself. The Turkish carrier is called "Hamal." He wears a leather hump on his back to facilitate his carrying immense loads. We saw men staggering under burdens weighing several hundred pounds and bent nearly double. Perspiration was pouring down their livid faces, while every muscle and nerve were strained to its utmost tension.

A couple of these men carry a barrel weighing 500 pounds suspended between two poles resting on their shoulders. Fresh meats strung on poles are hawked about the thoroughfares and bread, circular in shape, is peddled at the street corners.

As the Turkish government does not hesitate to open letters coming through its mails, Great Britain, Germany, Italy and other nations have post-offices of their own and mail and distribute the letters sent to and received by their subjects. This concession was granted under the Berlin treaty.

The panoramic view from the Arabic was fine. The shores of the Bosphorus are lined with the palaces of the Sultan. He has twenty-two in all, and we suppose a number of wives in each. It is understood he never sleeps two nights successively in the same bed. The Sultan has 360 wives. When it was asked why he did not have 365, or one for every day in the year, Dr. Jordan very ungallantly replied, "Do you not think His Majesty needs a little peace and rest?"

Whenever the ruler of another country notifies His Majesty that he will pay him a visit the Sultan has a palace built especially for the accommodation of his guest.

A magnificent structure was pointed out as having been built at a cost of many thousands for the King of Italy. This palace was occupied only four days by the royal guest, and still remains vacant, but is guarded by military. Along the shores are the summer hotels and palaces of the representatives of various nations.

The Shah of Persia had one built especially for his representative. The governments of England, France, Germany and other nations each have princely edifices for their ministers and ambassadors. Many wealthy merchants likewise have their summer residences and villas along the shores of the Bosphorus.

The city of Constantinople is divided by the Bosphorus and the Golden Horn into three parts—Galata and Pera, north of the Golden Horn, occupied chiefly by Europeans; Stamboul, the old city in which the Turk predominates, and Scutari, on the Asiatic side, which is cosmopolitan.

The Galata bridge, as a work of art, is a poor affair, but the crowds that cross and recross it equal, if they do not surpass, the tide of humanity that goes over old London bridge. Here we see people from every nation, clad in all kinds of costumes of every color, riding, walking, begging, laughing and crying; and, to add to the hurly burly, fakirs offering all kinds of curios for sale and exhibiting signs and placards in many languages, appeal to you.

We steamed up the Bosphorus into the Black Sea beyond Robert College, an American missionary school, where we were saluted as we passed, both going and returning, with cheers and waving of flags and handkerchiefs by the scholars and inmates.

The college is situated on the European side of the Bosphorus, a few miles from Constantinople. It was founded in 1863 and is doing a wonderful work. The students number about 300, with a list of graduates numbering about 400, and partial course students nearly 2,500. Its property and endowments are valued at $450,000.

The students are mostly Armenians, Greeks and Bulgarians. The college, through its charter, is a part of the University of New York. Mr. Robert gave $30,000 towards the foundation of this mission. It is now self-supporting and is a magnificent monument of Christian education.

The same may be said of the American School for Girls at Scutari, on the Asiatic side, which is being conducted by Americans. Members of the Alumnae of this college visited the Arabic the night before we left and gave a delightful entertainment of songs and recitations. It was the privilege of the tourists to contribute to the fund for the support of this institution. This school has a faculty of thirty-one, chiefly Americans, and about 160 students. It is religious but non-sectarian.

We left the city of Constantinople without regret and have no desire to see it again. When we think of it hereafter the place will be associated with recollections of nameless odors and unsightly scenes, while discordant sounds will arise in our ears. But let me say, apropos of Constantinople, that we were impressed with the profundity and apparent sincerity of the Turks in their religion. Their belief is that "prayers are better than sleep." Five times a day the faithful prostrates himself with his face towards Mecca. The Muezzin's call to prayer is frequently heard from the minarets of the mosques. Translated, it is as follows:

"God is great. (Repeated four times.)
I bear witness that there is no God but God (repeated twice);
Come to prayers, come to prayers;
Come to salvation, come to salvation;
God is great; there is no other God but God."

The Sultan is not only a political autocrat, but also the religious head of Islam; yet notwithstanding the fact that it is against Moslem law for foreigners to have places for their worship, there are in Constantinople a Bulgarian Church, a Church of England, a Jewish Mission Chapel, a Free Church of Scotland, and the American Board (Congregational).

In their Oriental language, Smyrna, the chief town of Asia Minor, is called by the Asiatics "The lovely, the ornament of Asia." On arriving we saw the city spread out before us like a picture, beginning at the margin of the bay and climbing the hills in a series of terraces, with high ranges of mountains in the background. The town's dark groves of cypress, its painted balconies, the minarets of its mosques and its church spires make a beautiful and alluring picture.

Smyrna is a city of considerable size, having a population of some 225,000. It was the home of the fabled Croesus, whose name was the synonym for wealth before the infamous American combines and trusts created the Rockefellers and Carnegies *et id omne genus.*

Charles Dudley Warner has characterized Smyrna as an "Asiatic city with a European face; it produces nothing and exchanges everything; it is hospitable to all religions and conspicuous for none, and it is the paradise of the Turk, the home of luxury and of beautiful women." It is also one of the seven cities claiming to be the birthplace of Homer.

Although the followers of Christ were first called Christians at Antioch, Christianity took deep root here, and Smyrna became one of the seven churches referred to in the Book of Revelations. Here, too, Polycarp, the second Bishop of Smyrna, suffered martyrdom. His remains are buried here. The Bishop's last words, when pressed to recant his faith in Christ, have become famous—"Eighty and six years have I served Him, and He has never done me wrong; how then can I blaspheme my King that saved me." These noble utterances came from his lips about 155 A. D.

After many conflicts between Arabs and Turks on the one side and the Knights of Malta on the other, Smyrna passed into the hands of the Turks, who still retain it.

There are two railroads giving access to the interior of the country. This, combined with its beautiful harbor, makes it a prominent and wealthy city. But these innovations of railroads and electric street cars have not retired into innocuous desuetude the old "ship of the desert," of whom it may be truly said—

> "Steam may come and steam may go,
> But ye camel goes on forever"—

for most of the merchandise to this day finds its way into the city on the backs of these patient beasts, and in the streets may be seen caravans laden with goods. Evolution has not reached the camel.

The East is not famous for its iconoclastic ideas. The Oriental folk are noted for being a people opposed to change, and are very much on "the-same-yesterday-and-to-day-and-forever" order.

Smyrna is known the world over for its figs and dates; it is also celebrated for its raisins, opium, spices, silks, sponges and especially for its Oriental rugs, carpets and embroideries. Here, as elsewhere over the world, can be seen the ancient Roman aqueducts, built in the third century before Christ, which brought water from a spot fifteen miles distant.

The bazaars, while not so extensive as those of Constantinople, yet contain quite a variety of wares of all

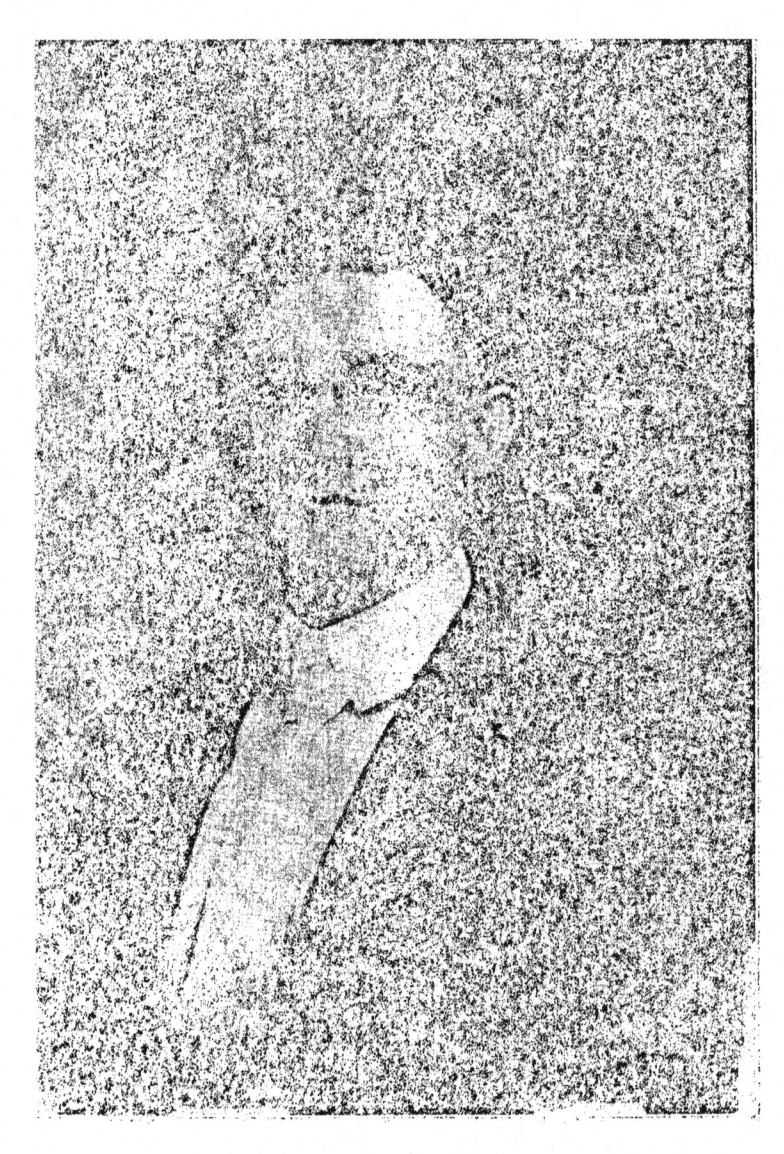

HARRY TALMAN MOORE ("THE YOUNG VOYAGER").

into innocuous desue
whom it may be trul

steam m:
But ye ca

for most of the merc
the city the back
-treets may be seen c
has not reached the

The East is not fa
Oriental folk are n
change, and are ve
to-day and forever"

Sunset is known
it is also celebrated
sponges and especia

HARRY TALMAN MOORE ("THE YOUNG VOYAGER").

kinds, and prices are more reasonable than in Constantinople. Smyrna is a great market for rugs. There are said to be about 5,000 persons engaged in the manufacture of carpets and rugs in the city. Many of our ladies bought themselves rich—or rather poor—in the rug line. Over forty mosques rise heavenward in the city and there are quite a number of Greek, Roman, Armenian and other churches in the city. There is also an American mission in Smyrna and an American college for boys and girls.

From Smyrna we journeyed to Ephesus. Going to the railroad station we took street cars drawn by horses, with traces made of ropes.

The distance from Smyrna to Ephesus is about fifty miles, and the compartment cars are very comfortable. Most of the route is along a beautiful valley, with lovely verdure and blooming fruit trees. We saw the peasants at work in the fields, and as we beheld them scattering the seed the parable of the sower came to mind, for there he was before us. "Behold a sower went forth to sow," as he did when our Lord uttered this beautiful allegory.

The land is quite fertile. We saw fine wheat, figs, olives, dates, grapes and almonds, as well as the so-called English walnut, growing in profusion, while the hills in the background cast shifting shadows over the landscape in a beautiful hide-and-seek fashion, that accentuated its beauties and added to the picturesqueness of the scene.

Licorice root is also grown here quite extensively, this being the largest market in the world for this product. And here, too, we found the agent for that great octopus, the American Tobacco Company, negotiating for the whole output, and thus shutting off competition and driving another nail into the coffin of individual enterprise and personal initiative.

The city of Ephesus of to-day is of very small propositions. Its ruins, its historic reputation and its sacerdotal memories are its chief attractions.

Arriving at the station, where there are a few scattered houses, we were told that the ancient site of the city is about a mile off, but an Asiatic mile and an American mile are two distinct and different propositions; in other words, we concluded the distance was about four miles, interspersed with rocks, stones, mud and the debris of ancient temples, up hill and down, into boggy land.

We, however, got over the ground very well, considering we met with a stiff breeze from the Arctic regions or some other cold source.

The first ruin we came to was that of St. John's Church, of which nothing now remains save a few pillars and masses of cemented brick and stone. Between one portion of the walls a large tree has grown. It is unpleasantly suggestive of the many divisions in the Church. We next went past the Cave of the Seven Sleepers, whose repose we made no attempt to disturb. After this we viewed the remains of the Gymnasium, and beyond, a trench full of white marble blocks, the remnants of a Roman temple. Next we saw the Circular Temple, erroneously called the Tomb of St. Luke. Farther on were the ruins of the Wool Market, as shown by the inscriptions found there.

The most interesting of all the ruins now presented themselves—the theatre mentioned in the nineteenth chapter of Acts. As we stood within the circuit of its marble walls, the marble seats rising in tiers one above the other on each side, we could imagine the scene so graphically described between St. Paul and Demetrius, the "silversmith, which made silver shrines for Diana" that "brought no small gain unto the craftsmen." Demetrius was afraid Paul's teaching would put him out of business, for the former represented a craft that sold temple models to the people.

Here Paul pleaded for two hours for a hearing, but the rabble drowned his voice with the cry, "Great is Diana of the Ephesians," in the same way as the modern patriot's voice is sometimes hushed by the vulgar herd. The seating capacity of the building was 25,000 persons. Among the other ruins are the Greek Tower, or Prison of St. Paul, the church in which the third Ecumenical Conference was held (481).

Last of all we went to the ruins of the Temple of Diana itself, which was one of the seven wonders of the world, and was considered one of the most magnificent structures of ancient times. Pliny tells us that it was 425 feet long and 225 wide, and that 127 columns gave support to the roof. Only the remains of the substructure and of the pavement are now left.

There are a great mass of marble fragments, and here one of our ministers—a man of an archæological turn of mind—came to grief. He attempted to conceal a fragment of marble under his coat and was arrested by the guard, but was eventually released. Many of the marbles of this splendid building have been carried to the British Museum.

After viewing these ruins in a piercing cold wind, which chilled us to the marrow, "The Young Voyager" and the writer decided to make the return trip on a donkey, so I hired one a little larger than the ordinary goat. The diminutive creature would doubtless have protested at the imposition, as did Balaam's beast, had he been endowed with the power of speech. But as he could utter no complaints, he trotted along very nicely, picking his steps gracefully and carefully over the rocks and stones and through mud and water, with admirable patience and caution. When within about half a mile of the station, however, he let out a blast from his trumpet that went forth with a resonant sound upon the lambent air, if not musically, certainly sonorously and with far-reaching effect. In a few seconds this blast was returned by his father, mother, brother, wife, sister and other relatives—

"For, while he spake, a braying ass did sing most loud and clear."

No sooner did the replies reach my donkey's ears expectant, than he raised his tail high in the air and started off at full gallop. In vain I screamed "Whoa," "whoa," "wah!" The more I pulled and "hollered," the faster he went, for the blasted beast did not understand English. The wind was blowing about forty miles an hour, while one of my stirrup leathers was useless. And there I was, holding on like grim death, to the donkey with one hand and with the other pressing my hat down on my ears, as my raincoat flapped in the wind like the sails of a ship in a gale. The ride of John Gilpin was nothing to compare to this Ephesus ride. Finally, we got to the station, but for several days I found it pleasant to dine at a lunch counter and to sit down as little as possible.

"The Young Voyager's" beast, whose name was "John," was a slow animal, disposed to ruminate by the roadside, picking a tuft of grass here and a thistle there. The rider protested against these dilatory movements by sundry kicks and complaints aimed at the animal's owner, who always trots along beside his beast. The owner of the donkey could not speak English, but made signs to "The Young Voyager" to grasp the animal's tail and give it a twist, which the rider did with prompt, if not satisfactory, results. This course acted like a "live wire," for his donkey started on a run with heels in the air.

"The snorting beast began to trot, which galled him in his seat,
So, 'Fair and softly John,' he cried, but 'John' he cried in vain;
That trot became a gallop soon, in spite of curb and rein;
So stooping down, as needs he must, who cannot sit upright,
He grasped the mane with both his hands, and eke with all his might."

The people seeing me in the lead, and "The Young Voyager" evidently trying to overtake me, thought we were running a race, and as we went through the village—

"The dogs did bark, the children screamed, up flew the windows all;
And every soul cried out 'Well done' as loud as he could bawl."

The result was that "The Young Voyager" also had to do penance in an upright position.

Great are the asses of Ephesus! Both of our little donkeys were like Rosinante, the famous steed of Don Quixote—poor in flesh. A strong man could have carried both, one under each arm or on his shoulders.

At Ephesus we found the fulfillment of Revelations, "I will remove thy candlestick out of its place," for not even a single place of worship of the Christians remains.

Ephesus is a mass of ruins; its harbor, where fleets once moored in safety and received and discharged cargoes, is now filled up and overgrown with weeds. Desolation broods where once was a city of considerable importance. This is evidently a visitation from God, as St. John uses the words, "Because thou hast left thy first love."

The run from Smyrna to Ephesus was made with an American locomotive. We noticed Oliver chilled plows and other Yankee machinery in use in this fertile section. Our party passed a caravan of seventy or seventy-five camels en route to distant Persia. They were laden with Syrian merchandise, which was to be exchanged for the valuable products from the hand looms of that beautiful land of Cyprus and the Queen of Sheba. It takes six months to make this journey.

Going to Smyrna from Constantinople we steamed through the Greek Archipelago, stopping in the Bay of Acree opposite Caifa and Mount Carmel. We also passed the site of ancient Troy, where our mind naturally reverted to the great epic of Homer, who recounts so graphically the ten-years' siege by the Grecians and the city's ultimate fall and destruction. Nothing but an undistinguishable mass of ruins now remains to mark the spot. We likewise steamed by the Island of Rhodes, once the headquarters of the Knights of St. John, and Cyprus, one of the largest islands of the Mediterranean. On the east we could see the Mountains of Lebanon, while Taurus appeared on the north.

Cyprus was celebrated in antiquity as the birthplace and abode of Aphrodite, the Goddess of Love and Wedlock, in Greek mythology.

The splendid cedars that flourished in the days of Hiram and Solomon, and that were used in the building and adornment of the temple, have long since disappeared, and the mountains at a distance look bleak and desolate, a cap of white resting upon their loftiest peaks.

Carmel is intimately associated with the romantic adventures of David. In this section dwelt Nabal, whose wife David married. Poor Nabal had hardly gotten cold before the ardent David wrote her a note or sent her word that he would like "to take her to him to wife." Of Abigail it might truly be said:

> "Frailty, thy name is woman!
> A little month; or ere those shoes were old,
> With which she follow'd her poor husband's body
> Like Niobe, all tears,"

And she at once consents, and becomes one of the better halves of the son of Jesse, for it is recorded in Holy Writ: "And Abigail hasted and arose, and rode upon an ass, with five damsels of hers that went with her, and she went after the messengers of David, and became his wife."

Mount Carmel is celebrated in the Old Testament as the place of residence of the Prophets Elijah and Elisha.

It was here the old prophet made that impassioned address and said unto the people: "How long halt ye between two opinions? If the Lord be God, follow Him; but if Baal, then follow him." And it is recorded, "the people answered him not a word."

The very place is pointed out where Elijah mocked the Baalites, and said to them concerning their god: "Cry aloud, for he is god; either he is talking, or he is pursuing, or he is in a journey, or peradventure he sleepeth and must be awaked."

The place of the sacrifice also is pointed out, as well as the place at the Brook Kishon, where the false prophets were slain. Over Elijah's cave in which he dwelt is built the monastery of Mount Carmel. The mountain itself is barren, but the slopes have been settled by a German colony, who make good wine from the grapes grown in their vineyards. From the ship to the shore the distance is about a mile, and we took the trip in small boats pulled by Arabs, all clad in their peculiar costume, and barefooted. They pull the oars standing up, putting one foot against the bench or seat in front of them, and the other on the bottom of the boat, which gives them good vantage ground to pull from. While working the oars the Arabs chant one of their plaintive and melancholy airs to the beat of the oars.

The greatest elevation above the town is pointed out as being the place from which the servant of Elijah, after going the seventh time, discerned "a little cloud out of the sea, like a man's hand." Guides also call the attention of strangers to the place where Jael committed her cruel and inhuman act in smiting Sisera. Beyond lies the great fertile plain of Esdraelon, where Barak and Gideon won their victories, and where Saul and Josiah fell. Jews, Gentiles, Saracens, Christians, Crusaders,

Frenchmen, Egyptians, Persians, Druses, Turks and Arabs—warriors of almost every nation—have pitched their tents in the plain of Esdraelon.

Dr. Power, in one of his letters, says: "It is a vast meadow, rich as an Illinois prairie, twenty miles in length, or more, by perhaps ten in width, largely owned by one man in Beyrout, who pays his peasant farmers a franc a day, and revels in wealth, while the poor are oppressed. The people here are beggars in a land which should blossom as the rose, because of the burden of taxation and the hard hand of the oppressor. One cannot find more fertile soil; wheat, barley, grapes, figs, olives and pomegranites yield abundantly. It is spring and the peasants are ploughing and the fields are covered with tens of thousands of lovely flowers. Our guide said: 'We do not cultivate flowers. We do not need to; God gives them.'"

CHAPTER IV.

Dr. S. D. Bartle's Description of the Holy Land—Two Days at Nazareth—Missionary Work Among Native Children—Weakness of the Turkish Government—Sea of Galilee—Scenes in the Home of Our Lord—Dr. John D. Jordan's Visit to Places Made Sacred and Historic by Christ—Nazareth of To-Day—Traditions Told the Traveler—Valley of Esdraelon—Mount of Transfiguration and Hills of Gilboa—Place of the Sacrifice—Jacob's Well and the Mount of Olives—Tomb of the Sons of Levi—Dr. F. D. Powers' Beautiful Rhapsody on Nazareth—Cradle of Religion—Pestiferous Children.

Our immediate party of three did not take the Galilee and Samaria trip. Those going on this journey left the cruise at Caifa and rejoined us later on. I submit a delightful account of this trip, written by my versatile friend, the Rev. S. D. Bartle, of Mechanicsville, Iowa. It follows:

"We, who were to take the overland trip through Galilee and Samaria, did not think much about dinner on March 7th, for we were on deck looking at the land in the distance, and at noon we landed at Caifa, under the shadow of Mount Carmel. It seemed as if the entire town had come out to meet and welcome us with their salutation for 'baksheesh,' which, being interpreted, means 'give me a present.' All the natives must have thought that the Americans were gold mines, for it was 'baksheesh' from the time we landed at Caifa until we took the steamer at Joppa for Egypt.

"Our overland trip transcended all my most glowing expectations. I have ridden over the Alps and Rockies, through the forests and over the plains of our great country, yet this trip was infinitely more fascinating than anything I had ever seen. At every turn we came face to face with realities of history more wonderful than dreams. Up on that mountain Elijah triumphed over Baal; yonder Gideon won his first victory; there Bárak defeated the army of Jabin; not far beyond Saul and Josiah met ignominious death; under that tree, or its ancestor, Jael drove the nail into Sisera's head; in that village John and James were born; this is the home of Jesus' childhood; on the horned Hattin yonder Jesus preached that wonderful 'Sermon on the Mount'; that rounded mount is Tabor; this village is Cana; we are now on the road where Jesus healed the nobleman's son; off yonder is the home of Magdalene; that queen of mountains with snowy hair is Hermon, and this is the Sea of Galilee—all these came under our observation from Caifa to Tiberias. And over all these hang the spell of a history of four thousand years.

"If a person adjust himself to the changes from the grandeur of America to his now surroundings, he can see beauty that cannot be described by pen—beauty to which justice cannot be done by paint and brush. It is a land of flowers. The cultivated ones are usually grown behind stone walls, and very few can see them; but there the wild flowers grow everywhere. To gaze upon them set my soul on fire, and I could not help but exclaim with Christ, 'that even Solomon in all his glory was not arrayed like one of these.'

The City of Nazareth.

"We spent two nights in Nazareth, a city despised by Jesus' contemporaries, but dear to the hearts of all Christendom as the home of our Redeemer's boyhood. The natural features of the town are precisely such as are pictured in the Gospel narrative; built in terraces 1,100 feet above the level of the sea on one of the rocky hills enclosing the valley basin and overtopped by precipitous heights, from which we got a most commanding view of the country from the sea to the Jordan Valley, and from Hermon to Tabor, and the southern highlands. No thoughtful man or woman can look over this territory unmoved, for here the world forces have frequently contended for the world-wide ideas in the fierce debate of battle. And many of the students of the prophets think that here is to occur the last great fight between the forces of good and evil.

"The town is certainly picturesque, many of the houses being built right up against the perpendicular rocks, and overlooking the roofs of those on the streets below. Undoubtedly most of the traditional sacred places here are apocryphal, such as the carpenter-shop of Jesus and the synagogue in which He preached, as well as other places. Yet there are certainly two places where the Holy Child did go—namely, the crags overlooking the city and the ancient fountain where the whole community for many generations has drawn its water. You cannot approach any sacred locality here without running up against the tables of money changers, and without an inglorious battle with a swarm of human mosquitoes, which sing their pestilential songs while seeking to suck a drop of your blood. Tradesmen and beggars are everywhere.

"While in this city we had the great privilege of spending the afternoon with Miss Frances E. Newton, Superintendent of the Church Missionary Society of England, which conducts several day schools here—Cana, Er-Reinen, Ma'lul, Yafa and Sharjarah. These schools are doing a grand work for the native children, and I believe that in the future, as the outcome of this great work, Palestine will be a better and cleaner land. We saw the change it made in the native homes for the better.

"In carrying on this educational work they are following very closely in the Master's footsteps, for 'He went about all Galilee, teaching.' Most probably he taught in some of these self-same villages. One scene touched our hearts as we came into a room where there were twenty-four girls from thirteen to fifteen years of age. Miss Newton asked them to sing the song of welcome. They sang it well. Here are the words:

"'Welcome to Nazareth, thrice blessed spot;
Jesus our Saviour did here fix His lot,
Shall we not venerate the very sod
That once was walked by the dear Son of God?

"'Welcome to Nazareth gladly we sing,
Home of our Shepherd, our Saviour, our King;
Welcome, yes welcome, oh! word of good cheer
To the bright land of our Saviour so dear.

"'Welcome to Nazareth, sing we to-day;
Welcome kind friends from a land far away,
Remember when home with your children so dear
To pray for the children who welcomed you here.'

"The weakness of the Turkish government is shown in an incident that happened in a village near Cana two days before we arrived there. A young man went out into the fields to plough, taking with him eight oxen. There is a village near there that has a bad name because all the people there are exceedingly wicked. Some of these people murdered the young man and stole his oxen. When the parents found their son dead in the field with his head battered to a jelly, they notified the government officials at Nazareth. Several officers were sent to find the murderers and oxen. After they discovered the oxen in this village they returned and told the parents what they had found, but added: 'We can do nothing because we are afraid of the people.' Such a government! The poor people are taxed to death, having to pay not less than 33 per cent. on all products and sometimes as high as 62 per cent.

The Sea of Galilee.

"If one comes to the Sea of Galilee expecting to find the human conditions in any way like those created in his mind by the Gospel story, he will be sadly disappointed. There is not a place made sacred by the feet of Jesus left to welcome us. The city of Tiberias, where we spent a night, was never entered by our Lord; and that alone of the once many happy towns along this shore is able to give us shelter.

"And its citizens are a wretched set. About the only thing here which seems to be alive is the wicked flea. The Arabs say that this is his capital, and that here he reaches his tallest stature. I believe them. Most all of our party carried home unmistakable proofs of his villany.

"The country on the western shore of the sea, which was the scene of the happiest period of our Saviour's ministry, is blighted beyond all description. Yet it was once, as Josephus describes it, 'an earthly paradise.' A portion of it was called, because of its natural treasures, Genesreth, which means 'garden of riches.' On these shores were flourishing towns, such as Capernaum, Bethsaida, Magdala and Tiberias, besides many happy hamlets. Its hillsides were covered with vineyards, olive orchards and fields of yellow grain. Now bare rocks, fruitless wildernesses and hot sands are there. Nearly all the people have fled, and the few who remain are, for the most part, worn and wasted by poverty and disease.

"During our eight days' overland trip there is one thing we suffered, and we shall never forget it. The water is very impure. No doubt the water is pure at the starting place, but if you saw what it went through and how careful (?) the natives were in getting it you would do as we did—go without it. For eight days I never drank one glass of water in any form—no tea, coffee, or anything else. The most of us ate our meals without anything to drink but we had all the oranges we wanted and the juice was our water. The first two or three days it seemed that we must drink but by the time we arrived in Jerusalem we did not mind it. Just as one of the boys put it, 'it was hard luck.'"

NAZARETH AND THE NAZARENES OF TO-DAY.

Some wiseacre has said, "In a multitude of counsellors there is wisdom." This trite old saw is generally regarded as true. Having this in mind, I next give the graphic account of the same trip by the Rev. John D. Jordan, D. D., of Savannah, Ga., to be followed by the narrative of Dr. F. D. Power, D. D., of Washington, D. C., who have kindly contributed the same for my use.

"NAZARETH, GALILEE, March 9th.—I greet you from the home of our Lord. I presume that this little city of 8,000 motley inhabitants looks little like the Nazareth of His day, when its reputation was so bad that it was thought that no good thing could come out of it. The general outline of the country must be pretty much as it was in His day, for it is stone. Nazareth is a city built on a hillside, which curves as a half moon, opening toward the south. There are two modern hotels here, where guests are made fairly comfortable. The Victoria is the better. Its proprietor and most of his help can speak some English. The people are chifly shepherds, craftsmen, vine dressers and farmers.

"I saw here an old-fashioned corn-mill which reminded

me of the days when I was a boy and went to mill. We saw many workshops, no doubt like the one in which our Lord worked, for the customs of the people as to dress and manner of life have not changed in all the centuries. One can hardly believe it, but it is so, and when he sees things as they are, he no longer doubts.

"There are many Christians in Nazareth, chiefly of the Greek and Latin churches, but they impressed me as little ahead of the heathen or Mohammedans. They have so much superstition and falsehood as to make them appear in great and pitiful contrast with Christians of America. They have erected their churches on the supposedly sacred places. Unfortunately, each of the two churches claims a separate and distinct spot for each incident. In one Latin Church they show the exact spot where Mary stood when the angel appeared to her and announced that she should become the mother of the Messiah. Of course, they call this the Church of the Annunciation. Back under this same church is a kitchen, claimed to be the very kitchen in which Mary did her cooking. In that kitchen is what is claimed to be the original door or gate to the Lord's workshop.

"Solemnity ceases to be serious when, a few hundred yards further on, is a Greek Church into which there gushes a great fountain of water, and they tell you it was on this spot, while taking water from the fountain, that the angel made his announcement to Mary.

"The Latins have another church, a part of which they claim is the walls of the synagogue in which our Lord preached from Isaiah LXI., 1-3, as narrated by Luke, IV., 18-19. Then they take you nearby to a place called the 'Hill of Precipitation,' where the people of this town tried to destroy Jesus after the sermon, as recorded in Luke IV., 29-32. This might impress one more favorably, but for the fact that a few hundred yards away the Greeks have a church and hill of which they tell the same story. Just how two Christian churches can tell such opposite stories, and both be infallible, I cannot determine. What miserable liars the heathen must believe us Christians to be, and this belief is not without some foundation.

AT THE FOUNTAIN.

"There is a splendid fountain or spring in Nazareth, out of which gushes great streams of water coming down from the mountain side. By this spring or fountain is the place to see the village people. They are coming and going all day, of all ages and sexes, but chiefly women and children. You see them washing their feet, hands and faces, their dirty clothes, the entrails of a goat or sheep and filling their water pots all from the same spring. What a fine, pure water they might have if they would only keep it clean!

"The same thing is true of all these towns and cities. The question arises as to what the traveler is to do for water to drink. Some do without, drinking beer or light wine, and others have the water boiled. We requested our hotel people to have care in getting the water, and then boil it for us, and it was quite good and perfectly safe. Many who claim to 'touch nothing at home' take their wines and beer freely and with apparently good relish here. Each follows his own bent and no questions are asked 'for conscience' sake.'

"We had our first view of Palestine early in the morning. Mount Hermon was sixty miles away, 11,000 feet above the sea and covered with snow. Soon Mount Carmel was in sight, then the Valley of Acre, then the towns of Acre Haifas and Cesarea. In the afternoon we landed and took carriages for Nazareth, eighteen miles away, where we arrived at night.

"On the journey we drove for some hours alongside Mount Carmel. Just before dark we hit upon a spot called 'Herosheth of the Gentiles.' Here one can see on Mount Carmel, the place of sacrifice, where the contest took place between Elijah and the prophets of Baal, and the place of the killing of the latter on a hill below beside the River Kishon.

"To the south lies the plain on which Barak of Israel overcame the hosts of Sisera, the Canaanite general. East of us lay the far-famed Valley of Jezreel, more commonly called by the Greek name Esdraelon. Far away across the valley we could see Little Hermon, the town of Jezreel, once the city of Ahab and Jezebel, and the sights of Nain, Endor and Shunem. On this spot we rested our team and ate a lunch. I took occasion to read the Scripture bearing on the events noted.

"My great teacher, the late Dr. John A. Broaddus, advised me two years ago if I ever came to Nazareth not to fail to get the view from the highest point above Nazareth. So to-day I ventured up to this point to have, perhaps in many respects, the greatest view from any one point in the world. Here we could see clearly for fifty miles in each direction, giving in a circle a radius of 100 miles.

"To the east was Mount Tabor, the Mount of Transfiguration, many believe; south of east and beyond the Jordan we saw the Mount of Moab; southeast we saw Little Hermon, Heights of Gilboa, Plains of Esdraelon, and beyond these the mountains of Samaria; to the west was Mount Carmel and the Mediterranean Sea, with our steamer in full view; north we saw snow-capped Hermon and the mountains of Lebanon. The depression of the

Jordan Valley and Sea of Galilee were in sight, though the water we could not see; we could see far beyond the Jordan.

"Never before could I appreciate so fully some of the maps which I have seen representing the topography of this ancient land. What views our Lord Himself must have had as a boy and young man from this very spot. We hated to leave the place.

"Mounted on Arabian steeds, a party of us set out for Tiberias and the Sea of Galilee at 6 A. M. yesterday. My good friend and typical Southern gentleman, Col. C. C. Sanders, of Gainesville, Ga., decided to go, too, but he would not ride on horseback. He had arranged before leaving home for a palanquin to be carried by two mules.

"Seated in his Arabian chariot, the Colonel set out in advance of those on horses. When he reached the top of the hill, the mule in front, whose business end was toward the Colonel, opened up a siege on the palanquin. The vehicle fell under the rapid fire and the Colonel fell with it.

"By this time the aft mule, whose head had been toward the Colonel, broke loose, changed his position and opened fire from the rear, while his mate kept up a steady fire in front. The Colonel, who was a gallant Confederate officer and fought in forty battles, hastily beat a retreat, neither to the front nor to the rear, but to one side, and came off, strange to say, without a wound, except in his pride.

"The palanquin was demolished and left by the roadside. As the Colonel looked on the scene in disappointment and grief, the driver of the warrior-like mules asked him, in the best English at his command, what he wanted to do. The Colonel said he would like to go to the Mount of Precipitation, where Jesus stood after His humiliation at the hands of His brethren and townsmen.

"About this time the party came upon the scene, so Colonel Sanders was given a seat in an emergency carriage, and made the trip the jolliest, happiest man in the bunch, many times laughing himself into tears as he told of the scene of his downfall.

From Caifa to Nazareth.

"In making the journey from Caifa to Nazareth and Tiberias, one makes the curve of a crescent, with the first and last forming the points. The distance is forty miles, with Nazareth in the center. Some miles before reaching Tiberias, you come to the Mount of Beatitudes, where the Sermon on the Mount was preached. From there one sees Mount Tabor to the south, Mount Hermon to the north, the Sea of Galilee and the valley in which the last great battle between the Crusaders and Turks was fought. Over against the Mount of Beatitudes is another mountain with a city on its top. How forcibly the words of our Lord, 'A city set on a hill cannot be hid,' came to me.

"We reached Tiberias at noon and had a lunch at the Hotel Tiberias. This is a city of some 5,000 people, Syrians and Jews chiefly. Great poverty and ignorance prevail here. In the afternoon we sailed on the Sea of Galilee and visited the ruins of Magdala, the home of Mary Magdalene; Bethsaida, the home of Peter, Andrew and Philip, and Capernaum, the home of our Lord after His departure from Nazareth.

"The afternoon on this famous sea was very delightful and full of sacred memories. On our going out the sea was as glass. The boatmen had to row us. As in a moment there was a breeze, then a heavy wind and almost a storm, until many in the boat feared and some were seasick. The Lord seems to have given us just the afternoon. We had a sail of twenty-five miles and the last half of it was an exciting race. After a night's rest we left in the early morning and arrived here at noon. I put one steed out of business yesterday, and to-day I asked for one strong and spirited. They gave me a fine fellow that one gentleman had given up as unmanageable. I handled him with ease, and was the first to reach our hotel to-day.

"We are in a land of one word, and that word is 'backsheesh.' You hear it everywhere and always. The beggars use it, the children use it, the guides use it, the women use it. When they see the American or European coming, the people meet to say 'backsheesh.' This means 'tip me' or 'give me something.' Our horsemen say it when they help you mount and when they help you dismount. One of our party dropped his cap and a little girl was standing near. The guide called to the girl to hand the gentleman his cap. She said, 'Let him give me backsheesh first.' Our boatmen would stop rowing and sailing to ask us for 'backsheesh.'

"This has become so common that it has got into the story of our Lord's walking on the water. It is said that after He had sent His apostles away, He engaged a man to take Him across the sea and the fellow would say 'backsheesh' until the Lord got tired of him and got out and walked rather than ride with such a man. I do not vouch for the truth of this story, but I do declare that if the minds and hearts of the people were as open to truth and light as their hands are open to receive 'backsheesh' they would soon be saved—a nation could be born in a day.

"This is a land where the women, donkeys, camels and

children bear the burdens. The women wear bloomers and the men wear skirts. These people are a cowed people, poor and oppressed. The Turk is a blight on the world. His government is a disgrace to civilization and decency. The people are taxed 33 per cent. of all they can produce. There is nothing to encourage enterprise or the importation of capital.

"An English gentleman bought a piece of ground on one of Nazareth's highest hills and built a nice house for a residence, and then the government would not let him live in it, but bought it from him, lest he might want to put a fort there for Great Britain.

"Before leaving our ship we were asked to select roommates for our stay in Galilee and Samaria. I had gotten well acquainted with a gentleman from Kentucky of the name of Ham, so I said 'Give me Ham.' The manager said, 'Why Ham?' I replied, 'This is one time I prefer Ham to the whole hog.' My selection did not prove a bad one by any means.

"I should have said that a few miles from Nazareth, on the way to Tiberias, we visited Cana, where Jesus performed His first miracle, making water wine. It is a small village. We visited a Latin Catholic Church, under which they showed us the well from which the servants drew the water that was made wine. Some of our party were amazed and full of holy wonder.

"Just across the street we visited a Greek Catholic Church, which, they assured us, was over the spot where Jesus made water wine. They did not have the well from which the water was drawn, but they had the pots that contained the water which became wine. And there were the pots before us. And there was more wondering. How could there be two exact spots for the same event? Let some wise head answer.

"After all, I rejoice in that saying in the Scriptures, 'The Lord preserveth the simple.'

"We now depart on a journey of sixty miles through Samaria to Jerusalem, the city of our God. With greeting to all, JOHN D. JORDAN.

THROUGH THE FAMED VALLEY OF ESDRAELON.

"FROM NAZARETH TO JERUSALEM, March 13th.—March 10th we started south for Jerusalem, a distance of ninety miles, as we had to ride it, visiting the places of interest along the way. We passed down a steep, rough and winding way into the Valley of Esdraelon. From the mountain top before descending the whole valley looked like a vast lake. A heavy fog spread like a great carpet over the entire country. We were here reminded of the mirage of the desert that so often brings hope to the weary traveler. Soon we were in fog and could not see 100 yards in any direction. The fog settled and we continued our journey under a sky without mist or cloud.

"Our first traveling in the Esdraelon was with great difficulty on account of the mud. Colonel Sanders' palanquin had been repaired and he started for Jerusalem in his Oriental chariot. Soon his mules stuck in the mud and one fell broadside. The Colonel was discouraged, and abandoned all hope of ever seeing the ancient city of the King, unless he could obtain other means of transportation. He was given a good horse and proved one of the finest riders in the company of thirty-five, besides guides and muleteers.

"On entering the valley, we had Mount Tabor in full view on our left. This is claimed by many to be the mount on which our Lord was transfigured. It is indeed a great 'mountain apart.' In front of us and to the left lay Little Hermon Mountain. A few miles away, and on Little Hermon's northside, we could see the city of Nain, where our Lord raised to life again the dead son of a widow. The town is now called Nein. Farther east, and near the northern end of Little Hermon, we could see the site of ancient Endor, where Saul went to consult with the old witch.

"Bearing gently on the western end of the mountain, we passed around to the southwest and hit upon Shunem, where Elisha had his chamber in the home of the Shunammite family, and where he restored to life the Shunammite child after it was dead, or resuscitated it after a deep swoon from a sunstroke. We had quite a discussion between two preachers just here as to whether the boy was really dead or in a state of coma.

"Shunem is now a dirty, modern village, called Solam. There is no place in it that would prove an inviting chamber to a prophet. Here David's nurse was born, and here the Philistines were formed in battle array against King Saul, just before his great defeat and tragic death.

"A little farther to the south are the hills of Gilboa, where the Israelites were encamped to fight their foe. In full view were the grounds where the battle was fought and where Saul and his son, Jonathan, died. In the distance we could see the town Bethshan, to which the bodies of Saul and Jonathan were taken and fastened on the city's wall till brave Israelites went and took them down and cremated them.

"About an hour and a half after passing Shunem we came to Jezreel, the summer home of Ahab and Jezebel. One would never judge it to have been a royal city of great wealth. Here Jezebel, the woman who did more to hurt Israel than other woman, was thrown from her mansion and killed. There was no crime of which she was not capable or at which she would hesitate if it lay in the way of her purpose. Here we were in the path where Jehu did his fast driving to avenge Israel of the defeats that brought on the death of Ahab.

"At Jezreel we had our first outdoor lunch and it was a good one and greatly enjoyed by a hungry party. The natives swarmed around us like the people of Savannah swarm to the street parade of a circus. They seemed anxious to have some token as a souvenir of our having passed their way. They would take anything, dead or alive, cold or hot, and the larger the better they like it. They preferred money, and their first choice was not the penny. They are Mohammedans, poor, dirty, ignorant and oppressed.

"After lunch, and while our horses rested, we walked to the eastern side of the town, where we could see Gideon's fountain—a great spring coming from the ground and forming the head waters of a small river that flows east into the Jordan. It was at this stream Gideon tested his men as to whether they would stoop to drink, having laid aside their arms, or whether they would hold their arms in one hand, dip water with the other and drink from it, keeping a sharp eye out for the enemy all the while—a thing that those who stooped down to drink could not do.

"These vigilant fellows were the chosen of God to win a great victory. Let it not be forgotten in this connection that the proper translation of the Scripures makes it quite clear that the spirit of Jehovah clothed Himself with Gideon to win this fight. In other words, the spirit of Jehovah put on Gideon as a military garment and fought through him.

"At mid-afternoon we arrived at Jenin, the Scriptural Enganim, at the southern edge of the Valley of Esdraelon.

It is a modern village of dirty huts and dirty people. We stopped here over Sunday. There is a modern hotel in Jenin, owned and managed by the Hamburg-American Line of steamers. We rested, had service and wrote to our homes. At night our dragoman, Shukreg Hichmeh, took a party to an Arabic coffee house. It was interesting as he interpreted for us. These Mohammedans are polygamists. It was amusing, and sad, too, to hear them tell why they had more than one wife. One old fellow brought down the house when asked how many wives he had, by replying, 'I am sorry to say I have one. I had rather have none.'

Pit in Which Joseph Was Thrown.

"Monday we were off on our way and in a few hours came to the ruins of Dothan and saw the 'dry pit' into which Joseph's brethren are said to have put him before selling him to the caravan bound for Egypt. The pit was full of water. I waited to hear the remarks that must needs come. I did not have to wait long. Our dragoman was pounced upon for showing us a pit full of water for a 'dry pit.' The enthusiastic and exact theologian had forgotten that this is the wet season, and that many places now full of water will be dry in a few months. I ventured the suggestion and all was well.

"While we were by the pit we saw a large caravan of traders come around a hill on the main road that leads to Egypt. We recalled the Scriptural narrative, and how impressive it was to remember that such a sight in the distance suggested to Joseph's brethren the idea of selling him into slavery rather than leaving him to die in the pit.

"Our journey for some time made it clear why Joseph's brethren left the unfertile and drier country of Shechem and went to the rich and well-watered plain of Dothan. Such scenes and events make the wisdom and force of the Scriptural narrative throb with life.

"We soon came upon the hill of Samaria, a magnificent hill, rising terrace upon terrace with all the comeliness and beauty of nature and art combined. It stands 500 feet above the valley surrounding it on all sides, and is itself surrounded in the distance by other mountains. A more splendid position for a city would be hard to find.

"On the top of the hill Ahab and Jezebel had their 'Ivory Palace' and lived in the greatest pomp of royal estate. Here also Herod had his magnificent palace and theatre. We saw the barley and beans growing, and the farmers ploughing amid the very foundation of all these great buildings. One hundred great marble columns stand as nude and forlorn reminders of a glory departed. Many others have been thrown down and built into parts of a crude fence.

"All over this hill and among the great marble pillars could be seen half-nude natives working the soil in the crudest way. Down on the hillside is a rude little village of dirt houses, without a single article or inviting feature. Ahab and Herod would hardly know the site of their ancient glory. It was their wickedness that has brought this once magnificent place to naught. As we read the Bible we were impressed with the force of prophecy. All regretted to leave the Hill of Samaria, so beautiful in situation, graceful in form and queenly in its bearing.

"In the afternoon we galloped into Nablus, the ancient Shechem, which lies between Mounts Ebal and Gerizim on the edge of the latter. Our party went at once to the Samaritan Synagogue, built 700 years ago. It is an humble building, crowded into a dark corner, with no light except from the roof and the door. We were shown copies of the Pentateuch, one said to be 2,000 years old and the other 3,575 years old. I thought these rather striking dates, but held my peace. We met the Samaritan high priest, 'Jacob, son of Aaron.' He is an elderly man with a pleasing manner and kindly face. He reminded me strikingly of the late Dr. Isaac P. Mendes, of Savannah.

"There are only 195 Samaritans now. There are more men than women and they cannot marry outside their people. No woman can have more than one husband, so there are several men on the waiting list. They are a poor, industrious, pious people. We took up a collection for the high priest and were thanked.

"A few of our party ventured to walk to the top of Mount Gerizim and to the place of sacrifice. It was an undertaking which many attempted and failed, stopping by the way or returning. Here the Samaritans observe every year the feast of a passover, killing seven lambs, according to the seven families now of the Samaritans. For nearly 2,000 years, or since the destruction of Jerusalem, A. D. 70, this is the only place in all the world where the paschal lamb has been regularly slain. I looked on the place where they are slain and cooked.

"The next day found us early on the road, passing between Mounts Gerizim and Ebal to "Jacob's Well." This is one of the well-known and well-authenticated spots of sacred history. Here it was that our Lord, wearied with His journey, sat on the well and talked with the Samaritan woman. To enjoy it read the fourth chapter of the fourth Gospel.

"After leaving the well, we passed near Aphek, where Eleazer and Phinehas, sons of Levi, are said to be buried, and came to Levonah. Here we met one hundred Russian pilgrims making a tour of the country on foot. They are a worse looking people than the natives.

"Soon we were at the ruins of Shiloh, and, in fact, all is ruin. Only one tree and one wall remain on the site of the ancient city of power and greatness. Here again prophecy has been fulfilled. We lunched on the main carriage road from Nabher to Jerusalem and visited the ruins of Bethel. Here we passed over the roughest roads and through the most barren country yet traversed. No wonder Jacob had unrest after traveling over this country.

"Here, ten miles away, we saw for the first time, and very distinctly, the city of Jerusalem and the Mount of Olives. Standing on the ruins of Bethel and looking at Jerusalem and the Mount of Olives gave me emotions beyond description.

"We turn aside to the main road at Ramallah and spend the night at a good hotel, owned and managed by our dragoman, Shurkey Hishmeh. He showed us every kindness here, as elsewhere.

"The next morning we looked from the front porch of the hotel toward the west and saw Mizpeh, where Saul was made King of Israel. Just below, on the hillside, is Emmaus, and a little to the north of Emmaus is Gibeon. From our hotel we could see Joppa, twenty-seven miles to the northwest.

"We spent the forenoon visiting some mission schools in Ramallah. All persons opposed to foreign missions should see what these Protestant mission schools do for the communities in which they are located. The chief school here is a Quaker institution and has been in operation seventeen years. It has thirty-four girls and twenty-five boys. They sang for us several songs, including 'America.'

"At lunch Mr. Hishmeh had a lamb cooked whole, full of rice, and brought it on the table. All greatly enjoyed it, for it was good and signified the greatest hospitality.

"In my next letter we will take in Jerusalem and Jericho, the Jordan and the Dead Sea and Bethlehem."

Dr. F. D. Power's Narrative.

Who could ever forget the ride to Nazareth on a bright, glad spring days? Who can sleep his first night in Nazareth, whatever may be the comfort of his couch or the weariness of his frame? Who can ride through these absorbing scenes and view the upland mountain-rimmed plain where nestles the city of our Lord's life for so many years and not be thrilled and silenced? Who can walk the streets, narrow and dirty as they may be now, and thronged with children where He once played as a child, and mingle with the shepherds and craftsmen, vine dressers and tillers of the soil, of whom He in His young manhood was one, and climb the hill which gives the widest sweep of vision in all Palestine, which, no doubt, was one of His most frequented and most delightful resorts, and not feel nearer to Him and most supremely blessed?

There are a thousand things of interest in Nazareth. Besides the strange people and customs, the shops and bazaars and market places, the camels and donkeys, the caravansaries, such as our Lord was born in, and camel trains with which He no doubt somteimes journeyed, there are the Cave of Annunciation and the kitchen of Mary, the carpenter-shop of Joseph and stone slab on which He dined with His disciples, and the synagogue in which He stood up to read the Scriptures, and other supposed places associated with Him, all of which, however doubtful, have a great fascination for the visitor. Two places there are we may be quite certain about—the fountain on the edge of the village, which has been from time immemorial the one unfailing source of water supply, and the ridge which rises 500 feet above it, known as Neber Said. The fountain is called the Virgin's Fountain, and is the center of the social life of Nazareth, where women and maidens gather for gossip, and fill their earthen pitchers, as they did, no doubt, in Mary's time. I took one of these pitchers, which the women balance so gracefully on their heads, resting on a little Jaffa cap, and lifted it to my shoulder and it must have weighed forty pounds. They carry them, apparently, with the greatest ease, and without touching them with their hands. The water is clear, and cold, and beautiful, and though they tell you never to drink the water of Palestine, we did so with perfect comfort and confidence.

The other point of certainty is the hill top. Who can look from this eminence and not be moved? To the north towers Hermon, snow-capped, 10,000 feet above the sea; the mountains of Lebanon, the land of Zebulon and Naphtali. To the west the blue waters of the Mediterranean were visible, with our ship lying in the harbor, plainly seen with the naked eye, though twenty-three miles away, and Mount Carmel and the place of sacrifice, and the Valley of Kishon and beautiful Plain of Esdraelon. Eastward lay Mount Tabor and south Little Hermon and the mountains of Gilboa, Samaria and the plain of the Jordan.

A dozen famous villages are pointed out—Sepphoris, where Mary's mother was born; Nain, where Jesus raised the widow's son from the dead; Endor, where Saul had his experience with the witch; Megiddo and Jezreel, where Ahab had his summer capital and palace—his Versailles, the scene of revelry and tragedy, for here was Naboth's vineyard, and here Jezebel was eaten by dogs, and here the Israelites were defeated by the Philistines and Saul and Jonathan fell. We may hear David sing,

"I am distressed for thee, my brother Jonathan; very pleasant hast thou been unto me; thy love to me was wonderful, passing the love of women. Saul and Jonathan were lovely and pleasant in their lives, and in their death they were not divided."

We may look at Nain and hear the touching story: "Behold a dead man carried out, the only son of his mother and she a widow! And when the Lord saw her, He had compassion on her and said unto her, weep not. And He came and touched the bier, and they that bare him stood still. And he said, Young man, I say unto thee, arise. And he that was dead sat up and began to speak. And he delivered him to his mother."

We may look on the broad Plain of Esdraelon, famed for great armies, and see kings and conquerors passing over it, from Assyria and Babylon on the east and Egypt on the south, the Israelites coming down from the hill country and binding the Canaanites who dwelt "in the land of the valley" with their "chariots of iron"; Barak, inspired by the song of Deborah, rushing down from the hills, and sweeping away the nine hundred iron chariots of Sisera; the army of Sennacherib, when—

"The Assyrian came down like the wolf on the fold,
And his cohorts were gleaming with silver and gold,
And the sheen of their spears was like stars on the sea,
When the blue waves roll nightly on deep Galilee."

Here Roman fought Crusader and Turk, and Napoleon was checked by the English when marching from Egypt by way of Jaffa seeking the conquest of Syria to march on Constantinople and "enter Europe by the back door," and here in the Apocalypse we are told is to be fought the last great battle of the world which is to precede universal peace—Armageddon—the battle of Megiddo, the ancient name of Esdraelon.

Tabor, wooded and green, tells of the transfiguration; Carmel of Elisha and Elijah; Gilboa, rocky and barren, speaks of the beauty of Israel slain upon its high places; Hermon, lordly and snow-crowned, pictures the eternity of God's promises and the calmness of God's peace. But at our feet lies Nazareth—Nazareth which testifies as to the Life—the Life that was lived there; the Life which is the Light of the world.

This was the place. Here the Life began. Over these hills rambled the Holy Child. Down there at the Virgin's Fountain the mother came often leading Him by the hand. Nazareth was His home. "And He went down with them and came to Nazareth, and was subject unto them. And Jesus increased in wisdom and stature and in favor with God and man." The Jesus who is the way, the truth and the life was Jesus of Nazareth.

Nazareth has little beauty. Not one of our Lord's people—not a Jew—is to be found to-day in Nazareth. Christians are there. We were received warmly into a Christian home and saw their family life. Moslems are there. Greeks and Latins have their churches and contend for its sacred places. But there was lived the Life, and this makes it sacred. The houses are homely. Every one is a perfect cube—"the length and the breadth and the height of it are equal." They have as much variety as so many blocks of stone hewn out of a quarry and have no virtue but in their masonry. The people are not handsome nor cleanly, but mostly poor and mean. They pester you. The smallest children cry "Backsheesh! backsheesh!" until you fairly run wild because of their importunities. But there was lived the Life. It is the cradle of our religion. It was the home of its founder. It has witnessed the beginning of a great history. In the Himalayas there is a stream which flows forth from under a glacier. It may be no more than others which issue from the region of eternal snow, but it is the source of the Ganges, a river which to hundreds of millions is like the river flowing out of the throne of God. So from this little mountain town of Galilee has gone forth the stream which is for the healing of the nations.

"He always kept close to nature," says Renan. It is easy to picture Jesus on this height, the marvelous boy, looking with great eyes upon the boundless plain below, beyond which lay Jerusalem and its great story for Him; and off, far off, to the sea, which rolled from upon the horizon, emblem of immensity, infinity, eternity, beyond which lay the great world for which He was to suffer. And so in silence and communion with nature, and with His Father His soul grew to its immeasurable greatness. He must still love Nazareth—these hills, these poor people, these little children He must still care for tenderly. These that come from the ends of the earth to see the home of His childhood, and young manhood, because they honor Him—He must see them and feel kindly toward them.

> "What means this eager, anxious throng,
> Which moves with busy haste along;
> These wondrous gatherings day by day?
> What means this strange commotion, pray?
> In accents hushed the throng reply,
> Jesus of Nazareth passeth by."

CHAPTER V.

Jaffa, the Joppa of Scripture—Queer Antics of Oarsmen in the Harbor—History of the Town—Our Author Speculates About Noah's Ark—The Orient the Cradle of Some of Civilization's Bad Features—An "Obiter Dictum" on Trusts—Rose-Bedecked Hills—Ekron—First Sight of Jerusalem—As to the Site of Calvary—Supposed Tomb of Jesus—Church of the Holy Sepulchre—Mount Olivet and its Associations—Two Competing Churches.

From Caifa our good ship steamed to Jaffa, the Joppa of the Bible. The harbor is a poor one and we had to land in small boats. When the sea is rough it is sometimes two or three days before a landing can be effected, as it is a rockbound coast. Here Hiram, King of Tyre, brought the cedars of Lebanon for the building of the temple.

We found five ships and many small craft in the harbor. The oarsmen, like those at Caifa, go barefooted and pull their oars standing, seating themselves to recover, then rising and pulling again, and singing to the dip of the oar. The sea breaks over the rocks in great waves and travelers have to pass between immense boulders, a feat which these boatmen perform with the skill of experience.

It was from Jaffa that Jonah sailed on his whaling expedition. This was also the city of Simon, the tanner, whose house we visited. Upon the top of this structure Peter had the vision related in the tenth chapter of Acts. Here, too, Dorcas was restored to life by Peter. But judging from the raggedness of the children, she at present has no followers in the making of "coats and garments," which rendered her so dear to the widows, who stood by weeping in the upper chamber.

This ancient city was the base from which Godfrey de Bouillon, the famous Templar, the paladin of the East, operated during the first Crusade, in the capture of Jerusalem. The city was captured and destroyed by Saladin, the celebrated Sultan of Egypt and Syria, in A. D. 1188, but was rebuilt by Richard, the lion-hearted. It has always been noted for the manufacture of soap, but this product is doubtless exported, as there is no evidence from external appearances that much of the article is used by the inhabitants—certainly the children are not liberal patrons of this great civilizer.

Joppa's oranges are fine and its gardens and citron groves are fragrant and fertile. Tradition says this is the spot where the old patriarch, Noah, dwelt, and that here he built and launched on the troubled waters of the great deluge that ark which served to preserve the human race during the great inundation.

It is not stated in Holy Writ how long Mr. Noah was employed in his enterprise, but as the ark was as large as a modern man of war, being 525 feet long, 87 feet in breadth and 52 feet in height, it was quite a big undertaking, and probably consumed several years in the building.

During this period one can well imagine the ridicule and derision the old man endured—the gibes and jests uttered at his expense. I doubt not that his neighbors, being unbelievers, regarded him as crazy. So entirely absorbed were they in mundane affairs, and so continuously did they indulge in all manner of wickedness that we are told "It repented the Lord that he had made man on the earth, and it grieved Him at his heart."

These frivolous sinners saw no indications of an overflow of the waters or any danger that the fountains of the great deep would be broken up. The rocks in the harbor were so dangerous, and the distance from the shipyard and deep water so great, that they believed it would be impossible to launch successfully, in the ordinary way, so great a craft. And as poor old Noah's fellow-citizens did not credit his predictions of the coming deluge, they ceased to interest themselves in his work, and in all likelihood regarded his story as a standing joke.

As time wore on they probably stopped asking him how he was getting on with his boat, when he looked for the flood of waters that was to float it and on what date he expected the windows of Heaven to be opened. The boys, after the manner of their kind, in going and returning from school, doubtless invited him, in sarcastic tones or jocular vein, to "come out of that ark." And probably the urchins asked him a thousand times when the deluge would arrive, and why he did not put on his gum boots and raincoat, and raise his umbrella and "come in out of the wet."

But the old man knew what he was about—he was in communion with his God and had faith in His promises.

The inhabitants of the doomed city were not only irreverent, but so wicked that they paid not the slightest attention to Noah's warnings and admonitions. This is evident from the fact that God regarded only Noah and his immediate family as being sufficiently righteous to be worthy of preservation.

But there came a day, after Noah's work had been completed, when a strange and panoramic scene presented itself——one that excited the wonder and curiosity of the people of this ancient city. An ordinary circus always arouses the interest not only of children, but of adults, yet there was never, before or since, congregated so complete an array of quadrupeds and birds and reptiles and insects as this venerable man got together, for we are told that under his supervision was "every beast after his kind, and all the cattle of their kind, and every creeping thing that creepeth upon the earth after his kind, and every fowl after his kind, every bird of every sort."

We can imagine this huge procession headed by the stately elephant with solemn steps and slow; next comes "the old ship of the desert," with his swinging but steady gait; then the lordly lion, not rampant or couchant, but walking quietly and sedately with lowered brush, his fearful roar hushed into quiet and his savage, baleful eye with its lambent fires in repose. Now we see the feline race—the spotted leopard, the magnificent tiger and the mild-mannered and usually gentle grimalkin, not snarling, growling and biting, as is their wont, but typical of the state foretold by Isaiah, when "the wolf also shall dwell with the lamb, and the leopard shall lie down with the kid, and the calf and the young lion and the fatling together, and a little child shall lead them."

Then comes the gawky giraffe with his head in the clouds and by his side waddles the short-legged hippopotamus, doing his best to keep up with his long-limbed companion; the wild ass of the desert and the farm horse amble along side by side; the wild boar of the jungle and the house pig grunt in happy unison; the bison of the plains and the pet cow trot along in confidence together.

Without attempting to name the animals, suffice it to say that the organization of the first menagerie was a complete and triumphant success—neither P. T. Barnum nor John Robinson has ever been able to rival Noah's menagerie and circus.

Whilst these animals are walking quietly into the ark and taking their allotted places—the clean and the unclean, each after its own kind—there approach more slowly the creeping kind—the snakes and the lizards, the terrapins and the turtles, the caterpillars and the ants, the earwigs and the snails, the earthworms and the fireflies, the ubiquitous fleas and the comparatively motionless slugs. Then we hear a buzzing of bees and wasps, hornets and yellow jackets, and of flies of all sizes and species, from the tiny gnat to the blood-sucking gadfly. And as Noah journeys along the locusts sing their plaintive air, and the mosquitoes emit their friendly notes of attachment.

It must have been a wonderful, yet a terrifying, sight to behold this motley array—sworn enemies to one another—ambling, crawling or creeping along side by side, and, as it were, by instinct making for the same goal; in quiet and peace assembling at the same headquarters or rendezvous.

But, on the other hand, it must have been pleasing to note the concert of action in the same direction of wild and tame animals, the gentle and the vicious, the order and system observed, the storing of supplies, the transfer of household goods.

And verily the unusual commotion and preparation of Noah and his family were well calculated to excite interest and arouse not only the curiosity of the people of the city, but to awaken their fears and occasion their repentance. The indifference of these folks can only be accounted for upon the supposition that, like Ephriam of old, "they were joined to their idols" and God determined "to let them alone."

While these things are going on the sky is darkened and the sun obscured by the flight of thousands of birds, all winging their course with eyes focused upon a certain point. They move in the same mysterious way that marks their annual pilgrimages through pathless space in obedience to some unknown law or instinct implanted in them by an All-Wise Providence.

As these birds are strung out for miles upon the distant horizon, like a ribbon stretched from pole to pole, their forms and plumage at first are an indistinguishable mass, but as they get nearer and their individual forms are silhouetted against the sky, it is observed that the van is led by the king of fowls, the noble and lordly eagle. His pinions are outstretched and his piercing eye is centered upon the common goal. In his wake follows the huge condor and the fleet-winged albatross, the long-necked stork and the various species of the heron—white, purple, blue, green—with their long legs straight behind them. Then come the swans, ducks, geese and other wild fowl after their kind; after them the various species of owl, winking and blinking in the bright sunlight; then the raven and the hawk family. The swift, the swallow and the martin likewise appear, as do Robin Redbreast and the bullfinch, the querulous parrot, the contentious jay, the sweet-voiced nightingale and the hooper with its wierd and melancholy cry. The gaudy lyrebird, the gorgeous hummingbird, the tiny titmouse, the merry little wren are also in evidence—in fact, all the fowls, by sevens, are embraced in this magnificent gathering—the first and the greatest aviary ever collected on earth, and one that would have delighted an ornithologist and been invaluable as a collection.

As the birds settle with weary wings upon the top of the ark and preen their feathers into decency and order, preparatory to entering the window and being shut in for seven days before the threatened destruction comes, they present a wondrous sight.

Never before since Adam "gave names to all cattle and to the fowl of the air, and to every beast of the field," has there been such an assemblage.

And now they all are gathered in the mighty vessel,

the window is shut and the door is barred, when suddenly the forked lightning rends the darkened sky and the detonations of peal after peal of reverbrating thunder shake the very heavens and make the earth quake with fear. Then it is that amidst the commotion of the heavens "all the fountains of the great deep are broken up and the windows of Heaven are opened" and the city of Joppa, with all its inhabitants except righteous Noah, perishes from the face of the earth!

This old country of the Bible, the Orient, which cradled civilization, which nurtured the arts and sciences, which gave birth to our religion and the most perfect code of morals, upon which the jurisprudence of all nations is founded, is a wonderful land, apropos of which "the preacher" has said, "There is no new thing under the sun."

In our Anglo-Saxon conceit "we think we know it all." We imagine, too, that we have perplexities unheard of by the Orientals—problems, the solutions of which, are untried; polemics and questions in political economics undreamt of in their philosophy; but it is because we have not studied these matters by the light of Biblical history.

For instance, we think Socialism is a new fad—an untried quantity in social polity—whereas, the first society of this character was founded by our Lord's Apostles themselves, when they "had all things in common" and "neither said any of them that ought of the things which he possessed was his own." Yes, the Apostles tried this experiment, but they found it did not work and, therefore, abandoned it. And the latter-day disciples of this theory will learn the same lesson in time.

We also complain about the modern "trusts" and deride them as a product of our civilization and a result of our environments—the Standard Oil monopoly, the American

Sugar octopus and the American Tobacco combine, with all their ramifications. But their destruction of individual initiative, their war against personal effort and their powerful and heartless machinations do not compare with the first gigantic "trust" instituted by Joseph, who has been designated "the only gentleman named in the Bible."

This ancient trust was instituted, organized and perfected in Egypt thousands of years ago, when Joseph, taking advantage of the necessities of the people, captured their money. And when their money failed he took their cattle, their horses, their flocks and their herds. Then, as the famine waxed sore and the second year's distress fell upon them—when wives and children were crying for bread—he seized their lands. And when he held a title deed to their estates he took their bodies for bread and they became the servants of Pharaoh.

The story is well worth reflecting upon. Unless our government takes some drastic step and enacts laws to curb American combines and trusts, like conditions will produce like results.

On landing at Joppa we found the wharves filled with Syrians, Greeks, Turks, Arabs, negroes and other peoples, and with strings of camels laden with oranges, coffee and like things. This country is noted for the delicious flavor of its oranges. Baskets, apparently holding a peck, were offered for twenty-five cents. Several of us bought, but on investigation, we found that even these people were up to Yankee tricks, for the baskets had false bottoms, and instead of holding twenty or twenty-five oranges, only contained ten or fifteen, the rest of the measures being filled with paper.

The country from Joppa to Jerusalem, the Holy City, for a part of the way is very fruitful, and oranges, olives, figs, wheat and barley may be seen in the fields. Along the hills grow white and red roses—the rose of Sharon—the narcissus, the carnation and other flowers, while in the meadows one sees the famous lily of the valley.

The first town of importance after leaving Jaffa, or Joppa, is Lydda, which in olden times belonged to the tribe of Ephriam. This is the place where Peter healed Aeneas of palsy. Yonder is Ramleh, with its historic Crusaders' Tower 120 feet high. Here Samuel judged the people and the children of Israel asked for a King.

We next came to an old Arab village, the Ekron of the Old Testament, where the Ark of God was taken by the Philistines. After this in importance is the Hill of Gezer, which was presented to Solomon by his father-in-law, Pharaoh, as the dowry of the latter's daughter. The next place to the right contains the ruins of the ancient Bethshemesh, a city of the tribe of Judah. Here some of the inhabitants looked into the Ark of the Lord and He destroyed 50,000 of the common people and seventy of the principal men of the city, according to Samuel. About two miles away is Zorah, the birthplace of Samson. A little farther on is a gorge called Wady es Sarat. The house in which Samson and Delilah dwelt is pointed out and high up among the rocks is a grotto which is alluded to as the Strong Man's cave. Our attention was also called to the supposed spot where Samson turned loose the 300 foxes with firebrands attached to their tails. These firebrands, it will be remembered, consumed the corn of the Philistines. The field between two mountains, from which David got the stone with which he smote Goliath of Gath is likewise to be seen along this route, and at the next station the boys offer for sale slings, represented as fac similies of the one David used. We can well imagine the scene described in the Scriptures—

"One struggle of might, and the giant of Gath,
With a crash like the oak in the hurricane's path,
And a clangor of arms, as of hosts in the fray,
At the feet of the stripling of Ephratah lay."

And as they witnessed the catastrophe—

"—a shout like the roll of artillery rose,
And the armies of Israel swept on their foes."

The next place pointed out to us is the spot where Samson is alleged to have destroyed the Philistines with the jawbone of an ass. Philip's fountain, where he baptized the eunuch, is also shown; in fact, every foot of the ground is historic and replete with Biblical associations and sacred narratives.

Passing many interesting points we enter a more desolate region, barren of trees and with scanty herbage. The hills are covered with goats seeking a precarious living from the barren soil. Occasionally we come to small and verdant pastures dotted with flocks of sheep, which are attended by their shepherds as of old.

We continue to wind along the Judean hills, there being a gradual rise in the ground until the city—the Holy City—bursts upon our view. No Christian's heart can fail to be stirred when first he beholds this place, hallowed, as it is, by a thousand sacred memories. As the pilgrim enters through the gates he exclaims with the Psalmist, only changing the tense of the verb, "My feet do stand within thy gates, O Jerusalem." And his heart utters a prayer of thanks that he is permitted to walk within its holy precincts, while his soul is moved to its profoundest depths at the prospect before him. Doubtless also he recalls the lines—

"Jerusalem! alas! alas! of old,
Deaf to whate'er prophetic seers foretold,
Assailing all, whom Heaven, in mercy sent,
And murdering those that warned thee to repent.

"How oft hath God, still gracious, striven to bring
Thy devious brood beneath His sheltering wing."

This is the city in which our Lord dwelt; He walked these streets; here is the site of the temple in which He worshipped and taught and from whose gates He was taken to Calvary. Here on His entry the multitude "took branches of palm trees and went forth to meet Him and cried, 'Hosanna! Blessed is the King that cometh in the name of the Lord.' And this same rabble in a few days cried, 'Crucify Him, crucify Him.'"

Jerusalem has been destroyed by sixteen different seiges, and the city of the present is really the eighth built on the ruins of its seven predecessors. After its destruction by Titus it remained uninhabited for more than fifty years, not a single person dwelling within its boundaries. Its restoration after this period as a Christian city was by Helena, the mother of Constantine. Jerusalem has been under Moslem dominion since 637 A. D. with the exception of the century of Crusader occupation. At present it has a population of about 60,000—40,000 Jews, 13,000 Christians and 7,000 Moslems. Jerusalem has eleven gates, five of which are closed. The two main streets are David and Damascus, which traverse the city at right angles and mark the different quarters of the town. The thoroughfares are narrow and filthy; the houses all small and dilapidated, and the drainage the worst imaginable, for sanitation is unknown.

Among the first places we visited was the Church of the Holy Sepulchre. Whether this is the true site or not is uncertain. It looks improbable that the same site should be both the Calvary and sepulchre of our Lord. When the fact is considered that the site of old Jerusalem is filled with the rubbish of centuries, and that to find the original foundations it is necessary to dig down over a hundred feet, it can readily be realized that it is mere conjecture as to the true locations.

The present site is recognized because it was the seat of Hadrian's temple to Venus and the place indicated by the vision of Empress Helena. Whether it be the true site or not, we do not know. We do know, however, that somewhere within a certain area our Lord suffered death, was buried and rose again on the third day.

As we looked upon the spot, which for fifteen centuries has been regarded by pilgrims as the most sacred in the world, and beheld believers prostrating themselves and kissing the marble slab under which they believe our Lord lies, we felt like exclaiming, as did the father of the son who had a dumb spirit, "Lord, I believe; help thou mine unbelief."

No place on earth is so sacred and dear to the Christian as Calvary and no spot so hallowed by holy thoughts and associations as His sepulchre. My eyes, readily responding to the flood tides of emotion that swept through my mind and touched the chords of my heart, like the wind breathing upon an Æolian harp, became suffused with tears. I bowed my head in adoration and prayer of thankfulness that I had been permitted with reverent soul to do homage to His beloved memory.

After we have read that Joseph of Arimathaea took the body of our Lord "and laid it in his own tomb, which he had hewn out in the rock, and he rolled a great stone to the door of the sepulchre and departed," we naturally expect to find the same environments as those indicated by this description, and at first there comes a sense of disappointment—a doubt about the matter. The tomb chamber is entirely lined with marble and has no resemblance whatsoever to a cave cut in a rock. There is no rock to be seen in this chamber.

On the right as you enter there is a marble bench. This, we are told, is the tomb of Christ. It is about two feet high, six feet long and three feet wide, and covered by a marble slab with a deep groove or crack running across its center. Through this narrow opening we are told that the miraculous fire issues. There is nothing about the pictures presented to suggest the simplicity of the Gospel narrative.

And yet, if this be the real spot, consecrated with His blood, embalmed in the hearts of His adherents and watered with the tears of His disciples, why should it not be beautified and adorned by the loving hands of His followers, even as we decorate and embellish the last resting places of those near and dear to us?

As I stood, as it were, beneath the shadow of the cross on which He suffered, I recalled the words—

> "Behold Him now
> Suspended on the cross! On His pale brow
> Hang the cold drops of death; through every limb
> The piercing torture rages; every nerve
> Stretched with excess of pain, trembles convulsed."

And yet amidst this agony He speaks and

> "Wafts His last prayer to all approving Heaven;
> 'Forgive them, for they know not what they do.'"

Some condemn the display and decorations and the burning of lamps and incense at His tomb, contrasting these with the simplicity of His character, the humility of His nature and the modesty of His life. But do not these very objections increase the love and affection, the adoration and devotion to which He is entitled and which it is not only our privilege, but our duty, to render and emphasize?

The central point of interest in the city is the Church

of the Holy Sepulchre, the alleged Calvary and the supposed site of our Lord's tomb, but there is no certainty as to the authencity of this statement. If my opinion be worth considering, I should say that latter-day surmises about the spot are incorrect. From the reading of the Scriptures one is induced to believe that the crucifixion took place *outside* of the city. The Church of the Holy Sepulchre is within the walls. It is possible, but not at all probable, that the tomb of Joseph of Arimathaea, "which he had hewn out in the rock," was situated at the place where executions ordinarily took place, for Joseph was "a rich man" and would hardly have selected such a location for "his own new tomb."

St. John is the only one of the Apostles who suggests that "there was a garden where He was crucified; and in the garden a new sepulchre, wherein was never a man yet laid."

But be that as it may, the saddest reflection upon Christianity is the fact that here Latin, Greek, Armenian, Syrian, Copt and Abyssinian has each his own particular shrine within the enclosure; all calling themselves Christians, but ready to cut one another's throats, and requiring a Turkish guard to keep them from so doing. What a commentary upon our Lord's teachings!

As we cross the threshold of the church we notice that three marble columns flank the door on either side. One of them has a crack in it, and it is believed that from this rift, on Judgment Day, will leap forth the fire that is to destroy the world. The surface of this riven shaft is as sleek as glass from the kisses of the pilgrims.

The Church of the Holy Sepulchre is not so much a church as a sacred exposition building. Under the same roof or series of roofs, are a multitude of shrines, chapels, stairways and caves—in fact, all the sacred places and things mentioned in the Bible.

About the first object that attracts our attention after entering the building is the Stone of Unction, on which, it is asserted, the body of Jesus was placed by Nicodemus to be anointed for burial. Before this stone is a painting and a row of gilded lamps.

A few steps from this is the spot designated as the place where the mother of Jesus stood while His body was being anointed. Nearby is another shrine, known as the "Chapel of the Parted Raiment." This is supposed to indicate the exact spot where the garments of Jesus were disposed of by lot. Then come other chapels denoting, respectively, the places where Christ was crowned with thorns, where He was scourged, where He was nailed to the cross, where He appeared to Mary Magdalene after His resurrection and where the Roman centurion stood during the crucifixion.

Then we are shown a stone bearing the impressions made by our Lord's wounded feet, after which we go down a stairway some five yards to see the place where the true cross was found, after it had been buried for three hundred years. It is said that in the same pit were found all three of the crosses, those upon which the two thieves were crucified, as well as that of our Lord.

The good Empress Helena, under whose direction these excavations and discoveries were made, was puzzled to know which was the sacred one. To determine this they were taken to the bedside of a devout woman who was very ill. When she beheld the first cross she became demented; when she saw the second she had terrible spasms, but when the third, which proved to be the true cross, was brought to her bedside she was completely restored to health. This was, therefore, declared to be the true cross.

We regard the "invention of the cross" as a fraud on

the credulity of the Christian, almost equal to the imposture called the miracle of the "holy fire," to be witnessed at the Greek Easter in the Church of the Holy Sepulchre every year, when thousands rush madly over one another to light their torches by the flame of the Holy Ghost.

The Church of the Holy Sepulchre, as it stands to-day, is a comparatively modern structure. The original magnificent bascilica erected by Constantine in 335 A. D., was destroyed in 614 A. D. Two years after a group of buildings was erected by the Patriarch of Jerusalem. This was destroyed in 1010 A. D. When the Crusaders came to Palestine they found on the site a collection of small chapels which had been built in the year 1048. These chapels were incorporated by them into a great cathedral, and new shrines added. In 1808 this cathedral was destroyed by fire. The present church, as it now stands, is the result of this restoration and reconstruction, which took place in 1810.

In another part of the church is the Chapel of the Crucifixion, where is shown the very rock of Calvary. In this stone is the rent made by the earthquake that occurred when Christ was crucified. One can even look down into the very hole in which the cross was placed.

The next place of interest is Adam's grave. What authority there is for supposing that Adam was buried here I cannot imagine. They seem to have overlooked in this *"omnium gatherum sanctorum"* the spot where grew the tree of knowledge; the place where the serpent deceived our first mother; the locality where Cain slew his brother Abel; the last resting place of Eve, and the spot upon which Noah's ark rested.

We made our entry into the Holy City by the Jaffa Gate, which is near the center of the city on the west side, with the ancient Tower of David to the right. To the right is the Armenian quarter; on the left the Christian. The Mohammedan quarter lies to the north, and the Jewish to the south, near the temple area.

In the middle of the Greek chapel a short marble pillar is fixed in the pavement. This is shown as the center of the earth, and is alleged to mark the precise spot from which was taken the earth that helped to form Adam.

There are no electric or horse cars and no electric or gas lamps in the old sections of the city. Darkness envelopes the scene, and little can be perceived by night, even if there be a moon visible. The stores are pretty generally closed when night falls.

While Jerusalem is not progressive, as compared with the present up-to-date cities, either of America or Europe, or even with Cairo, in "Darkest Africa," yet it is improving. In 1838, the estimated population was only 11,000; now it has about 60,000.

Modern Jerusalem, outside the old walls, has many beautiful buildings, good hotels, hospitals and schools. The great Jewish philanthropist, Montefiore, settled a colony of his own race in one hundred and fifty houses. About one thousand people occupy them, and these quarters are given to the occupants, rent free, so long as they lead decent and cleanly lives.

Jerusalem is built upon Mount Zion and Mount Moriah, on either side of which are valleys replete with profane and sacred history.

The Tyropean or Cheesemonger's Valley which, in the time of Christ, was spanned by a bridge, is now so filled with the debris of centuries as to have almost disappeared.

The Valley of Hinnon, which lies to the west, is marked by very steep sides. It has formed a most admirable defense for the city, having literally been filled with the bodies of attacking beseigers. It is also known as the

Valley of Gehenna, or "pleasant valley," a misleading name, as it was, in later times, used as a crematory for the refuse of the city. In this same valley is the spot called Tophet. At this place sacrifices to Baal were made.

A considerable portion of the city is still surrounded by walls, battlements and towers, thirty or forty feet high. In one part of the wall is a projecting stone some twenty-five or thirty feet from the ground. This is to be the judgment seat of Mohammed on the Day of Judgment, according to Moslem tradition. On the momentous occasion in question all the people will be gathered in the valley below. From this point, it is believed, there will be erected a bridge across the valley to Mount Olivet—a bridge as narrow as the blade of a sword. To pass over this structure will be the test of orthodoxy. None but the followers of the prophet are expected to meet the crucial test and land in safety on the other side.

The Valley of Kedron, also called the Valley of Jehosaphat, lies east of the city. The rock-ribbed hills on both sides are filled with tombs. Amongst others, are pointed out those of Isaiah, Hezekiah, Zechariah, St. James, Joseph and Mary. The tomb of the Virgin is the most prominent, and its identity is established by another vision of the Empress Helena. (I fear the Empress was a visionary person.) A church was built over the place about the twelfth century.

A conspicuous tomb is that of Absalom, which is still pelted, according to ancient usage, by the Jews, as an evidence of their contempt for an unfilial son.

Of all the hills that encompass Jerusalem the Mount of Olives is the most interesting and the most sacred. The dear old name warms every Christian heart. It is thoroughly enshrined in true, pure, religious sentiment.

In the times of the patriarchs Jehovah was worshipped here. It was here also that King David fled from his ungrateful son, Absalom, when the latter attempted to supplant him. But it is the Mount of Olives' association with Christ that makes it sacred to the Christian. Here it was He spent whole nights in prayer. From this holy spot He made His ascension. At this place

> "Majestical He arose—
> Upborne, and steered a flight of gentlest wing
> His native Heaven to gain; whilst from their eye,
> That to its center fixed, in mute survey
> Pursued the ascending glory, a bright cloud,
> Of bidden access, his latest presence caught:
> By angel forms supported, who in song,
> Not unperceived, and choral symphony,
> Through Heaven's wide empyrean loud rejoiced."

In full view from the summit of the Mount of Olives are many places closely identified with Christ's life. Below us lie Mount Moriah and Mount Zion. We stand on the spot designated as the place where He stood, when, with tear-bedimmed eyes, our Lord looked out upon Jerusalem and uttered that most pathetic of lamentations—"O, Jerusalem, Jerusalem, thou that killest the prophets, and stonest them that are sent unto thee; how oft would I have gathered thy children together, even as a hen gathereth her chickens under her wings, and ye would not." Here He was wont to retire at evening for rest and devotion after the trying ordeals of the day; here he went early to offer up His morning prayers; here He met with His disciples, instructed them and communed with them; here He delivered His parables and foretold the destruction of Jerusalem.

The view from the Mount of Olives is not only interesting, but far-reaching. We see hills and valleys that are all intimately associated with sacred history. To the east we get a glimpse of the Dead Sea, nearly 4,000 feet below, as well as of the Jordan winding its way along the valley, whilst in the background are the mountains of Moab, which bring to mind the beautiful story of Ruth and Naomi. On yon historic peak stood Moses, "and the Lord shewed him all the land of Gilead * * * and the plain of the Valley of Jericho, the city of palm trees unto Zoar." And the Lord said unto him, "I have caused thee to see it with thine eyes, but thou shalt not go over thither." And the great law-giver of the Israelites breathed his last on this desolate mountain with the promised land in full view—the then beautiful and fertile valley of the Jordan inviting and smiling enchantingly before him in all its verdant beauty.

> "God made his grave, to men unknown,
> Where Moab's rocks a vale unfold;
> And laid the aged seer alone,
> To slumber while the world grows old."

To the north are the rugged mountains of Benjamin, and to the south the wilderness of Judea, in which our Lord spent "His fast of forty days, after which He was an hungred." This is the most desolate region in all Palestine; not a blade of grass, it is said, grows upon the hills and not a living sound is to be heard or seen throughout all their extent. It was, therefore, a physical necessity that the angels should minister to our Lord when he dwelt in this barren wilderness.

The Russian Tower that crowns the summit of Olivet is quite an impressive structure, the best of all the views above referred to may be obtained from it.

The Greek Church, not to be outdone by the Russian, has rather marred the summit with chapels, shrines and official residences, while the Latin Church, not to be surpassed by either, has erected a paternoster chapel, upon whose walls the Lord's Prayer is inscribed in thirty-two different languages.

In the church over the alleged place of the ascension an impression in the rock is shown as a footprint made by our Lord just before His final departure from this earth.

The Mount of Offence, where Solomon in his degeneracy built an altar for the worship of Moloch, is also visible from Olivet.

The Hill of Evil Council is opposite Mount Zion. It is so named from the tradition that Caiphas, who resided here, made the agreement with Judas to betray Christ into His enemies' hands. The Aceldama, or Field of Blood, bought with the thirty pieces of silver—the price of Christ's betrayal—is on the other side of the Brook Siloam.

A chamber excavated in the rock is still the charnel house of the poor of Jerusalem. It is stated that the earth of this field will in forty-eight hours consume the flesh from the bones committed to it.

We were also shown the so-called Judas tree upon which, it is alleged, the traitor hanged himself.

CHAPTER VI.

Mosque of Omar Occupies Site of Solomon's Temple—"The New Calvary" and its Authenticity—Persistent Cry "Backsheesh" Heard Even in Sacred Places—Disputed Points About the Garden of Gethsemane—Jews Bewailing the Desolation of Israel—Via Dolorosa—John Doorsy and His Wee Son, "Jorge"—Semi-Domesticated Ravens—A City That was Accursed—River Jordan—Desolate Dead Sea Neighborhood—Bethany—A Glimpse of the Mount of Temptation—Birthplace of Jesus.

Whatever doubts may exist about the other sites of Jerusalem there is no cavil or question that the Mosque of Omar, or as it is called, the Dome of the Rock, stands where the magnificent Temple of Solomon once stood, and where afterwards the Temple of Herod was erected. This is also said to be the spot where Abraham attempted to offer up Isaac as a sacrifice.

The temple area is venerated alike by Jew, Moslem and Christian. It is truly the greatest of all "holy places." The enclosure contains about thirty-six acres; about one-sixth of this space is inside the city walls.

Owing to the words of our Lord—"there shall not be left one stone upon another that shall not be thrown down"—it is generally believed that even the foundation stones of the temple and the city walls were removed; but those who have viewed, measured and examined the locality are of the opinion that the original walls of the temple and some portion of the ancient city walls still remain. The anathema of our Lord was doubtless intended to apply figuratively, not literally, to the superstructures and the buildings.

So far as one can see, there are ten or twelve courses

of stone nearly opposite the Mosque El Aksa, about thirty feet high, and constituting part of the original foundation walls, which have been cleared of the debris of centuries; near the foot of this part of the wall is the place where the Jews assemble for prayer. They regard it as holy ground.

Under ground there is an immense cathedral called the "Stables of Solomon." It is supposed to be an ancient granary or storehouse, but was used as a stable by the Crusaders. We found it a cold and cheerless place, inhabited only by the pigeons, which are permitted to occupy it unmolested.

The Mosque El Aksa is the largest individual structure in Jerusalem, being 272 by 184 feet. At one time it was a Christian Church. In the mosque are some ancient marble pillars from the Temple of Herod and a beautiful carved wood pulpit.

The Mosque of Omar, or the "Dome of the Rock," is considered the finest building in Asia. It is octagonal in shape, each side being sixty-six and one-half feet wide, and fairly glistens with richly colored marbles and tiles. Its dome is of such exquisite proportions that it is regarded as a model of symmetrical art. The Mosque of Omar was built by the Moslems before the Crusaders, but was enlarged by the latter. It was completed, as it now is, in 1561 by Sulieman, the Magnificent. The interior is richly decorated with marble pillars of various colors, marble mosaics and tasteful decorations. There are also some beautiful stained-glass windows, which date back to 1528. The dome is 115 feet high and gracefully proportioned. Marble floors, covered with magnificent rugs, blend harmoniously with the splendid windows. The chief feature is the rock itself, which is directly under the dome and marks the site of the great altar of burnt offering. It is fifty-seven feet long by forty-three wide.

A high iron railing guards it and no one is permitted to trespass upon its sacred precincts.

The Moslems believe that Mohammed made his last prayer on this rock, and that when he ascended to Heaven the rock started to follow him, but was kept back by the Angel Gabriel. In proof of this the finger marks may still be seen. Another Moslem superstition is that Mohammed drove into the rock certain nails, which are gradually to work through the stone and fall into the cavern below. This cavern, it is thought, leads to the Kedron Valley, but the Moslems are too superstitious to remove the stone that fills the exit, and thus test the matter. When all these nails work through the end of the world will come. As there are said to be only three left, we were cautioned by the guides to walk softly lest a jar might cause another to go through.

A graceful pavilion bears the name of "David's Judgment Hall." The Moslems claim that King David hung a chain here as a test of men's veracity. All who were truthful could touch this chain without ill effects, but as soon as it came in contact with a liar a link fell off at once—one link for every lie. Had it been an endless chain it would doubtless have been exhausted ere this. Suffice it to say, not a link remains at present; even the staple to which the chain was attached has disappeared.

Amidst the "dim religious light" that pervades this sanctuary there emanates from some of the priests "an odor of sanctity" not altogether pleasant to the olfactory nerves.

This magnificent structure is built to guard and consecrate a mass of unhewn stone, for this is the summit of Mount Moriah, the site of King Solomon's Temple. Here Abraham and David knelt in prayer. The Ark of the Covenant rested on its surface. Beneath it are cisterns into which the blood of the sacrifices flowed.

The new Calvary, or Gordon's Calvary, so called in honor of General Gordon, who, during his visit, expressed his belief in it, is now accepted by many as being the true Calvary. Certainly it seems more likely to be the true Calvary than the spot which has been recognized as such for so many centuries.

Those who favor this location point to the fact that it is outside the old walls. It is an elevation not far from the Damascus Gate. The shape of the hill is not unlike that of a skull. This and many other reasons are adduced to prove that this is the true Calvary.

An unanswerable argument, settling beyond all doubt the question in its favor, was embodied in the reply of a guide to one of our party, who asked, "Why do you suppose this to be the real place?" "When the tomb was opened," replied the guide, "the bones of our Lord were found there!" Evidently this guide had never heard of the resurrection and ascension of our Lord.

But the pleasure of visiting the Holy City, and, indeed, all places of interest in Palestine, is marred by the persistent cry for "backsheesh, backsheesh." One hears it even at the gate of the Garden of Gethsamane and at the holy sepulchre. At every point persistent and insistent beggars appear. Worst of all we were importuned at Gethsemane by a small army of lepers. Their fingerless hands, shoeless and toeless feet, whitened faces, slightless eyes and haggard features excited both pity and disgust.

The demand for a concentration and consolidation of all and everything that Biblical history calls for or suggests, has been created by the morbid curiosity of the pilgrim and tourist, and the effort to supply this demand is commensurate with the requirements of travelers. Laudable economy, therefore, has been shown in husbanding everything under the roof of the Church of the Holy Sepulchre and within the zone of the temple area.

There is no place that appeals so forcibly to one's religious feeling as the Garden of Gethsemane; but alas! we have two supposed Gethsemanes, whose competitive claims are strongly urged by both the Greek and Roman churches. There is no doubt that the original garden was somewhere in this belt.

> "Here He led
> From the last Supper, when the hymn was sung,
> His few grieved followers out in that drear night,
> When, in the garden, on the mountain's slope,
> His agony wrung forth the crimson drops."

The generally accepted spot is that called the Latin Garden, because of the eight large and hoary olive trees within the enclosure. These trees assuredly are very ancient, as is attested by their size and gnarled appearance. Their age certainly cannot be less than a thousand years, and they may have sprung from the original roots of the trees under which "His sweat was as it were great drops of blood falling down to the ground."

The garden is about 300 by 200 feet and is enclosed by a high, whitewashed wall. Its trees are protected by a high iron fence. A contribution to the attendant monk procured us a few leaves that had fallen from one of the olives and a few flowers grown on one of the borders. The place is laid off in flower-beds and looks like a modern flower garden. In this respect it is disappointing.

The Greeks have their Garden of Gethsemane a little higher up the slope of the hill; they are just as confident as the Romans that theirs is the right one. Standing in the Latin Garden with Olivet before us, we are certain, beyond a reasonable doubt, that this is the very hill and we know that the garden is not far off; and it really matters not whether Greek or Roman be right as to the identical spot where our Lord prayed that "this cup pass from me."

It was at this spot, according to St. John, that "Jesus entered, and His disciples; and Judas also, which betrayed Him, knew the place, for Jesus ofttimes resorted thither with His disciples." Here it was that, withdrawing from His disciples, He offered up that sublime prayer of resignation, "Not My will but Thine be done."

The most pathetic scene we ever witnessed was at the Wall of Wailing. Outside and below the temple, near Robinson's Arch, which is an abutment of the bridge that spanned the Tyropean Valley, this wall is one hundred and fifty-six feet long and fifty-six feet high. Here, especially on Fridays, the Jews gather to bewail the desolation of Israel.

The place is an open, paved court, filled with Jews of all classes and ages, male and female, who recite from the Lamentations of Jeremiah and the Psalms. They also put into the cracks of the walls slips of Hebrew Scripture passages, as well as nails, which have been sent by friends at a distance, who desire thus to be vicariously represented.

For centuries the Jews have mourned over the desolation of Israel. There are no people on earth who sacrifice as much as they do for conscience' sake. They have adhered to the religion of their fathers with unswerving loyalty and a faith that knows no doubt. All these centuries they have kept the observance of the Passover, instituted to remind them of their deliverance from the Egyptians; the Feast of Tabernacles, to recall to their memory the weary wanderings of their forefathers in the wilderness, and the Pentecost, in token of the receiving of the law amidst the thunders of Sinai. Other religions have grown, flourished and decayed, but Judaism remains as firmly rooted in the Hebrew mind as the Rock of Gibraltar in its ocean bed. Other systems of religious faith have changed and have called new councils to amend and alter their creeds. Other people, like the Celts, the Saxons and Normans, mingling their blood by marriage and intermarriage, have lost their identity. Nations and peoples mentioned in Holy Writ have passed away; have perished from the face of the earth, and are known only in song and story. The Egyptian, the Babylonian and the Persian empires rose, flourished and vanished, but "God's chosen people" remain to-day as they were hundreds of years ago.

While the Jews are a remarkable, a peculiar and an extraordinary race, they are, above all things, religious. They are noted also as being a law-abiding people. They are one as the ocean in their obedience to the laws of the country in which they live, but as distinct as the billows in their social distinctions. The Jew thrives where others scarcely live. He knows no decadence, no infirmities of age; no weakening, either physically or intellectually.

It has been truly said, "All things are mortal but the Jew; all other forces pass away, but he remains." And yet—

"That people once
So famed, whom God Himself vouchsafed to call
His chosen race, and with a guardian hand
Deigned to protect, from Palestine exiled,
Are doomed to wander; although scattered thus
Through all the globe, there is no clime which they
Can call their own, no country where their laws
Hold sovereign rule. Irrefragable proof
That every oracle of Holy Writ
Was given by Heaven itself!"

Cowper has truthfully said in this same connection—

"They, and they only, amongst all mankind,
Received the transcript of the Eternal mind;
Were trusted with His own engraven laws,
And constituted guardians of His cause!"
* * * * * * *
"Their glory faded and their race dispersed,
The last of nations now, though once the first."

The Pool of Siloam is near the southern end of Jerusalem. This is the pool where Christ bade the blind man "go wash" after He had anointed his eyes with clay. It no longer yields restorative and healing waters, but is partially filled with rocks and garbage.

The most sacred thoroughfare in Jerusalem is the Via Dolorosa, said to be the street along which our Lord bore His cross to Calvary. But there can be no certainty about this, even if this is the route, as the Jerusalem of the time of Christ, except the temple area, is buried beneath the rubbish of centuries, anywhere from a depth of thirty to a hundred feet.

In this street is shown the house of Pontius Pilate, and thence, past the Ecce Homo Arch, one has pointed out to him the place where Pilate is supposed to have said, "Behold the Man." A spot is indicated where Jesus took the cross on His shoulders; another where He fell in weakness; another still where He addressed the women of Jerusalem, and yet another where Veronica, it is said, wiped the perspiration from His brow.

Some distance farther on is a depression in the wall, caused, it is alleged, by Christ's elbow, as He pressed against it in His fall.

Amongst other holy sites on this street are the houses of Veronica, and of Dives, at whose door Lazarus begged. There is also exhibited the stone near which the thirty pieces of silver were counted out to Judas. If one were satisfied that this were really the street through which our blessed Lord passed, and that the statements about these sites were authentic, one's heart would be wrung with anguish and one's eyes bedimmed with tears. But there is always the element of doubt.

We also see the Tower of David, the Pool of Hezekiah and the Pool of Bethsaida, where the waters were troubled for the healing of the people and where Christ healed the impotent man, who was unable to get into the pool. It was 372 by 126 with a depth of sixty-eight feet. Other reputed sacred places are too numerous to mention.

One night during our sojourn in the Holy City, as president of the Masonic Association of the Steamer Arabic, I called the craft together and we all proceeded to Solomon's Quarry near the Damascus Gate. The quarry extends about 700 feet under the city. Our party was photographed by flash light.

From this quarry was procured, it is said, the stone out of which the temple was built by King Solomon. The stone is almost white and when first cut is quite soft, but becomes hard on exposure to the air. A tradition exists among Masons that the order was instituted by King Solomon himself in this quarry.

The Jews, Mohammedans, Greeks and Armenians have distinct quarters, each with their characteristic costumes and habits of life. There are other nationalites, too, for forty languages are spoken in Jerusalem. If all the inhabitants were to attempt to talk at one time what a babel there would be!

While in Jerusalem our party of three employed as dragoman one John Doorsy, who signs himself "wrightter Erabic letters and Pittishens in the streat of the Holy Sappillkeer." Doorsy is a native of Jerusalem, a Christian and a teacher of English, "as she is writ" in Jerusalem. He was for many years a teacher in Bishop Gobart's School, but owing to bad eyes, an affliction from which a large number of the inhabitants suffer, he had to give up the position, so he now follows the vocation above indicated, and in addition pilots visitors around. We found him intelligent, prompt and courteous.

On the second day of our visit, after a hard day's

tramp and ride, he invited us to his house to take some refreshment, saying he would consider it a great honor and pleasure to entertain us. Entering his door, we were greeted by his wife, who kissed our hands. This ceremony over, we were introduced to the thirteenth baby, a buxom brat of about six months, who exhibited his first tooth with the incipient pride of unsophisticated youth.

George, or as his father writes it, Jorge, is a very bright little chap, who "swam" on the floor and crowed for our entertainment with great gusto, much to the delight of his fond mother and to the profound satisfaction of his aged father. This boy, it should be understood, is the Benjamin of the father's old age.

After "Jorge" had again and again exhibited his first tooth and gotten through with his acrobatic performances, our host brought in a bottle of wine, which we discussed with enjoyment. The baby took a spoonful of this and Madam accepted a glass at my hands. We then partook of some cakes and confections, the repast ending with Turkish coffee. The house, which was cold and had floors of marble or stone, sadly needed a fire, but neither the baby nor his parents seemed to feel uncomfortable, although we had to keep on our overcoats to be comfortable.

Since our return home I received the following letter from Dragoman Doorsy, which is a good sample of phonetic spelling:

FROM JERUSALEM IN (24) MAY 1906.
DEAR MR. J. S. MOORE:
Sinse your Magesti left Jerusalem till now you do not appsent from my mind if you plies as to let me no that you poth ritch your homp safe in good health and in great beace.
Then also I beg to say that befor (1) month God from his Marcyfuly tammted me in that time that I am ought syed the Jaffa geat it poshet me from behind me one carriage and in my bag to the ground and from this rision untill now I am remened

tramp and ride, he invited us to his house to take some refreshment, saying he would consider it a great honor and pleasure to entertain us. Entering his door, we were greeted by his wife, who kissed our hands. This ceremony over, we were introduced to the thirteenth baby a buxom brat of about six months, who exhibited his first tooth with the incipient pride of unsophisticated youth.

George, or as his father writes it, Jorge, is a very bright little chap, who "swam" on the floor and crowed for our entertainment with great gusto, much to the delight of his fond mother and to the profound satisfaction of his aged father. This boy, it should be understood, is the Benjamin of the father's old age.

After "Jorge" had again and again exhibited his first tooth and gotten through with his acrobatic performances, our host brought in a bottle of wine, which we discussed with enjoyment. The boy took a spoonful of this and Madam accepted a glass at my hands. We then partook of some cakes and confections, the repast ending with Turkish coffee. The house, which was cold and had floors of marble or stone, sadly needed a fire, but neither the baby nor his parents seemed to feel uncomfortable, although we had to keep on our overcoats to be comfortable.

Since our return home I received the following letter from Dragoman Doorsy, which is a good sample of phonetic spelling:

FROM JERUSALEM IN (24) MAY 1906
DEAR MR. J. S. MOORE:
Sinse your Magesti left Jerusalem till now you do not appsent from my mind if you plies as to let me no that you poth ritch your homp safe in good health and in great beace.

Then also I beg to say that befor (1) month God from his Marcyfuly tammted me in that time that I am ought syed the Jaffa geat it poshet me from behind me one carriage and in my bag to the ground and from this rision untill now I am remened

"LITTLE JORGE" OF JERUSALEM.

REXBURG, IDAHO

in the badstad. My Son Jorge just he swim on the floor as to fatch on you for to kiss your hand and for to give you a capp of wine from his hand and he also recommend himself to be a Son for you then on this matter we believe that your Magesty his Fatheer therefor because you are the Fartheer of Marcy as to do with your Son from time to time in eny kind of favour for the sake of his Motheer and because she has a sore eyes. And instad of that we all ask God to keep you all as well and to giv you the Inheritins of his Kingdom. And also by this letter I send to you the pictior of my Son Jorge as to remember him by your Marcyfully.

Lastlay) as to accept from me from my wife our great regerds to your Shilldern and to your all Famala and to my friend Mr. J. V. Perley, and also I hope from your kindness for to manshind my name to your Parens and to your Frands in eny seazen they wish to come to Jerusalem as to be a Dragoamn for them; I am be opplidged as to sand for me the answer.

This es my address,   JOHN DOORSY.
Wrightter Erabic Letters and Pittishens in the Streat of the Holy Sappillker.

"And a certain man went down from Jerusalem to Jericho." We never before realized the significance of the little word "down" until we took this trip. The distance from Jerusalem to Jericho, in an air line, is about thirteen miles and by the ordinary route about sixteen, but the road is very precipitous and rough, and the Plain of Jericho is over 3,600 feet below Jerusalem; hence the significance of the word "down."

Our method of travel was in an open carriage with three horses. The sun was hot; the road, where not hilly, dusty and the poor beasts were unmercifully lashed by the drivers.

We had not traveled more than half the distance when "The Young Voyager," who sat in the front seat just behind the coachman, showed signs of distress by coughs and nose-blowing. After a while he remarked that he did not believe the driver had taken a bath since his birth, and that the odor emanating from him was awful, but we subsequently discovered that this unpleasant smell came not from the driver, but from the horses. These animals are fed, not like the horse of "Captain Jinks of the Horse Marines," on oats and beans, but on barley and cauliflower, and when they perspire the ensuing scent is like a combination of gunpowder and asafœtida, or the stink pots used by the Chinese in their naval engagements.

Jerusalem produces the finest cauliflower in the world, and at first we were very fond of it, but we could never relish it after our trip to Jericho.

From our observations we concluded that the drivers of Palestine were the most cruel we had ever met. On one occasion our horses balked at a hill, whereupon the brutal jehu got out and hit one of the animals on the head with a large stone. He thereby lost his "tip," for we told him that on account of his cruelty we would give him no "backsheesh."

A pleasant contrast to these brutes are the cabmen of Naples, who drive their horses without bits in the mouth, guiding them by pulling the rein in the direction they wish the animals to go. We commend them to the tender consideration of the S. P. C. A. Associations. In Naples, by the way, the horses and donkeys hitched to carts sometimes have a wisp of hay tied to the cart saddle, so that when not traveling the beasts can reach around and get a nibble.

The road to Jericho is through the winding Valley of the Jordan, with the gray and desolate-looking mountains of Moab in the distance, and the whole region treeless and barren; yet these bare, billowy hills and great ravines are not without their impressiveness and grandeur. After traveling some time we came to the Wady-el-Had, or Valley of the Watering Place, the only spring of water between Bethany and the Jordan Valley. It is called the Apostles' Spring, and there can be no doubt that our Lord and His disciples drank from it.

We continued our descent through the barren waste until we passed the spot where "a certain man went down from Jerusalem to Jericho, and fell among thieves," and pretty soon we were comfortably housed in the Khan Hadrur, or Good Samaritan Inn. This hostelry is about half way to Jericho. Here we partook of refreshments with a good deal of enjoyment and relish. We, however, did not try the oil which was poured into the wounds of the unfortunate who fell among the thieves, but we did drink a bottle of very indifferent wine, evidently not. of the vintage of which the unfortunate partook, unless age adds to acidity and insipidity. The thieves of this section were in evidence in the shape of fakirs with curios and antiques offered at high prices.

Among the curios exhibited here is the shirt of Goliath of Gath. It is about ten feet long and four feet broad. When we saw it there were no blood stains on the garment, so it could not have been the one Goliath wore when David smote him in the forehead and slew him.

We next journeyed to the Brook Cherith, where Elijah, the Tishbite, was fed by the ravens. Ravens are still seen flying about this section. In Palestine, in Egypt, and even on the Continent, the raven is a semi-domesticated bird; he resembles in shape our common crow, but in the Orient his plumage is not entirely black like our bird's. His breast is rather a whiteish-brown. These Eastern ravens are quite tame and do not fear man.

In Cairo, just in front of Shepard's Hotel, we noticed a raven's nest, and also found numbers of their abodes elsewhere. On the "Continent," too, we have seen them following a few feet behind the ploughmen and picking up the grubs unearthed.

Elijah must have had a very lonesome time at the Brook Cherith. It is a very uncomfortable looking place, and we do not blame him for changing his quarters to the house of the widow of Zarepeth.

In the ravine is a Greek monastery. It is built against the side of the cliffs; how any one gets in and out of the place, unless he is let down and pulled up by a rope, is a mystery. We were told that no woman had ever been across its threshold. Sensible women! One immured within its walls would soon be dead to all mundane affairs.

The site of ancient Jericho is indicated by a large mound, and as one looks at this mass of earth one can but exclaim: Are these the remnants of the walls that fell at the blasts of the trumpet? And viewing the desolation, where once stood the city of Palius, one naturally recalls the awful words pronounced by Joshua: "Cursed be the man before the Lord that riseth up and buildeth this city Jericho." Jericho in its day evidently was a city of importance; its walls were so considerable that houses were built upon them.

It was the first city in Canaan which fell into the hands of the Israelites. Jericho, for a considerable period, was the second city of Judea, and, according to the Talmud, contained twelve hundred priests. It had its hippodrome and amphitheatre, and in its royal palace Herod the Tetrarch died.

Near the eastern base of the mound is Elisha's Fountain—the one the prophet salted, and whose waters he made sweet, so that they "were healed unto this day." We drank of them and found them sweet. It is a beautiful stream, with water enough to turn a mill wheel, and it irrigates the whole Valley of Jericho. Wherever its waters touch fertility prevails. Near the fountain is the Cave of Elisha, and over against it beyond Jordan, Elijah "went up by a whirlwind into Heaven"—when Elisha possessed himself of Elijah's magical mantle.

At this famous fountain we met with the Governor of Jerusalem and his suite. Perley, who is always anxious to make acquaintances, gave one of the party a military salute, and entering into conversation with the man, proceeded to give his "military experience." Later Perley came to us and reported that he had been invited by the Governor to call on him at Jerusalem. We asked him to point out the Executive to us, which he did. The man, however, proved not to be his Excellency, but the corporal of the squad, so after that we frequently asked Perley when he intended to call on the Governor and when he expected to dine with him.

According to Josephus, the Plain of Jericho was the most fertile and delightful in the world; but then, there was a pretty good slice of the world that Josephus never saw. Therefore, due allowance must be made when he says: "He who should pronounce this place divine would not be mistaken. It will not be easy to light on any climate in the habitable earth that can be compared to it."

In our judgment the climate must have undergone a wonderful transformation since the time of this Jewish historian.

A dilapidated building is pointed out in Jericho as the identical house where Jesus was entertained by Zaccheus. The only reason why the sycamore tree into which Zaccheus climbed on that occasion is not shown, is because the only tree in the vicinity is a palm, supposed to be the sole survivor of the famous grove that gave ancient Jericho the name "City of Palm Trees."

Modern Jericho consists of a few wretched hovels, inhabited by an unattractive people. The only object of interest in the village is a ruined tower, built as a protection against robbers. Here it was in the days of the ancient Jericho that our Lord restored the sight of blind Bartimeus.

A half-hour's ride brings one to Gilgal. Here the twelve stones taken from the Jordan were set up as a memorial, and here, by Divine command, the Passover was celebrated.

The custom of measuring distances by time is still observed as in ancient days; distance is always spoken of as so many hours, not so many miles, as with us.

Several times on this trip all of us had to get out and walk, owing to the steepness and roughness of the roads and to the fact that our horses were not able to carry us up or down the ascents and declivities with safety. During the whole journey, both going and coming, we were guarded by a detail of armed Bedouins under one of their Sheiks; otherwise the trip would not have been safe. We were made to realize the truth of the old song, "Jordan is a hard road to trabble, I believe."

From Jericho we drove to the Jordan. We were disappointed at the stream, for its waters were muddy, and although the river had overflowed its banks, it was not more than fifty or sixty yards wide. The Jordan's banks are low and the view unattractive.

We took a boat ride on the river at the place pointed out as the identical spot where Christ was baptized. He could easily have been immersed, as I presume He was.

As I stood musing on the shores of this famed river that old hymn came into my mind—

> "On Jordan's stormy banks I stand
> And cast a wishful eye
> To Canaan's fair and happy land,
> Where my possessions lie."

And I wondered, too, if the writer had ever seen the Jordan except in his imagination. The hymn, I suppose, was a figment of the fancy, but it is not without force. Witness these lines—

"Baptized as for the dead, He rose
 With prayer from Jordan's hallowed flood;
Ere long by persecuting foes,
 To be baptized in His own blood."

Both on our trip down and back we encountered many caravans of camels tied together with strings, head to tail, and of donkeys in groups of three or four, laden with oranges, flour, faggots and produce.

The Jordan, to the imagination of the Jew, is a magnificent river. He invests it with a poetic imagery to which it is not entitled, except upon sentimental and religious grounds. Divested of its associations, it would be an ordinary stream of water, in no wise comparable to thousands of streams elsewhere.

From the Jordan we drove to the shores of the Dead Sea—the Salt Sea of the Bible. It is quite desolate, but not wanting in some beautiful aspects towards the purple mountains of Moab, which rise on the horizon. It is generally customary for pilgrims to bathe in the Jordan and the Dead Sea, but when our party was there it was a very bleak day, and not one of our travelers, to my knowledge, availed himself of the opportunity.

The Dead Sea is forty-seven miles long and from three to nine miles wide, and its greatest depth is 1,310 feet. Its surface is about 1,300 feet below the Mediterranean. No living thing is found in its bitter waters, and no vegetation exists on its barren shores. It is estimated that about six and one-half million tons of water flow into it every day, all of which are carried off by evaporation, as the sea has no visible outlet.

In going from the Jordan to the Dead Sea we passed through miles of barren land formerly covered by the water, which is receding year by year. The entire surface is covered with incrustations of salt that sparkle in the sun like thousands of scintillating diamonds.

The trip to the Jordan and Dead Sea is one we would not have missed but we have no desire to take it again— one is *quantum sufficit*.

We passed on the way many camps of Arabs. Their tents consisted of two or three poles and a piece of canvas—sometimes an old quilt or coverlet stretched on four poles. These people still seem to lead the same nomadic life they have lived for so many centuries. Some of the Arabs we saw had a few cattle, but most of them looked poverty-stricken and grovelling in want and nakedness.

Somewhere in this section stood Sodom and Gomorrah. Whether they actually lie covered by the waters of the Dead Sea, as some writers suppose, is unknown; but as the Bible speaks of them as cities of the plain it does not seem necessary to believe they are covered by these waters.

On our return from Jericho and the Dead Sea we stopped at Bethany, where dwelt Martha and Mary, and where Lazarus lived. It was on Christ's return to this city that the incident of the barren fig tree occurred. It was here, too, in the house of Simon the leper, that "there came unto Him a woman having an alabaster box of very precious ointment and poured it on His head at He sat at meat," at which seeming waste His disciples complained. And it was from this village He sent forth two of His disciples to "find a colt tied, whereon never man sat"—the animal upon which He rode into Jerusalem.

Here Perley—the irrepressible—being thirsty, asked for some water, but as his articulation is not generally distinct, the Arab to whom he addressed his request turned to me and asked, "What language does your friend speak?"

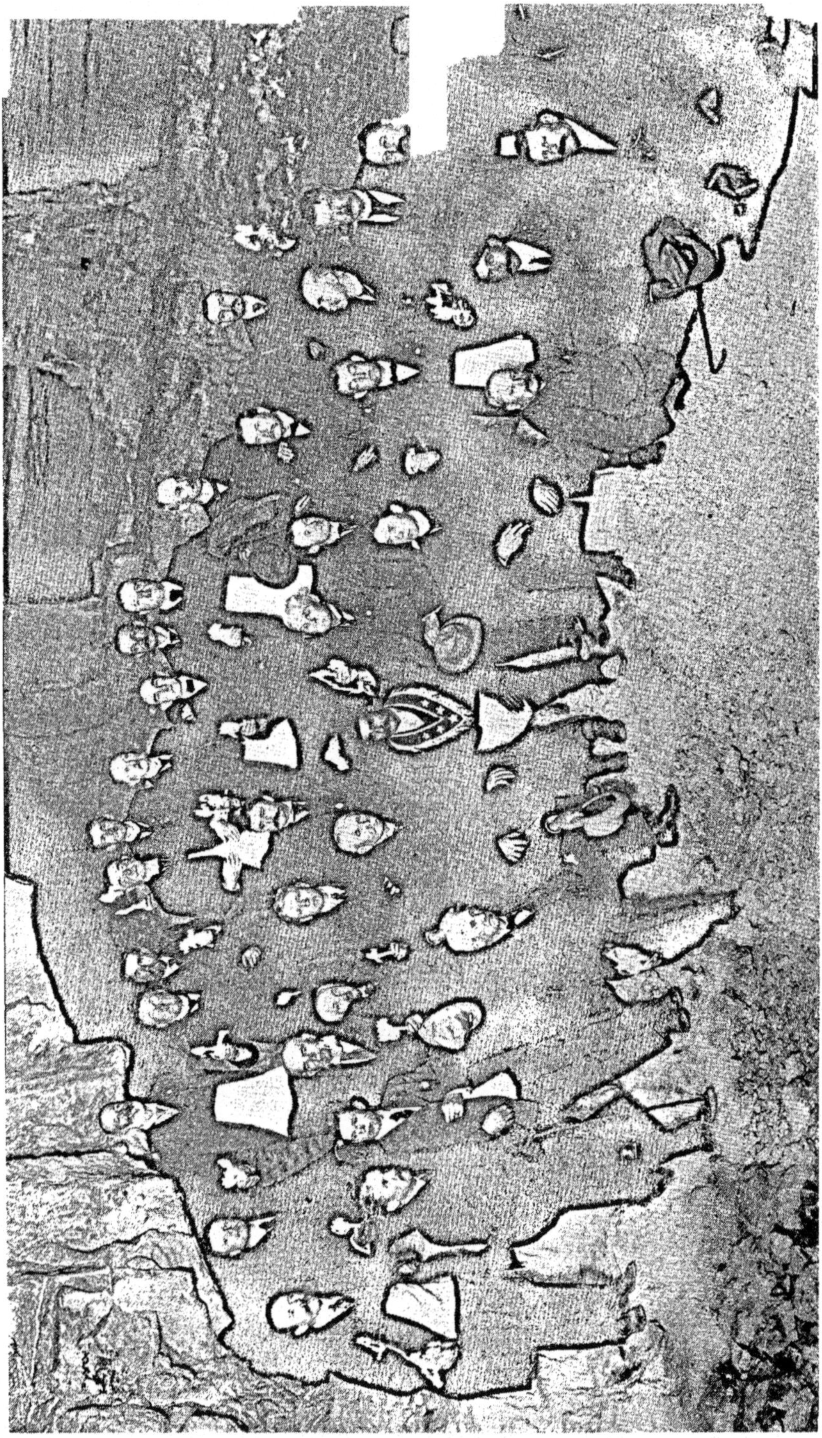

REXBURG, IDAHO

Near Bethany we saw many flocks of sheep attended by their keepers, and the sight recalled the descriptions in the Bible, "And there were in the same country shepherds abiding in the fields, keeping watch over their flocks by night." Hard by was what the natives call the "Eye of the Sun," which marks the boundary between the mountains of Moab and the Judean Mountains.

It was in this section that Jesus found His friend, Lazarus, whom He raised from the dead. We were shown a ruined tower, said to be the remains of the house of Lazarus and his sisters. The tomb of Lazarus is on the edge of the village. It is of considerable size and has an arched chamber and four niches for the reception of bodies; moreover, there is an unbroken sarcophagus remaining.

The mountains of Moab and the Judean hills in this vicinity are bare of vegetation. There is absolutely no timber. The slight growth of to-day is consumed tomorrow by the many flocks of goats and sheep that graze on the sides daily. The limits of the fields are marked by neither fences nor enclosures, but by a narrow strip of unploughed ground or a heap of stones—not even a hedge. The cattle are all tended.

Many caravans of camels and donkeys passed us on our return to Jerusalem. In the prime of Rome all roads led to the Eternal City; in Palestine all public highways led to Jerusalem, the Holy City.

On our return from Jericho to Jerusalem we passed the Mount of Temptation, which overlooks the plain and faces Jericho. But if the prospect presented to Christ was not more alluring than the scene before us, He deserved no particular credit for resistance to the wiles of the arch fiend. When the devil, doubtless looking down the slope of the mountain, asked that "these stones be made bread," he called for a greater miracle than the mere words would indicate, since the whole side of the mountain, as well as the plain, is a mass of broken boulders and rock, which, converted into food, would have served the whole of Judea for years. Along the face of the mountain are caves, once used by hermits.

Barring the cold, we were fortunate in having lovely weather during our stay in Palestine—the days sunshiny and delightful and the nights cool, but lit up by a resplendent moon and by a bright and scintillating galaxy of stars.

The sunsets of Jerusalem, by the way, are very beautiful—the yellow, the violet and the rose, all mingling, form a most gorgeous combination of colors, rivalling the rainbow in its many and varied tints; the blending of scarlet, green, gold and crimson with blue and emerald, is lovely beyond description; and the effect is heightened by the outlines of the sacred hills as they merge with the shadows of the distant mountains.

On this trip we also saw the sun rise over the mountains of Moab and beheld Aurora as she mounted their summits in her chariot, dispelling darkness and clothing the landscape in the tints of the morning; kissing the dewdrops with the fragrance of her presence, and bathing hill and valley in the soft rays of the rising sun, until she "sealed up the stars." We never before had so fully realized the poetic beauty of those Biblical words, which say: "There is one glory of the sun, and another glory of the moon, and another glory of the stars."

One night during our stay in Jerusalem it was so cold and the hotel so uncomfortable, owing to its lack of fires, that we retired to our rooms, and recalling the experience of Col. Mulberry Sellers, lighted a couple of candles; but finding no appreciable change in the atmospheric conditions we cut the candles in two, thus making four lights. Our scheme, however, was all in vain. We, therefore, put our overcoats on the bed clothes and covered up to keep warm.

The hotels at Jerusalem, be it said, are of the poorest quality; the accommodations miserable; the service of the worst kind and the fare indifferent. One of our friends, who was stopping at another house in the ancient city, came to our hotel and boasted that he had had fowl at his hotel once a day ever since his stay there. "That is nothing," said I, "we have had three *foul meals* every day we have been here."

Speaking of fowls, reminds me that Judge Masters made due research, but found no records of the importation of any foreign poultry into Palestine. He, therefore, concluded that we were fed from the lineal descendants of that celebrated cock that crowed to arouse Peter, when he denied his Master. If such a thing were possible, judging from the difficulty we found in masticating a certain bird on our table, we think the same old cock was served at the Hotel de Park.

The bread also was ancient and indigestible. Most of the water used in Jerusalem comes from cisterns, but some is brought in from neighboring springs in leather skins. Goat and pig hides are used, and in size and shape the receptacles remind one of the water bottles referred to in the Bible. "The Young Voyager" discovered some mollywigs and polliwigs in his wash basin, and suggested that the Israelites, on their return from Egypt, must have brought some of Pharaoh's frogs along with them.

The hotel waiters are a mongrel set, composed of Arabs and negroes and a mixture of both. All are poorly groomed and careless in the discharge of their duties, but anxious for "backsheesh" just the same.

Our next trip was to Bethlehem. We passed the Hill of Evil Council and then came to the Well of the Magi, where the Wise Men saw reflected in the water the Star, which in their journey they had lost sight of on the road to Bethlehem.

Many of the houses in Bethlehem are built of sunburnt brick—miserable abodes—and the occupants appear to be poor and destitute. Men, women and children go barelegged and barefooted. But in some places the fields and hillsides are carpeted with poppies, buttercups, daisies and other wild flowers.

About three miles from Jerusalem one comes to the well from which the Holy Family is said to have drunk in its flight into Egypt. Here may be seen the Field of Peas, so-called from the legend that our Lord once inquired of a man what he was sowing, and on receiving the curt reply, "Stones," forthwith turned the peas the farmer was scattering into stones. This tale does not strike one as being in keeping with the gentle nature of our Lord.

Bethlehem in the early morning presents a pretty picture—a scene long to be cherished in memory. "The little town of Bethlehem" on the hillside with its houses clustered together, offers a pleasant sight. The streets are cleaner and the women and children better looking and more decently dressed than in any other place in Palestine.

In Bible history, Bethlehem is associated with the lovely romance of Ruth and the youthful home life of David. It is also notable as the birth place of Joab, Asahel and Abishai, but its crowning distinction is that here our Saviour first saw the light. Beautifully has the poet said:

"At His birth, a star
Unseen before in Heaven, proclaims Him come,
And guides the Eastern sages, who inquire
His place, to offer incense, myrrh and gold.
His place of birth, a solemn angel tells
To simple shepherds keeping watch by night."

Many things in the Holy Land are apocryphal, but there seems to exist not a shadow of a doubt that this is the birthplace of Jesus. The Church of the Nativity, built over the grotto or manger where Christ was born, is the oldest church in the world, unless we except the Pantheon in Rome, which is still in good condition. The Pantheon was a pagan temple before the Christian era, but in the third century became a Christian house of worship. The Church of the Nativity, on the other hand, was not erected until the year 330 A. D. Its exterior indicates its antiquity. The interior has an impressive simplicity, in keeping with our Lord's character and simple life. It has forty-four monolithic columns with Corinthian capitals. In the crypt of the Nativity the tourist is shown the cave, or grotto, where it is believed that Christ was born. But there is nothing in the surroundings and environments which savors of a manger.

The church is about forty feet long, twelve wide and ten feet high. The walls are of masonry and the pavement of marble, with a silver star in the floor near the altar, with these words, *"Hic de Virgine Maria, Jesus Christus natus est."* Thirty-two lamps light the chapel.

A short distance from the Star of Nativity is the manger where Christ was first cradled. We go down a few steps into a room about ten feet square. The altar of the manger is on one side; that dedicated to the Magi is opposite on the other side.

The so-called manger is a block of white marble, hollowed out. It occupies a recess in the grotto, and is about two feet high and four in length. In the grotto is a picture of the Magi offering gifts to the infant Jesus.

The alleged original manger, or trough, was carried to Rome. There are various altars and chapels. One, dedicated to the Holy Innocents, marks the place where several children that were concealed, were found and slain by Herod.

A short distance from the town is the so-called Field of the Shepherds, where the shepherds were "abiding in the field, keeping watch over their flock by night," when the angel brought them "good tidings of great joy." Not far away, Ruth gleaned among the sheaves in the field of Boaz and set her triggers to entangle him in the net of matrimony—a feat which she successfully accomplished.

Bethlehem is the most hopeful of all the towns in the Holy Land. It has a population of about six thousand, all of whom are Christians, except about two hundred and fifty Moslems.

We were shown the spot where Saul lay asleep when David "took the spear and the cruse of water from Saul's bolster"; and also the Cave of Adullum, where David concealed himself. We also visited the Tombs of the Kings, where it is said that thirty-seven Jewish monarchs were interred. The chambers are cut in the solid rock, covering probably half an acre of ground, but each one has been despoiled of its coffin. Not even a bone is left. Emptiness reigns supreme.

To us was pointed out a well over which it is said the Star of Bethlehem stood, and also the Tomb of Rachel, where she wept over her children and would not be comforted. An arched stone sarcophagus covers the good woman's remains. Seven days in every year the Jews come to this tomb and hold services in her memory.

We were shown the Grotto of Milk, where lies the stone upon which, it is said, that Mary nursed Jesus. Some of the Virgin's milk spilt or flowed on the stone, which, according to popular belief, endows it with miraculous qualities. Women who are short in their supply of milk come here and sit on the stone or send for a few grains of it, which they pulverize and eat; and the happy result is an increasing flow from their breasts. (?)

We also saw the Well of David "that is at the Gate of Bethlehem." It was for this he "longed, and said, 'Oh, that one would give me drink of the water of Bethlehem, that is at the Gate.'" And three of his brave soldiers "broke through the host of the Philistines" and took it to David, but notwithstanding his great thirst, he refused to drink it, because these men had put their lives in jeopardy for his sake.

On the occasion of our visit the flocks were grazing on the same hills and were being driven along the same paths as of yore. Women and children were on the sides of the mountain gathering sticks. These, for the most part, they bound into bundles and bore on their backs, after having secured them by the rope with which they were bound across their foreheads. Some bore the bundles on their heads.

At Bethlehem the chief occupation seemed to be the making of crosses, beads, stars and other ornaments of pearl for sale to the tourists. We saw some shells, the workmanship of which was most delicate and exquisite.

On our last day in Jerusalem we took another trip to the Mount of Olives, the Garden of Gethsemane and the Church of the Holy Sepulchre—places we never expect to see again. Then we silently bade them adieu, profoundly thankful that we had been permitted to view these sacred places, hallowed by so many associations and sanctified by His presence. It was a profound satisfaction, after such a day's tramp, to get back to the hotel, poor as it was, and sink down into a comfortable chair.

"Boys will be boys" the world over. Witness the fact that we saw the urchins of Jerusalem playing marbles and pitching pennies, although they do not play marbles like our youngsters. They put the "taw" on the ground and shove it with the forefinger, instead of shooting it from the thumb. The cent-pitching was the same as ours.

The Jews in Jerusalem are a hard looking set; they do not compare with the Jews in our city. Among the common people the moral degeneracy is frightful. Their houses are filthy, their persons unclean. They are very heavily taxed, and it is said that their poverty is becoming more pitiful, while the beggars are growing more numerous and more persistent. The city of Jerusalem has neither bookstore nor newspaper, so that ignorance goes hand in hand with poverty and untidiness.

CHAPTER VII.

Alexandria and the Bay of Abukir—Rural Egypt a Land of Flies and Fertility—Irrigation Methods—Touching Scarab Beetles and Camels—Government Dispensary at Baliana—Ruins at Abydos—Egyptians of To-Day—Wished-for Crocodiles Never Appeared—Wonders at Karnack—Temple of Rameses—Thebes and its Colossal Guards—Kings who Built Pyramids—The Ascent of Cheops—Facts About the Inscrutable Sphynx—Sights in Cairo—An Ostrich Farm.

We left Jerusalem March 13th and reached Alexandria the next day. The approach to Alexandria reminds an American of Atlantic City, stretching as it does for miles along the strip of land which lies between the Mediterranean Sea and Lake Mareotis.

The first object that strikes the vision is the Pharos. This is "the direct descendant" of the earliest light-house in the world, the Pharos Tower, built in the reign of Ptolemy II., Philadelphus. The original tower was nearly six hundred feet high, and in it great fires were kept burning every night as beacon lights for mariners along the coast. It was regarded as one of the seven wonders of the world.

Not far away is the Bay of Abukir, where that noble youth, Casabianca, the son of the Admiral of the Nile, lost his life and won for himself the immortal encomium beginning—

> "The boy stood on the burning deck,
> Whence all but he had fled,
> The flame that lit the battle's wreck
> Shone round him o'er the dead."

The next most prominent object that attracts the eye

is Pompey's Pillar. This shaft is a single block of red granite about ninety feet high. Its name is a misnomer, as it was erected in honor of Diocletian, and has no historical relation to Pompey.

Owing to the prevalence of the plague, we were not permitted to visit the city. In the harbor we found three men of war flying the Stars and Stripes; a large flotilla of small boats and many merchantmen loading and discharging their varied cargoes.

Our journey by rail from Alexandria to Cairo was very pleasant, the service good, with modern accommodations, and quite in contrast with the railroads of Spain. We passed many mud huts and hovels, covered with grass and straw, in which the natives live. In the pastures were sheep and cattle and the peculiar looking Nile ox. The country is very level and the landscape is made beautiful by shapely and luxurious palms. Many brick kilns met our gaze, and as we looked on these we thought of the unhappy children of Israel and their relentless taskmasters, the Egyptians, who "made their lives bitter with hard bondage, in mortar and in brick."

There are no fences in Egypt; the narrow strip that lies on each side of the Nile is one continuous field of verdant green, whose boundaries are determined by the ancient landmarks of stones.

The fellahs working in the fields, in their unique and variegated costumes, present a novel and picturesque sight.

We found the dust very troublesome, but on the train was a "duster" in the form of a shapely Arab, who came regularly through the cars with his brush.

Hundreds of years ago, the historian, Herodotus, wrote: "Egypt contains more wonders than any other land, and is pre-eminent above all the countries in the world." This declaration stands to-day undisputed and verified.

From Cairo we traveled up the Nile to Luxor and Karnack, where we saw the ruins of ancient temples representing a civilization long since past and gone—a civilization that left its footprints on the sands of time in the shape of superb monuments, temples, pyramids and obelisks, unsurpassed in grandeur and beauty, as samples of sculpture and art.

Some of the paintings on the walls of the temples, in the mausoleums and chambers of the dead, or on the mummy cases, are as vivid in color as if put there yesterday, and yet they were made thousands of years ago. The shifting sands of the desert, the devastation wrought by man, the disintegration due to time and earthquakes and the gnawing tooth of the elements have laid many of Egypt's temples in the dust; but the paintings and the sculpture on what are left are perfectly preserved, so far as the freshness of the coloring goes. This seemingly imperishable work is now a lost art, as the pigment is unknown to the present generation. It is supposed that the ancient Egyptians made their pigments by dissolving the metals themselves.

Wonderful is the fecundity of the Nile! The Romans always spoke of their favorite river as "Father Tiber," while the natives of Egypt called their magic stream "Father Nile." We recall seeing in the museum at Rome a colossal recumbent statue, taken from Egypt when that country was under Roman rule, and called "Father Nile." In the hands of the giant are sheaves of wheat and barley; around his knees and on his body are children playing; cattle and sheep graze in the rich pastures and fish are laid at his feet on the banks of this wonderful river.

The Nile ranks as one of the four longest rivers in the world, being about four thousand miles in length. It is the Life-Giver—a stream of life between two continents of death—the great deserts. Some conception of this great river can be formed when it is stated (we suppose truthfully) that for more than a thousand miles no stream empties into it before the Nile reaches the Mediterranean.

Its waters are used to irrigate the entire length of its course, where the land is cultivated; it supplies the wants of neary ten million people; great quantities of its water are evaporated, and yet it is estimated that it empties into the Mediterranean 61,500 cubic feet of water every second.

In sooth, the fecundity of the Nile is most wonderful; wherever its magical waters touch, fertility exists; and where its waters do not reach, desolation and aridity prevail. This fecundity extends not only to inanimate, but to animated nature; not only to the vegetable, but to the animal kingdom. In the vast country traversed by the Nile the women all have children and the domestic animals breed rapidly, while the insect life is wonderfully prolific.

Many of the plagues introduced by Moses yet remain. The flies he invoked are still represented by a lively and active race. In vain do you sing "Shoofly, don't bother me," to them. At all times they can be seen on the faces and around the eyes of the children, who bear them with patience, as the Egyptian regards the fly as a sacred insect, and has great respect for the god of flies. Your scion of the Pharaohs does not wish to insult his majesty; and the fly, not being accustomed to being disturbed in his meditations or perambulations, resents the rebuffs of the irreverent traveler. Try your hand on the insect and he will come back at you with a persistent, determined buzz of indignation and surprise, so that you have to carry a fly wisp in your hand all the time, and must use it vigorously. Why these pests should annoy an innocent American, I cannot see; certainly it is not a case of the visitation of the sins of the fathers upon the children, because we are not of the same race.

The trip up the Nile in the steamer Victoria—a distance of about four hundred and fifty miles—was exceedingly pleasant and enjoyable. At last we had reached a land where the icicles and frosts of Jerusalem and Jericho were thawed into pleasant streams of perspiration.

The scenery along the Nile is striking and characteristic of the country. Crops are raised entirely by irrigation. We were told that it never rains, yet on our trip to the Tomb of the Kings "The Young Voyager" had occasion to remark, "It rains!" "Go away, boy," I said, "it has not rained here for thousands of years." But in confirmation of his assertion, I saw about two drops descend, one of which struck my hand. A lady also said she had heard a few drops pelting the roof of her hotel the previous night.

The same primitive methods that obtained during the days of the Pharaohs still prevail in Egypt. There are three ways in which the water is raised to the little channels through which it is carried off to irrigate the fields. The *shaduf* has been used from the earliest times. It is a kind of seesaw palm beam, or pole, with a lump of Nile mud at one end and a rod with a bucket attached at the other; it is worked by one, and sometimes by two men, who lift it eight or ten feet. When the river is very low, three, four and sometimes five-lift shadufs may be seen carrying the water to the fields.

The second medium is the *sakiya*. It is a huge

horizontal wheel, dragged round and round by a yoke of oxen or a donkey and a buffalo—sometimes by a camel. The animals turn a vertical wheel, on which is a rope connecting a number of earthen pots, that dip up the water as the wheel revolves, and then empty it into a trough at the top.

The third is the *Archimedean screw,* which revolves with a rotary and suction motion; but the shaduf and sakiya are in more general use.

We were told that higher up steam pumps were being introduced, but if brought into general use, these will do away with one of the most picturesque scenes on the Nile.

On our steamer the meals were served by Nubian waiters; they are a fine set of fellows, about the color of our mulattoes—lithe, graceful and agile as cats. They dress in pure white gowns, reaching nearly to their ankles; red fezes, red slippers, red sashes and black stockings, and present a most picturesque appearance. These Nubians are unusually polite and attentive to their duties.

In our ship's company we had an Egyptian fakir with a supply of scarabs, beads, rings, jewels and bracelets—all genuine (?) antiques. On our second day's journey he made his appearance on deck and placed his commodities on a table for inspection. After he had dwelt for some time on their beauty, and stated the different dynasties in which each article was used or made, he named his prices. The figures ranged from one pound to twenty-five pounds.

I stepped to the table, and taking up one or two scarabs, said, without cracking a smile, "Give me the three best you have for ten cents." I never saw a fellow so knocked out as he was. He said he had none of that kind.

Many persons paid extraordinary prices for these trinkets—prices far beyond what the things were worth, and a great deal more than they would have had to pay had they waited until they reached Luxor. A native never expects you to pay the first price asked.

The supply of scarabs is inexhaustible. It is to be presumed that they are shipped by the million from Germany or France. The scarab is made in the shape of a beetle and its material is of stone or clay. The backs of the imitation insects exactly reproduce nature, but the under sides are engraved like seals with an immense variety of devices, and are inscribed with charms or texts from the "Book of the Dead."

The scarabæid beetle was worshipped by the ancient Egyptians, who regarded it as an emblem of fertility and of the resurrection. It was the custom to place one under the tongue of the corpse and one over the heart. The beetles were also deposited in the mummy cases. Those sold are represented to be genuine—taken from the tombs and mummy cases—but not one in a thousand is the real thing.

The government of Egypt does not permit any one, except by special permission, to disturb the sepulchres of the dead; and every person found selling genuine scarabs, beads or other curios is arrested. Searches and exhumations are made by the government itself and whenever it comes into possession of a duplicate of any curio previously found in a tomb, it sells either the one on hand or the one found, in order to reimburse itself for the expense incurred.

Egypt owes its very existence to the Nile. Should this river cease to flow, or be diverted from its course, the whole cultivated section would lapse into the barrenness of the desert, by which it is bordered. In fact, only a circumscribed strip of land on each side of the river is cultivated. At some points, where canals are carried out from the river, these areas are enlarged, and in many sections the land irrigated is considerable.

So entirely dependent is the country upon the river that the year is divided into three seasons—*Nile,* inundation from August to November; *Shitwi,* from December to March, and *Sefi,* from April to July.

The population of Egypt is estimated at about ten million; three-fourths are fellaheen, or peasants; the rest Copts, Nubians, Turks, Laventines, Armenians, Jews and Europeans.

The fellah struck us as being a good and faithful laborer; all day long in the hot sun he will stand on the river bank working the shaduf, while his naked skin bronzes in the heat. The men wear full white cotton breeches and a blue cotton skirt, like the women's garment. A brown felt skull cap completes the costume. The Shekh will wear a black cloak, a red fez with blue tassel, white turbans and red or yellow shoes. The women are attired in a long, loose-sleeved garment of dark-blue or black, open at the neck, and usually have a long veil on their heads, but not over their faces. The better classes, however, do wear the face veil. In all the cities the Egyptians wear the red, flat-topped fez. This is the headgear of all except the poorest, from Khedive to donkey-boy.

The women of the towns wear voluminous black silk cloaks, which entirely envelope them, and black face veils with curious ornaments of brass—and sometimes of gold—that fit in the hollow of the nose where it joins the forehead. Some of the fair ones wear single, and some double, ornaments of this kind. We were told that those who wore one of these ornaments thus indicated that they were marriageable—ready, willing and waiting to be asked—while those who wore the double ornaments had yokemates already. The class who had none were neither married nor desired to enter into that state—will you believe me, there were very few of this contingent?

Our steamer goes slowly up the the Nile, as the water is low, and she has to feel her way cautiously, particularly at night, lest she run her nose into a sandbank. Now we experience a slight jar and we know we are aground; but as the vessel only draws two feet of water, and is flat bottomed, we soon get off again.

As we gradually ascend the breeze from the Lybian desert, purified by its passage over the hot sands, is delightfully refreshing; and before us is spread a beautiful panorama of natural scenery. Here is a flock of sheep grazing in the verdant fields and attended by their shepherd. There a drove of cattle quietly browsing or chewing the cud of content. Yonder, stretching along the banks, is a grove of stately palms, or a cluster of date trees, scintillating in the sun. Beautiful fields of wheat, clover and barley are waving in the breeze like rippling waters and we see acres of luxuriant cane shooting its spires heavenward to be kissed into sweetness by the sunbeams.

Here and there along the banks of the river are groups of natives in their characteristic costumes, squatting on the ground, working at the shaduf, or engaged in filling their huge water jars from the turbid, but life-giving, stream. Occasionally, in full view of all beholders, some simple-minded Egyptian appears in a state of nudity in the water; others are seen washing their clothes in the river as it meanders by their homes. The verdure of the fields is intense, as the rich alluvial soil produces the deepest green we have ever seen, "for the earth bringeth forth fruit of herself; first the blade, then the ear, after that the full corn in the ear." David must have been looking on such a scene when he exclaimed: "The pastures are clothed with flocks; the valleys are covered with corn; they shout for joy, they also sing."

The stream is here and there dotted with the craft peculiar to the Nile—boats with long, tapering, pole-like masts and bird-wing sails. They are the most graceful little ships in the world, as they dip or veer in the sun, according to the shifting of the wind. At night these sails glide by like phantoms. In the day they load and discharge their cargoes of wheat, onions and barley; we noticed many freighted with chopped straw for cattle.

Yonder, along the road that runs parallel with the stream, goes a drove of camels, laden with grain, provender or merchandise and slowly plodding their weary way to some town. These ungainly, but useful, animals continue to "carry the burdens of the Orient." They have been associated with the East from the beginning of time, and will never be supplanted by steam or electricity. True, these may somewhat lessen his burdens, but the camel in the Orient will always appear in evidence. Even before man was rocked in the cradle of civilization he was, and amidst all the wreck of matter and the crush of worlds he will still be there. The camel is the most patient of all beasts. At the command of his master he still piously kneels, as he has done for thousands of years, ever faithful and rarely refusing to bear the heavy burdens imposed on him.

The sight of a caravan carries one back to the days of Abraham and the Patriarchs. They did not believe in undue haste in those days; everything was done slowly, quietly, deliberately; we are even told that King Ahasuerus "sent letters by posts on camels."

The trip up the Nile at night was delightful, for the stars shone brightly, scintillating like diamonds, and the full moon, lighting up the waters for miles, was brilliant as it appeared in a perfectly cloudless sky.

The villages, as we passed, were wrapped in sleep, and the stillness, save for the noise of the steamer, was profound. Occasionally a light in some distant village could be seen, but nothing disturbed the quiet, save the ripple of the waters against the banks, or the barking of a dog in the distance. It was a scene alike peaceful and soothing, gently quieting mind and heart.

As the heavens stretched above us into boundless space, and the desert, in its profundity of silence, lay before us with all the mysteries of its wondrous past, I could but exclaim with the sweet singer of Israel, "When I consider Thy heavens, the work of Thy fingers, the moon and the stars, which Thou hast ordained; what is man that thou are mindful of him? And the son of man, that Thou visitest him "

We noticed that in the midst of the river, wherever the waters had receded sufficiently, patches of melons were planted, and we were told that the crop would mature in sixty days from the time it was put in the soil. We also saw many sugar factories, the largest in the world being on the Nile.

In ascending the river, we passed the Island of Roda, the place where the daughter of Pharaoh went down to take her bath and discovered the infant Moses sleeping among the bullrushes. The exact spot was pointed out, but I regret to say the rushes have long since disappeared.

Hard by is the old Nilometer, dating from 716 A. D. It is in the form of a well, sixteen feet square, with an octagonal column, inscribed with Arabic measurements, in the center. When the river is at its lowest point the

Nilometer covers seven ells, and when it rises, about fifteen ells. An ell is twenty-one and one-third inches.

We also passed the fine palace of the Khedive. We likewise had pointed out to us at a distance the mountains beyond, which offered the road by which Moses conducted the children of Israel to the Red Sea.

Many boats are kept loaded with stone to fill up weak spots in the river's banks. The soil is so rich and so lacking in clay or adhesiveness, that when the water rises vast inroads are made on the banks, and consequently there is a constant shifting of the bed of the river. The government lays the stone in the places where a sudden turn or bend in the river renders this necessary.

The city of Luxor originally was built on the side of the river opposite to that on which it now stands, a new channel having been made by this fickle stream. Both in loading and unloading the boats, the natives carry the stone on their heads in baskets. As a rule, the Egyptians live in small villages near the river. Their huts are flat-roofed and covered with straw, but shaded by beautiful palms, some of which grow through the roofs of the houses.

Each village, no matter how small, has its little mosque where the faithful respond daily to the muezzin's call to prayer, with their faces piously turned towards Mecca. Mohammedans believe the world is flat and that Mecca is its center. Mecca is the birthplace of Mohammed and the site of Kaaba, their venerated shrine.

The Kaaba is a cube-shaped building in the center of the Great Mosque at Mecca. It contains the sacred black stone, called *hajar al aswud,* said to have been originally a ruby, which came down from Heaven, but which is now blackened by the tears shed for sin by pilgrims. The black stone is in the southeast corner of the edifice and is the point to which all Mohammedans face during their devotions.

Sunning himself on the banks of the Nile, apparently in deep cogitation as he awaits the coming of his prey to satisfy the wants of nature, the long-legged crane can be seen. The blue heron, with outstretched neck, can also be seen winging his flight up the river as he is disturbed by the approach of the boat. Solitary and alone sits the pelican with his solemn features and distended pouch, as though pondering over the inscrutable mysteries of nature.

In many places the river's banks are honeycombed with holes made by the swallows and they can be seen darting in and out in countless numbers. In the mountainous section of the Nile, we saw perched upon the crags or circling around their summits, hundreds of eagles— probably the Gier Eagle of the Bible!

The old-time Egyptian was not without poetic fancy. Observing that the lotus showed its head above water at sunrise and sank again at Sol's setting, he conceived the idea of consecrating this flower to Osiris, or the sun. Moore has embalmed this conception in the following:

"The youthful day,
    Within its twilight bower,
 Lay sweetly sleeping
    On the flush'd bosom of a lotus flower."

Our first stopping place was at Baliana. Here we discovered a government dispensary. We entered and found amongst other liquids for sale Pabst American beer. We ordered a bottle, but as it was not iced we could not drink it. There is also a large sugar factory at this place.

Our object in getting off here was to visit the ruins of Abydos, distant some eight or ten miles. In order to avoid, as far as possible, the heat of noonday, we decided to get up at 4 o'clock the next morning. On arising we witnessed a curious and novel performance—the scrubbing of the decks by the Nubians. This feat is accomplished with their "pedal extremeties." A wisp of straw is held by some occult power in the middle of the Nubian's foot, and is artistically and effectively manipulated. Only one foot is used by each man, but all work in concert, accompanied by rhythmic songs and motions of the body.

It was a gay cavalcade that started on the ride through the desert to the ruins of Abydos. But before we set out we were treated to a sight of the "Battle of the Saddles." The conductor of our party had the saddles for our donkeys on the boat, having procured them in Cairo, and the natives were to furnish the beasts for the trip, so the effort of every donkey-boy in the neighborhood the next morning was to secure a saddle for his particular animal, thereby getting a customer and "backsheesh." These boys rushed pell-mell over the gang-plank, and a regular battle ensued. One would get a grip on the pommel of a saddle and another would sieze on to the stirrups, while a third would tussle at the girth. Such a jabbering and fussing was never before heard or seen.

Finally the captain, to quell the disturbance, had to call on the local police, who responded promptly. The police go armed with a cowhide or stick—the Egyptian is ruled entirely by the rod and the fear of the bastinado. Without mercy these African cops laid their lashes on the backs and legs of the boys, and actually threw several of them overboard. Order, by these means, was finally restored, and the saddles apportioned out among the claimants; but many of them not only had itching palms, but itching backs from the thrashings they had received.

We were greeted on our entrance into the town of Baliana by all of the children of the village and heard the usual cry, "backsheesh, backsheesh." Through the unpaved streets we took a walk, though we noted little of interest, save that the houses are built of sun-burned brick. The tourists amused themselves by throwing small coins to the crowd of Arabs, and there was so much scrambling that the police again interfered with their persuasive whips, which lashed right and left, and scattered the crowd in all directions.

The Arab policeman is a man of authority, even as was the Roman centurion, and exclaims, as did the latter, "I say unto one, go, and he goeth; and to another, come, and he cometh."

We had seventy-two on our Nile steamer and about sixty of these took the donkey ride. Each donkey was attended by a donkey-boy, who trotted along beside or behind his beast to keep him up and to attend to the wants of the rider. Without the presence of these boys behind or on the side the whimsical animals would have ceased to move.

The donkey-boys are a sharp set. They give their beasts pet names calculated to please the riders. My, donkey, for instance, bore the euphonious name "Yankee Doodle"; others were, respectively, called "America," "Dixie," "Jonathan," and the like.

We started from Beliana just as the sun rose over the hills bounding the deserts of Arabia and caused the dew-drops to scintillate like clusters of diamonds. The birds were caroling in the fields and our lungs expanded under the keen morning air. We passed through a beautiful valley. The camels were being loaded, kneeling obediently to receive their burdens for the day, and the shepherds were driving their flocks afield. We could see the farm laborers, both men and women, bestirring themselves for the duties that lay before them. Verily, our eyes gazed on an animated scene—one of pastoral beauty and life. It was like nature awakening from her sleep.

"The Young Voyager" came in contact with one of the Arab fortune tellers, and she told him he would attain wealth, live to be eighty-two and become the father of six sons and three daughters. Naturally he was much pleased with the tale she told.

In our ride across the desert to Abydos, the gentleman from St. Louis led the van. He rode without stirrups, and when the donkey trotted he held on to the crupper with one hand and to the mane of the beast with the other. His head made involuntary courtesies and bows of acknowledgement to all passers, his body swaying from side to side, first on the donkey's neck and then behind the saddle—

"Away went Bullock: who but he? his fame soon spread around,
He carries weight; he rides a race! 'tis for a thousand pound."

So all gave him free passage, and he was unanimously conceded to be the most polite man of the party, even excepting Perley, the invincible; but he remarked the next day that he felt like one of the martyrs who had been racked by the tortures of the Inquisition.

Next came "The Young Voyager," who sat his donkey with an uncertain poise. He had provided himself with a new native straw hat, "and he had bound a snow-white plume upon his gallant crest" in the shape of a beautiful silk scarf, which, like the oriflame on the helmet of Henry of Navarre at Ivry, floated on the breeze and rippled in the wind.

Then followed Perley, who bestrode a very small animal, so that his feet were constantly scraping the ground, and he came near ruining his patent leathers. Perley's donkey was disposed to buck, but Perley locked his long legs under him and the little beast could not dislodge his rider. As usual, Perley wandered off and got lost from the party, so we had to threaten to bell him. Some one suggested that he had probably stopped to count his postals, a duty he religiously performed several times a day.

The Judge and this chronicler rode well to the front, and here the accident, related in the beginning of these reminiscences, befell us.

In our party were many pretty girls who sat their donkeys gracefully and many gentlemen who rode cavalierly. There was one fat lady who could only mount from a wall or block. I shall never forget the pathetic look in the eyes of her donkey, as she first assayed to get on his back. The poor brute, as he felt her weight, turned his eyes as much as to say, "Have I this burden to carry?" The fat lady was going on quite merrily when the girth broke and she went down in a confused heap. But she mounted again and rode the balance of the way chaperoned on either side by an Arab. If she started to slide off on the right-hand side, she was held on by her right bower, while if she showed a tendency to go to the left she was supported by her left bower. By common consent the fat lady was given the right of way, and whenever she appeared the cavalcade veered over to one side of the road to admit her passage.

On the way we encountered a caravan of camels loaded with hay, and the huge mass took up the entire roadway. We had to dismount and take our donkeys down hill or get on the pile of stones by the highway until the caravan passed, else we would have been swept away as with a besom of destruction.

The first ruin we entered at Abydos was the Temple of Seti I. It is considered one of the most beautiful in Egypt, as it is built of fine white limestone. At one time it was entirely buried in the sand, but it has been excavated. The pylon and walls have almost disappeared, but there are some beautifully sculptured pillars. On the walls there are pictures representing Osiris, Isis and Seti I.

Passing through the entrance we came to a hall with twenty-four sandstone columns. On the walls were many curious carvings and sculptures peculiar to Egyptian art. The vaulted roofs of the finely decorated chambers proved interesting, the vault being of solid blocks. Here we saw the Tablet of Abydos, containing a list of seventy-six Kings.

Many of the pictures sculptured on the walls are in a good state of preservation. Their colors are vivid, notwithstanding the lapse of time, the throes of earthquakes, the vandalism of enemies and the disintegration caused by the elements. These temples were built 5,000 or 6,000 years B. C.

The next temple we visited was that of Rameses II., but we found very little of it standing. Some of the reliefs that survive, however, are very fine. In fact, there are acres of these ruins that possess great interest for the antiquary and the archæologist.

The ancient Egyptians had a book which they held just as sacred as we do our Bible. They called it the "Book of the Dead." From this they extract texts and inscriptions, which they placed on their tombs, mummy cases, monuments and temples. Their religion was an elaborate scheme of psychology. The human entity was conceived as consisting of seven different parts, of which the actual body was one, and upon the preservation of which, in some occult way, depended the ultimate reunion of the whole. It was for this reason that such care was taken to preserve the bodies of the departed from corruption and that they were made into mummies and hidden away carefully in tombs and pyramids. The destruction of the mummy might mean incompleteness of eternal being. The apathy and unconcern of the old-time Egyptian would seem to indicate that their aim in life was expressed in the words—

>"Death is the end of life; ah, why
>Should life all labour be?
>Let us alone."

The cherished doctrine was the metempsychosis; the soul, on leaving the body, was supposed to become a wandering spirit, entering into some bird of the air, beast of the field, or fish of the sea, and waiting for a regeneration in the natural body. This belief inculcated a pious regard for the security and preservation of the dead, and caused them to deify animals, reptiles and insects.

The Mohammedan faith consists of six articles, which constitute its creed—Belief in God, in His Angels, in His Scriptures, in His Prophets, in the Resurrection, Day of Judgment and Eternal Life, and Predestination. Among the believers the shibboleth is "Allah is God and Mohammed is His Prophet." The four practices required by their religion are prayer, alms, fasting and the pilgrimage to Mecca.

On the walls of some of the tombs are pictured pastoral and rural scenes—the reaping of wheat, the treading out of the corn; the winnowing, measuring and storing of the grain. The inscriptions give little songs of the laborers. One has been interpreted thus:

>"Hie along oxen,
>Tread the corn faster!
>The straw for yourselves,
>The grain for the Master."

The people of Egypt still use the antiquated and cumbersome wooden plow drawn by oxen and in some instances by camels; but the ancient method of driving a flock of sheep over the fields to trample in the grain is not now in vogue.

When I looked upon these and similar ruins and then saw the Egyptian of to-day—steeped in ignorance and grovelling in poverty—I asked myself the question: "Can these people be the lineal descendants of those who not only wrought such grand and imposing structures, but were adepts in sculpture and skilled in science; the builders of those grand pyramids that have excited the interest and the wonder of the world; the masters of a civilization that flourished when the world was in its infancy?"

And so, too, when I stood on the Acropolis at Athens, amid its acres of desolation—its sunken columns, its fallen pilasters, its ruined entablatures, its crumbling friezes, its broken cornices and its grass-grown architraves—the following questions suggested themselves: "Can the present people of Greece be the children of the heroes of Thermoplylae, Marathon and Salamis? Could their ancestors have been the masters of eloquence, the apotheses of liberty, the founders of classic art—the models of all time?"

As I reflected on the answers the breeze from over the blue Ægean seemed to whisper in accents soft and low—

"Fair Greece! sad relic of departed worth!"

But to return to my subject—our trip up the Nile was pleasant in every sense and our comparatively small company very sociable, while the officers of the boat, who were Scotch, proved cordial and genial. I shall never forget the delightful time we had one night, when we were entertained with song and music by the surgeon of the vessel and a coterie of congenial spirits. At the end of the evening we joined hands and all sang "Auld Lang Syne" with a pathos and tenderness long to be remembered. Although we were comparative strangers, when we came to the lines—

> "And here's a hand, my trusty fiere,
> And gie's a hand o' thine,"

we all felt it was a seal of real friendship.

Somehow we had always associated the crocodile with the Nile. Great was our surprise and disappointment, therefore, in not seeing any of these ungainly creatures sunning themselves on the banks or disporting themselves in the waters. Alas! in our trip of four hundred and fifty miles we did not see a single crocodile. The introduction of the steamboat has driven them away, but we were told some could be found beyond the cataracts.

In nearly every village we passed we noticed pigeoncots, built of mud in the shape of sugar loaves and whitewashed. Pigeons form an important item in the way of food in Egypt, and pigeon-pie is regarded as quite a dish with the natives.

The service and fare on the Victoria were far better than on the Arabic, and the trip was a delightful rest after our return from Abydos.

The immense quantity of stone that is being brought from the quarries by the boats or is being transported on the backs of camels for the strengthening of the river's banks and the building of dykes; the large number of small boats traversing the Nile loaded with cotton, cane, sugar, beans, wheat and other products; the tall chimneys of many large sugar factories silhouetted against the horizon along the banks of the stream, the whistle of locomotives and swift-passing trains, all indicate that Egypt is being moved by a new inspiration and is arousing herself from the lethargy of ages. Who knows? She may yet rehabilitate herself in the garments of a new era and of a living civilization.

If the old Pharaohs could come back and see the changes already wrought, and still going on, they would open their eyes with bewildered astonishment.

At the different stopping places the fakirs besieged us with all sorts of goods. Their offerings at Baliana were chiefly white shawls with gilt spangles, for which they wanted a pound, but willingly took half this sum if it was tendered.

After leaving Baliana we saw on one side very high mountains honeycombed with tombs, whilst on the opposite side were great stretches of sand. Farther up, we passed a unique town, evidently a monument to departed spirits, as it was built entirely of empty jugs and bottles. This was a curious sight, as the Moslems, as a rule, do not drink. It is against their religion, and they are the most religious of all people. Then, too, they are too poor to drink, even if they wish to. Moreover, they could not in a reasonable time empty enough jugs and bottles to build such a town. Taking all these things into consideration, we concluded that the whole of Egypt probably poured out its libations to build this town.

Our next stop was at Luxor, whence we visited Karnack. This is not a temple, but a city of temples, palaces, obelisks and immense statues. It is a growth of many centuries. The vast array of monstrous columns reminds one of the cathedral like isles of some great and magnificent forest. Karnack surpasses anything of the kind on earth, and when in its original condition the Great Hall must have been incomparable in its grandeur and majestic proportions.

Luxor is on the east bank of the Nile; it is a town of about ten thousand inhabitants. Here are to be seen the remnants of a temple of Rameses III., two obelisks, a pylon and the colossi. The entire structure originally was about eight hundred and fifty feet long and one hundred and eighty feet wide; only two of the six statues which stood in front of the temple remain.

Karnack contains the most wonderful pile of ruins imaginable. They seem to have been a series of connected buildings a mile long, and one can only conceive of their former grandeur by what remains. The Temple of Ammon has a pylon, or corner tower, three hundred and seventy-two feet wide and one hundred and forty-two high. The second pylon contains the Triumphal Monument of Sheshon I. (the Shishak of I. Kings, xiv., 25-26, and II. Chronicles, xii., 2, 4, 9), celebrating his victory over Rehoboam and his removal of the treasures from the Temple of Jerusalem.

The Great Hypostayle Hall is a stupendous structure, 338 by 170 feet. Its roof is supported by one hundred and thirty-four columns, arranged in sixteen rows, each of the central columns being eighty feet in height. The pillars and walls are covered with inscriptions and reliefs, many of them retaining the original coloring. Then there is another pylon and two obelisks and also avenues of sphinxes, to say nothing of other temples and columns too numerous to mention. All are elaborately carved. The stone was obtained at Assuan, only a short distance away, where there are immense quarries.

We next visited the remains of the famous city of Thebes, still guarded by the colossal statues of Memnon, which stand before the ruined temple of the King. Here they have stood since 1500 B. C., but now they are much weather-beaten and broken by earthquakes and vandalism.

They are about sixty feet high. The one to the north is the famed vocal Memnon, but when the rising sun kisses his face his lips are silent and no longer emit those vocal sounds with which, according to tradition, he was wont to greet the great luminary. Behind the statues rise cliffs honeycombed with tombs.

Of the hundred gates, about which the city once vaunted herself, not one stands to-day—they are all closed by the debris of her former grandeur and the shifting sands of Lybian desert. There remain only the remnants of one or two of the magnificent temples, with columns and pilasters half buried in the sand as if to accentuate the city's desolation and point out her sepulchre.

Thebes, the grandest city of ancient times, was twenty-three miles in circumference and extended beyond the Valley of the Nile to the base of the mountains of Arabia and Africa. It was connected with Luxor and Karnack by avenues of sphinxes; in fact, this territory was all one vast city. The whole is now strewn with the remains of temples, obelisks, columns and pyramids. As has been said by an eminent traveler, "the skeletons of giant temples are standing in the unwatered sands, in solitude and silence. They are neither gray nor blackened; there is no lichen or moss; no rank grass or mantling ivy to robe them and conceal their deformities. Like the bones of man, they seem to whiten under the sun of the desert." The prophecy of Ezekiel has been literally fulfilled—"I will destroy the idols, and I will cause their images to cease, and there shall be no more a prince of the land of Egypt." This once magnificent city was destroyed by the Persians under Cambyses.

We also visited the Tombs of the Kings—another donkey ride; in fact, we by now had become expert riders. These tombs are several miles from the Nile. To reach

They are about sixty feet high. The one to the north is the famed vocal Memnon, but when the rising sun kisses his face his lips are silent and no longer emit those vocal sounds with which, according to tradition, he was wont to greet the great luminary. Behind the statues rise cliffs honeycombed with tombs.

Of the hundred gates, about which the city once vaunted herself, not one stands to-day—they are all closed by the debris of her former grandeur and the shifting sands of Lybian desert. There remain only the remnants of one or two of the magnificent temples, with columns and pilasters half buried in the sand as if to accentuate the city's desolation and point out her sepulchre.

Thebes, the grandest city of ancient times, was twenty-three miles in circumference and extended beyond the Valley of the Nile to the base of the mountains of Arabia and Africa. It was connected with Luxor and Karnack by avenues of sphinxes; in fact, this territory was all one vast city. The whole is now strewn with the remains of temples, obelisks, columns and pyramids. As has been said by an eminent traveler, "the skeletons of giant temples are standing in the unwatered sands, in solitude and silence. They are neither gray nor blackened; there is no lichen or moss; no rank grass or mantling ivy to robe them and conceal their deformities. Like the bones of man, they seem to whiten under the sun of the desert." The prophecy of Ezekiel has been literally fulfilled—"I will destroy the idols, and I will cause their images to cease, and there shall be no more a prince of the land of Egypt." This once magnificent city was destroyed by the Persians under Cambyses.

We also visited the Tombs of the Kings—another donkey ride; in fact, we by now had become expert riders. These tombs are several miles from the Nile. To reach

"THE TRIUMVIRATE AND THEIR DRAGOMAN."

them one crosses a section of the desert and enters a winding, rocky valley, a wierd and desolate place. The old-time Kings showed no spirit of accommodation to future travelers in thus entombing themselves in such out-of-the-way places. This particular place in the Nubian mountains was selected by the Kings of the nineteenth and twentieth dynasties for their sepulture. There are supposed to be forty tombs in all, but only twenty-five are accessible, and only eleven worth seeing, as in many cases one is a reduplication of the other.

We visited the tomb of Seti L; its sculpture and coloring are very fine, and as the place is lighted up with electric lights it presents a splendid appearance. This tomb is made in the side of the mountain in the living rock. It penetrates 330 feet into the rock and consists of seventeen chambers, passages and staircases. The scenes depicted on the walls and ceilings are of a religious character. The chambers are entered by steps descending by a passage. Each chamber is beautifully ornamented by relief work, giving scenes and texts from sacred books. The tomb building was the work of the Kings of Egypt. It was a regal fad with them. When one ascended his throne he forthwith began to build his mausoleum and the work on it never ceased until his death. Each monarch vied with his predecessor in trying to make his tomb more beautiful and grander than the one that had gone before. Their constant effort, so far as a resting place was concerned, was to join—

> "The innumerable caravan that moves
> To the pale realms of shade, where each shall take
> His chamber in the silent halls of death."

At one period of Egypt's history the Kings built pyramids, the largest structure indicating the longest reign. The smaller the pyramid, the shorter the reign. But the very splendor these monarchs so lavishly displayed in the ornamentation and enriching of their monuments, was the cause of their memorials being disturbed and their sarcophagi plundered.

Only one royal mummy remains in these tombs, and access to it is not allowed. It can be seen, but not touched. This mummy represents the remains of Amenhetep II., just as he was placed on the day of his entombment. The lids of the fine sarcophagus and the coffin have been removed, and the mummy, decorated with the wreathes of flowers which have lasted three thousand years, may be looked upon from above.

There is nothing of the kind we have ever seen that is at all comparable with the tombs, temples and pyramids of Egypt.

At Luxor we were beset by a small army of curio sellers. They offered rings, scarabs, beads, images, mummy hands and feet; in fact, a small museum could have been supplied by these fakirs. The ever-curious Perley bought the mummied hand of some poor fellow who had ceased to have any use for it thousands of years ago. Perley asserted that it was a renewal of an old acquaintance.

Whole mummies were offered for sale, and as I looked upon the sightless eye sockets and the fleshless bones, I could but apostrophize these remains of humanity thus—

> "And thou hast walked about (how strange a story!)
> In Thebes' streets, three thousand years ago,
> When the Memnonium was in all its glory,
> And time had not begun to overthrow
> Those temples, palaces and piles stupendous,
> Of which the very ruins are tremendous."

After buying all the curios we cared for we were approached by a fakir with a beautiful string of beads.

We told him we did not want the beads, but he remained insistent.

"Well, what do you ask for them?" we asked. "Twenty-five dollars," was the reply. We turned away with disgust. "How much you give?" he asked. To get rid of him we replied, "We'll give you one shilling." "All right," was the reply, and so we bought for twenty-five cents what was priced at twenty-five dollars.

Another fakir came up with a fine scarab, apparently a genuine antique, and like one for which a certain member of our party had given several dollars. "How much you give for this genuine scarab?" asked the fakir? "Don't want it; have plenty." Still insistent. "What do you ask for it?" we inquired. "Five dollars; worth ten," was the reply. We got in our carriage to leave, when up the fellow came again and offered it for twenty-five cents. To get rid of him we said, "Will give you one cigarette for it." And, lo! he handed it over. These fellows always ask one price, but are prepared on short notice to take what they can get.

On our trip to the Tombs of the Kings we had to cross the Nile. The boats could not go within several yards of the shore, so each of us had to get on the back of an Arab and be thus carried to terra firma. The ladies were borne in the arms of the boatmen. Our trip on donkeys to the tombs was pleasant, but it was very hot on our return and the reflection of the sun was painful to the eye.

Perley got lost again, and we saw no more of him until after our return. "The Young Voyager" and this writer also got separated from the party and struck out for the river. When within a mile of the Nile we encountered a violent sand-storm. We could not see and could hardly breathe, so thick was the sand, so we decided to let our donkeys find the way, which they did, to our great relief.

Getting into our boats to cross over, we found the water very rough, the waves high and the spray dashing over the craft. Under the circumstances, we concluded that we had missed perishing in the desert to be capsized and drowned in the Nile. And, to tell the truth, if we had gone much farther we assuredly would have had a mishap; as it was, we were saved by the skin of our teeth.

The natives are a patient race. When not begging for "backsheesh"—there are many who do not beg—they sit quietly on the ground a la Turk. They have a sad, melancholic cast of countenance and rarely smile. The children, I believe, are the most patient on earth. It is very seldom that one hears them cry. They will sit all day, their faces covered with flies, without a whimper.

On our return to Cairo from Luxor we noticed that, in the suburbs of the city, the people deposit their refuse on the tops of their houses, whence it is liberally distributed among their neighbors by the winds of the desert. Many of the houses are covered with straw and twigs.

Of course, while at Cairo, we went out to see the Sphinx and the pyramids, among others, the famous Cheops, the largest the grandest, and in point of age, the father of them all.

The genus camelus is divided into two species—the Arabian and the Bactrain. The first-mentioned wears only one hump, while the latter is distinguished by two. We had the pleasure (?) of riding the Arabian animal. Charles Dudley Warner says of this beast:

"The long bended neck apes humanity, but the supercilious nose in the air expresses perfect contempt for all modern life. The contrast of this haughty 'stuck-up-ativeness' with the royal ugliness of the kindly brute, is both awe-inspiring and amusing. No human royal family dare be uglier than the camel. He is a mass of bones, faded tufts, humps, lumps, splay-joints and callosites. His tail is a ridiculous wisp, and a failure as an ornament or a fly-brush. His feet are simply big sponges. For skin covering he has patches of old buffalo robes, faded with the hair worn off. His voice is more disagreeable than his appearance. His gait moves every muscle like an ague.

"And yet this ungainly creature carries his head in the air, and regards the world out of his great brown eyes, with disdain. The Sphinx is not more placid. He reminds one of a pyramid. He has a resemblance to a palm tree. It is impossible to make an Egyptian picture without him. What a Hapsburg lip he has? Ancient, royal. The very poise of his head says plainly: 'I have come out of the dim past, before history was; the deluge did not touch me; I saw Menes come and go; I helped Shoofoo build the great pyramid; I knew Egypt when it hadn't an obelisk, nor a temple; I watched the slow building of the pyramid at Sakkara. Did I not transport the fathers of your race across the desert? There are three of us—the date-palm, the pyramid and myself. Everything else is modern. Go to.'"

To our other experiences we here added that of camel riding, and let me remark that the *modus operandi* is unique and peculiar. The patient and faithful beast, at the command of his driver, unhinges his forelegs and then unlimbers his hindquarters. You are thereupon invited to mount under protest from the camel in tones like the gurgling or babbling of many waters. You bestride the beast; he rises. ponderously on his forefeet and throws you over on his tail; about the time you are on the point of turning a backward somersault he clumsily lifts up his hind legs and precipitates you over his head. Just as you are about to drop between his ears he gives a timely and thoughtful shake that settles you in the saddle; he then strikes out with his right foot, which makes you think you are about to bite the dust in that direction; next he ambles with his left, which brings you back to your first position. He then "jollies" you backward and forward, sidewise and otherwise—particularly otherwise—circles, tangents and curvatures all get mixed together, until you can't tell where you are or whither you are going; but the real article of fun begins when he starts to trot. Then you shut your eyes and trust to fate, holding on to the pommel of your saddle until he stops, when you motion to the driver that you have had enough and do not care to play circus any longer. The driver now commands the obedient beast to unhinge himself for your descent and you get off profoundly thankful to be once more on terra firma. Thus ends your experience in camel riding, if you are wise. If you avoid the experience you are unwise.

On your arrival at the base of old Cheops you are immediately surrounded and taken in charge by the lineal descendants of the Forty Thieves, whose record is given in the Arabian Nights. They proceed to pull you first one way and then another, talking in incomprehensible jargon equal to the confusion of tongues at the Tower of Babel, until you hardly know your right hand from your left. You protest mildly at first, but this has no effect; you assert yourself more positively but in vain; then your ire rises, and you consign the whole gang to a place supposed to be warmer than the seven times heated furnace, in which Shadrach, Meshach and Abednego were immured, but without effect. We are assured, however, by the gentleman from St. Louis that nothing operates on the Arab so effectively as to tell them in plain Anglo-Saxon "to go to h—," delivered in a strong, vigorous manner. As the gentleman from St. Louis is a man of considerable age and experience he ought to know.

Finally, if you wish to ascend to the top of the vast pile of stone you designate five of the "forty thieves" by pointing them out and then commence the ascent. Two pull at each arm; two place your feet in position and the fifth shoves you in the back. The stones over which you climb are each about four feet high, and when you get to the top every muscle, sinew and nerve is strained and drawn to its utmost tension, and you sink down in an exhausted condition.

When you descend, all five of these same brigands pull your leg for "backsheesh" until you cry out against an insatiable extortion that knows no cessation, except in the complete depletion of your pocket-book.

The road by which you approach the pyramids and Sphinx is a beautiful drive. When you are within two or three miles of Cheops you think you are quite near, and when you believe you can almost touch it, it is still some distance away. You cannot grasp its vast size and dimensions until you look skyward and see the tourists crawling up its surface like ants. Or, if you are on pyramid, you look down where men and women appear like pigmies and donkeys like insects.

We had with us a jolly, good fellow, the Rev. S. D. Bartle, a regular shouting Methodist of the old school, weighing about 225 pounds, and from the far-away State of Iowa. On account of his extraordinary size the "forty thieves" required pay for an extra man. On the whole, it is to be doubted whether the demand was inequitable. This extra man had a rope around the parson and under his arms, and he would hold back, so that when the two who had hold of the minister's hand pulled forward the unhappy traveler was between two fires. Indeed, he was at times almost pulled off his feet. Brother Bartle made a picture never to be forgotten, and caused a great deal of laughter; but it was somewhat on the order of the boys and the frogs.

When the parson reached the bottom, we asked him how he enjoyed the trip. With that broad and expansive smile of his, he replied: "It was fun, and I laughed myself sore, but my legs are the 'sorest' from the stretching they got on the high steps."

The descent into the interior of the mammoth pyramid is attended by equal horrors and dangers—perhaps even greater. Instead of being pulled upward you are plunged downward into real Egyptian darkness—not your ordinary twilight or even the sombre shades of midnight, but a darkness that can be felt—a remnant of that gloom that spread over this ancient domain at the command of Moses in the days of Pharaoh. Then, amidst the obscurity of centuries and the silence of countless eons, you are ushered into the very center of this dismal charnel house, and are nearly smothered with the dust of ages and the shifting sands of the restless desert. Even though you be courageous, you fear lest you may never see daylight again.

The passages are very narrow and your discomforts are intensified by the close proximity of your Arab guides who freely breathe and liberally exhale garlic in the most generous and concentrated form. This, combined with the hideously obvious fact that they probably have not had a bath for years, makes the effluvia almost suffocating and unendurable.

Amidst dampness and darkness you flounder along the stifling passageways until you emerge again to sunlight—God-given sunlight—with feelings of profound and lasting thankfulness.

Cheops has a height of 451 feet (originally 483, but thousands of tons of stone have been taken from the top and sides to build mosques and other structures in Cairo) and a length of 750 feet, with cubic contents of 3,000,000 cubic yards. The Titanic structure covers an area of about thirteen acres. According to Herodotus 100,000 men were occupied twenty years in its construction.

It has been estimated by a French engineer that there is stone enough in this pyramid to build around the whole of France a wall one foot thick and five feet high. We think it very possible this is entirely correct.

A short distance from mighty and magnificent Cheops stands the mysterious Sphinx with its inscrutable features. Its sightless eyes have for centuries looked out upon the barren sands of the desert and have witnessed the rise and fall of empires, kingdoms, dynasties and religions. This mysterious monument has many times been covered by the restless waves of the Great Sahara, to be again and again exhumed from the sands. The Sphinx of Gizeh represents a male deity, having the body of a lion and the head of a man. It is said to prefigure the union of intelligence and power.

The Sphinx was hewn out of the solid rock and is sixty-six feet high. Its measurements are:

	FEET.
Length of body	150
Length of paws	50
Length of head	30
Width of mouth	7½
Width of face	14
Height of ear	4½
From crown to base	70

It has been greatly mutilated, but still preserves much of its nobility and majesty. Between its paws is an altar, and on its breast is a memorial statue of Thutmosis IV., placed there because the King, prompted by a dream, caused the Sphinx to be freed from the drifting sand of the desert.

John L. Stoddard, in his lectures on Egypt, says: "To-day the Sphinx appears as calm and imperturbable as it did six thousand years ago. It is probably the oldest relic of human workmanship that the world knows—the silent witness of the greatest fortunes and the greatest calamities of time. Its eyes, wide open and fixed, have gazed dreamily out over the drifting sands, while empires, dynasties, religions and entire races have risen and passed away. If its stony lips could speak, they might truthfully utter the words, 'Before Abraham was, I am.' It was, indeed, probably two thousand years old when Abraham was born. It is the antiquity of the Sphinx which thrills us as we look upon it, for in itself it has no charms. The desert's waves have risen to its breast, as if to wrap the monster in a winding sheet of gold. The face and head have been mutilated by Moslem fanatics. The mouth, the beauty of whose lips was once admired, is now expressionless. Yet grand in its loneliness—veiled in the mystery of unnumbered ages—this relic of Egyptian antiquity stands solemn and silent in the presence of the awful desert—a symbol of eternity. Here it disputes with time the empire of the past, forever gazing on and on into a future which will still be distant when we, like all who have preceded us and looked upon its face, have lived our little lives and disappeared."

"O, sleepless Sphinx!
Thy sadly patient eyes
Thus mutely gazing o'er the shifting sands,
Have watched earth's countless dynasties arise,
Stalk forth like spectres waving gory hands,
Then fade away with scarce a lasting trace
To mark the secret of their dwelling place:
O, sleepless Sphinx!"

We found Cairo a beautiful city—the Paris of the Orient, with its modern improvements, its gay throngs, its delightful climate, its splendid hostelries and its lively streets. It is an up-to-date city, and yet it is a city of wonderful contrasts; with over half a million inhabitants, all nationalities and types may be found within its limits. English soldiers, Arab lancers, Soudanese infantry and Egyptian cavalry—all in their varied uniforms—may be seen on the streets, and they add not a little to the picturesque appearance of this pleasant and fascinating city.

Cairo is nothing if not cosmopolitan. It is curious to see the old and the new order of things side by side—one the type of centuries long past; the other of the methods of to-day.

Along the river one sees the swift-moving railway train, while in the distance plods a caravan of camels—age and youth side by side. In the streets may be seen the patient ox moving slowly and steadily as of old, as there shoots by him the lightning-like electric car. Here comes an Arab in his little donkey cart; there goes a foreigner in his rapid automobile.

Many fine horses and carriages are to be noted in Cairo. On several occasions we saw the Khedive, who is quite popular, behind a spanking pair of bays. Occasionally may be sighted some rich pasha with his Nubian sais, or runner, who goes before the horse or carriage, no matter how fast the animals move, and shouts for the people to clear the way. We were told that these runners never live over fifteen years at this kind of work, the excessive exertion producing valvular disease of the heart.

Many curious street scenes attract the eye—snake charmers, Egyptian jugglers, organ grinders with their monkeys and boy acrobats, who go before you on the sidewalk and turn somersaults, which are accompanied by the usual request for "backsheesh." Among those seeking money may also be seen the flower venders, the sellers of postal cards and the peddlers of ostrich feathers, walking canes, beads, curios, etc. Bread is offered for sale on the street corners and carried about the streets on the head.

At Cairo, one of our party was importuned by a Persian to give him some medicine—the Arabs and Persians think all Americans are physicians or understand the occult science of the healing art. "What is the matter with you?" asked our friend. (This was a fine chance for Perley, but he had been lost for an hour.) The Persian replied that he had four wives, and they required a good deal of attention. He said he felt weak and wanted something to strengthen him. Our friend was unable to give him anything except his sympathy.

The old slave market still stands in the center of the city, but slaves are no longer offered for sale within its portals. When slavery existed the slaves were branded like cattle. We had a waiter at our table—an intelligent-looking African—who had three marks on each cheek and two just under the temples. He had been branded with a hot iron to indicate his ownership.

We were invited to a Greek Masonic Lodge where all the work was done in Arabic—it was all Greek to us. Here we were struck with a custom we had never before seen in a Masonic Lodge. When the incoming stationed officers were installed, the kiss of brotherly love and affection was bestowed by the outgoing officers. Kisses were bestowed on both cheeks.

Whilst we could not understand the language spoken, we could recognize the work by the old landmarks. The brethren who attended were admitted without personal examination on being vouched for by me. After the lodge closed a fine banquet at one of the hotels was served and much cordiality was shown, the talking being done through an interpreter.

About forty members of our Masonic Association, with their ladies, were invited by a Copt (a Mason) to his house at Helowan, some fifteen miles from Cairo and a mile or two from the Nile. It is a very pleasant little town and many persons of means live there. The Khedive also has a summer residence at Helowan.

This Copt who entertained us is the most prominent Mason in Egypt. He is the author of several works, written in Arabic, copies of which he kindly presented to Brother McAtee, of Philadelphia, who intends to devote the balance of his life—if he can find time—to deciphering the contents of these interesting books. Our erstwhile host is also the editor of a monthly magazine devoted to Masonry.

The party went by train and were met and escorted to the Copt's house and garden, where orange, fig, almond, apricot and other trees, as well as a great variety of flowers, abounded. A flowing fountain with electric lights in its center added novelty and beauty to the scene. The guests were escorted from their host's house to the lodge room, a neat, respectable stone building, with lodge, preparation, banquet and clothing rooms. The lodge was opened with the Brother Copt, Markarius Bey (a Christian), presiding as W. M. The S. W. was a Mohammedan; the J. W. a Jew, and the Treasurer a Persian. Our party was welcomed in Arabic by the master. His speech was translated so we could understand it.

Brother McAtee replied in English, which was translated into Arabic, so the local Masons could know our reply. This was, doubtless, a combination that never before met in this life—Christians, Jews, Mohammedans,

Turks, Nubians, Abyssinians, French and Americans; all differing in religious faith and creeds, but all bound together by a common tie.

This same hospitable Masonic brother also invited four of us to the theatre in Cairo. The performance was in Arabic, and we could only interpret the play by the actions and motions of the dramatis personæ. It was a love tragedy, and the forlorn lover sang most dolefully to the orb of night for fully an hour. Never before had we listened to such sad notes. We were not "sooth'd with the soft notes warbling in the wind," but enured "to thick-ey'd musing and curs'd melancholy."

The unmelodious melody of that wailing song will ever run like a sombre thread through our memory. It reminded us of a dog baying the moon. That actor ought to have been taken out and ducked, if not shot. An American audience would have hissed him off the stage in ten minutes; but the Egyptian audience thought the lugubrious fellow's "stunt" was fine, and when the rascal dwelt for five minutes on the most doleful of his notes, like the long-drawn-out howl of some moon-struck cur, they went mad, and encored him. And there we sat and had to hear it over again.

When the actor got to anything particularly pathetic, a sympathetic O! O! O! would run through the crowd, and we were reminded of the cooing of a turtle dove. Occasionally this non-impassioned "artist" would be encouraged by hand clappings from the audience. Then he would grow even more lugubrious. We never listened to such a performance before, and we hope never to be afflicted again in a similar manner. We could not, in deference to our entertainers, get up and leave, so we had to grin and endure it. The only relief we had was when our brother occasionally ordered beer and cigars.

There were present fifty or seventy-five Mohammdan ladies from the various harems, attended by the eunuchs. The boxes they occupied were covered with iron bars or grills, so closely put together that the women's features could not be discerned. They could see, but could not be seen by the audience. Now and then we could catch the glint of a bright eye, the sparkle of a gem, the shimmer of a jewel, or see the light from their cigarettes and a puff of smoke from their ruby lips.

"The Young Voyager" radiated his most seductive smile, made goo-goo eyes, and said he thought he saw a return smile, but the birds were caged. Perley got much excited (not lost this time) and became so greatly interested that he made inquiry of our entertainer if he could not "get behind the scenes?" On being informed that this was impossible, he took his opera glasses and began to ogle so persistently that he was informed he might excite the ire of the lords of these ladies if he kept it up; so he fell quietly to sleep and snored during the balance of the performance. The play had lost all interest to him. I would like to have joined him in the land of dreams, but I felt bound to do the honors to our brother, so we stuck out the five acts. The tiresomeness of the play was only exceeded by a performance we once witnessed at a Chinese theatre in San Francisco.

There are some splendid drives in and about Cairo, with magnificent rows of trees on each side of the carriageways. We visited the zoological gardens and found quite an interesting display.

The poorer classes have a curious way of carrying their children seated astraddle the left shoulder, the child holding on the head of its mother.

One of the centers of interest in Cairo is the beautiful Esbekiya Square; it is a charming pleasure ground filled with flowers, shrubbery, trees, lakes and ponds. Around it cluster many of the principal buildings of Cairo.

Perley and the writer got lost one night and wandered around the park's many sides for about one hour before we could get our proper bearings.

The better class of native women all wear black silk cloaks, but they make a display of their stockings, which are usually pink. They wear long veils and the ornaments before referred to on their noses.

The poorer women, who do not wear the veil, in order to make themselves hideous, tatoo blue lines on their chins. Frequently the blind beggar is in evidence. His usual cry is "meskin"—poor man.

Across the Nile runs a splendid draw-bridge on stout piers. When the draw is open you have to wait for the vessels all to go through, which takes about two hours. We were caught here once and had to amuse ourselves with the snake performers and organ grinders. On this occasion "The Young Voyager" met with another loss— the lovely white silk scarf that ornamented his hat on the donkey cavalcade ride was blown away by the wind.

The Cairo bazaars are very interesting, particularly the shops of the gold and silversmiths and of the braziers, where the work is done chiefly by hand. The citadel and mosques are fine buildings. There are 204 mosques in the city and no Christian wearing his boots or shoes is allowed to enter. He must wear slippers provided for the occasion, and for the use of these "backsheesh," of course, is demanded.

The Egyptian Museum is well worth visiting. At this institution we saw the mummies of Rameses the Second and Third. The hair of these potentates is still well preserved and the colors on the cases which enclose the mummies are as bright as they were thousands of years ago. Green, gold, pink, purple; and, in fact, nearly all the colors of the rainbow, are copied, and in some cases appear harmoniously and happily blended.

We were shown a mummy said to be the remains of the son of the Pharaoh who was drowned in the Red Sea when in pursuit of Moses and the Israelites; also the statute of Pepi I. and his son. Both figures are of beaten copper. Over a wooden case the ancient Egyptians wrought the face and figure of the King, inserting eyes of obsidian and white limestone. The bust, arms and legs consist of hammered plates joined, apparently, without solder. This venerable work of art was produced 3500 B. C. Many of the mummy cases have on their woodwork pictures of their occupants.

At the Museum, in pleasant contrast with the usual request for "backsheesh," we were confronted with notices saying, that by order of the Khedive, no tips are to be given to any one in the institution. It is stated that the better classes deprecate this custom of begging and the consequent bestowal of money. It is also said in this connection that the Americans have ruined the people and caused them to quit their ordinary vocations and crowd to the cities to live by mendicancy.

We took a drive out to an ostrich farm in the desert This enterprise has 800 birds of all ages and sizes, from the one-day-old chick to the patriarch of the flock. It is kept by a Frenchman, whose house is located on an oasis and generously surrounded by trees and flowers, but the pens in which the birds are confined are as hot as a torrid sun can make them.

In going and coming we passed the "Virgin Tree," under which the Holy Family rested (?) after their flight into Egypt. Driving to the ostrich farm we also passed Heliopolis, the On of the Bible. All that remains of the ancient site of the great seat of learning established here, on the borders of the Land of Goshen, is a solitary obelisk. It was here—doubtless by moonlight and under its very shadow—that the youthful David whispered the oft-told tale of love into the willing, perhaps eager, ears of Aseneth, the daughter of the priest of On, who became his wife. This obelisk was built in the time of Abraham. Under its shelter Plato wrote his poems and planned his academic school of thought. Here, too, Jeremiah communed with God and issued his denunciations of the sins of his nation, foretelling with prophetic ken the evils that would befall the Israelites. The obelisk on the Thames and the one in Central Park, New York, once were mates to the one now left solitary and alone to mark the site of the ancient city of On. In this connection, my old friend, C. A. Richardson, informs me he was present when the obelisk on the Thames embankment was placed in its present position.

It is generally supposed that there exists only the three pyramids shown in the pictures of Egypt, but there are a succession of these structures extending for about fifty miles and looming up in the distance. As one travels by rail along the course of the Nile he sees the remains of no less than seventy. An electric road runs to the great pyramid, Cheops, and to the Sphinx. One can almost imagine that the Sphinx would turn his long-gazing eyes from the waste of sands around him to look in wonder and bewilderment at the modern invasion.

At the base of Cheops and the Sphinx a town has sprung up, with hotel and other necessary requirements for the accomodation of tourists. Town lots can be had on the installment plan, and the same are staked out in the golden sands of the Sahara, as it were, under the very nose of the Sphinx.

Until we reached Egypt, we had no idea what the word "old" meant. We who write this book have been regarded as a sort of antiquarian, and have always felt an interest in archæological subjects. In fact, we have long been a member of the Virginia Historical Society, the Society for the Preservation of Virginia Antiquities and kindred organizations; in truth, we are getting old ourselves. We have looked upon "ye ancient capital," Williamsburg, with pride and pointed to the ivy-mantled tower at Jamestown as a synonym of old age. We have held in pious veneration old St. John's Church, erected in 1741, and admitted to be the oldest church in the oldest existing parish in the United States. We have looked upon the so-called headquarters of General Washington in our own city, Richmond, which is pointed out as the oldest house in the capital of the Old Dominion.

Some years ago when in England, we visited Westminster, St. Paul's and many other ancient buildings; and in Scotland, Sterling Castle, the castle at Edinburgh, and St. Margaret's, the oldest church in ancient Edinburgh. Even then we felt that our local antiquities, as "antiques," were not in it. And when we got to Rome, Naples, Pompeii and Venice, we found England and Scotland were youths in comparison to the "hoary headedness" of these countries. But when, forsooth, we reached Egypt we discovered that all the things we had ever seen or dreamed of before were as babes compared with the venerable landmarks of the Pharaohs.

When I left my Virginia home I asked my wife if there was any special thing she wished me to bring her. She said she had always wanted a dozen ivory napkin rings. So we began to inquire wherever we stopped for ivory napkin rings. At Madeira, Cadiz, Gibraltar, Algiers, Athens,, Constantinople and Smyrna we sought them, but all in vain. We were assured, however, there was no doubt about finding them at Cairo—that all things were to be had at Cairo. So when we reached Cairo we began our search again, but if there were a dozen ivory napkin rings in Cairo we could not find them, though we visited at least fifty stores and bazaars. On our way back home we tried Naples and Rome, without success. The search seemed like pursuing an *ignis fatuus,* but finally we found what we wanted in Brussels and London.

In Cairo we witnessed a Mohammedan wedding procession, headed by a drum corps, with kettle drum in full blast; then came the friends of the bride walking; next the bride herself in a carriage covered over with a fine rug; she could neither see nor be seen, which would have marred the pleasure of an American girl; then a number of carriages containing invited guests, followed by a "banner with a strange device," balanced on the chin of the bearer; then another banner carried on the head of an attendant. The bridegroom was not present, as he, according to custom, was not permitted to see his bride until after the ceremony had been performed. He then conducted her to his house and they saw each other for the first time. The courting in the Orient is done after the marriage, the whole affair being arranged by the parents. Even the love-making is done by proxy. Could anything be more horrible, my young friends?

CHAPTER VIII.

Mount Ætna, Naples and Vesuvius—Excavations at Pompeii—Among the Gamblers at Monte Carlo—Up the Rhine to Cologne—The Bishop and the Mice—Pilgrims See the Skulls of 11,000 at the Church of St. Ursula—Foul Canals at Amsterdam—Sights in Holland—The Hague and Antwerp—Perley Seeks the "Circus" in London—Adventures in Ireland—Shandon Bells and Comments on Old St. John's Church—Blarney Castle and the Irish Girls—Westward, Ho!—Betting on Shipboard—A Prince of Liars—Old Virginia the Best of All.

Leaving Alexandria for Naples, we steamed through the narrow Straits of Messina which divide Sicily from Italy. The mountains, bathed in a purple haze with a dark background and shifting, misty shadows, presented a beautiful picture, while the rocks looked like majestic castles inhabited by mighty giants and evil genii. We could imagine the hills invested with the creations of the old classic poets. Soon—

"Mount Ætna we spy,
Known by the smoky flames which cloud the sky."

The ancients believed this mountain the prison of a chained giant, Encelados, and the workshop of a swart god. The flames proceeded from the breath of the giant, while the thunderous noises of the mountain were his groans. When he turned upon his side earthquakes shook the island.

Our next stop was in the world-famed Bay of Naples. The ancient city of Naples was called Parthenope, after the fabled siren, who attempted, unsuccessfully, to seduce Ulysses, immortalized by Homer. In her rage and despair, she, together with her sisters, sought death in the sea.

Nightly, as our good ship Arabic lay in the bay, we would look at the stream of lava pouring through the immense crevasse down the sides of Mount Vesuvius, to burst forth in a few days as with a besom of destruction.

We visited the famous museum, where there is a fine collection from the ruins of Herculaneum and Pompeii. Among other curios we saw theatre tickets used in these ill-fated cities and made of thin marble. Those who went in free were presented with a small marble slab, on which was engraved a skull, hence the origin of the word "Deadhead."

We visited the zoological station, and found the aquarium of special interest. Here we saw the octopus, cuttlefish and other rare specimens of marine life. The Neapolitans did not particularly impress us, nor did the city's ragged barterers and beggars, or her smells and noises appeal favorably to our sensibilities.

Of course, we went to the resurrected city of Pompeii, which lay buried for so many years under the ashes and lava that destroyed it 79 A. D. Pompeii is about half excavated, and it is estimated that it will take forty or fifty years more to complete the work at the present rate of progress. The buildings are small, as a rule, and the streets very narrow, but well paved. The walls of the houses even to-day appear well decorated. One of the most interesting of the buildings is the Temple of Jupiter. A stairway leads to an upper story, from which is obtained a fine view, suggesting Shelley's lines—

> "I stood within a city disinterred
> And heard the autumnal leaves like light footfalls
> Of spirits passing through the streets; and heard
> The mountain's slumberous voice at intervals
> Thrill through those roofless halls."

In Pompeii there are many interesting buildings,

among others, the Ampitheatre, which could accommodate twenty or twenty-five thousand spectators.

The best advertised article of American manufacture in Naples—one found in every city—is the Singer Sewing Machine. It seems to be in universal use.

From Naples, where the party of the cruise was, to a great extent, disbanded, our trio went to Rome. We visited all the places of interest in the city, which have been described by me in my first book of travels, "A Transatlantic Itinerary." In the Eternal City we found the weather very cold, and had to build a fire in our room for comfort.

From Rome we returned to Naples, and from Naples we went to Villefranche (Nice). Here we bade our good ship the Arabic good-bye, and left the cruise. We do not hesitate to say that the trip, as a whole, was pleasant and enjoyable, barring the discomforts of the weather at many points, the indifference of the officers to the comfort of the passengers on the ship in not having the vessel properly heated, and the annoyance to which we were subjected in being compelled to tip the servants of the White Star Line.

Mr. Clark, the conductor of the cruise, and his charming wife, did all they could to render the trip pleasant. The same trip could not have been made individually for double the amount we paid. It is true that many of our guides were incompetent and indifferent; some were ignorant and had no information to impart, while others, who were well informed, spoke such poor English that they were not capable of intelligently imparting what they knew. With these exceptions, our pilgrimage was a delightful one.

The abstract of the log is as follows:

Date.	S. S. Arabic	New York to Funchal, Madeira.
1906.	Miles.	
February.		
8	65	
9	326	
10	323	
11	355	
12	346	
13	353	
14	328	
15	343	
	303	to Funchal. Arrived 9:13 February 16th.

2,742 Passage, 7 days 22 hours.

Villefranche is in the heart of the famous Riviera, the narrow strip of land which separates the Maratine Alps and the Appennines from the Mediterranean. It is celebrated for its fruitfulness and picturesque scenery. We had a delightful drive, in tourist coaches, to Nice and thence fifteen miles over the beautiful upper Corniche Road, to Monte Carlo. This drive is justly considered the finest in the world, as the road winds around the mountains, and one gets superb views of the scenery from different elevations. The weather was very cold and the wind keen, and during a part of our journey we were in a small snow-storm; yet, notwithstanding these physical discomforts, the drive was the most enjoyable we ever had.

Spread out before us, like an immense sea of molten silver, was the Mediterranean, its waters scintillating and changing into purple shadows or glinting with blue, green and gold. The roadway was lined with beautiful flowers and shrubbery, luxuriant roses and honeysuckle, while a splendid growth of aloes, palms, eucalyptus, lemon trees and geraniums flourished everywhere. The cold seemed so tempered by the winds from the sea as not to interfere with the vitality and luxuriant growth of vegetation.

On this ride we passed grand gorges and awe-inspiring precipices. We could see for miles down into deep valleys, where the cattle looked like crawling ants and men like specks on the distant horizon. Here, from an altitude of thousands of feet, and as we made a turn in the road, we had below us a last view of our good old ship. We all waved her a friendly farewell, which was returned by her many pennants fluttering in the breeze and rippling in the wind. As we wound around the mountains the villages and towns we had passed in the ascent, became mere specks or indistinguishable masses. The beautiful river that meanders about the base of the mountain, looked like a tiny silver cord, as it wound its way to the sea, and the distant train, as it sped along on its journey through the verdant valley seemed like a serpent pursuing its tortuous course. The constant shifting of the shadows as the sun appeared and disappeared under the clouds, wrapped the mountain in a beautiful haze, and clothed it in garments of blue and purple. Here and there, from greater heights, could be seen mountain streams rushing down the verdant hillsides, to loose themselves in the bosom of the sea. This splendid panoramic display continued until we reached Monte Carlo itself.

Monte Carlo is the chief town, or capital, of Monaco, which is the smallest of the soverign principalities of Europe, being not quite nine miles square. It has the smallest standing army in the world—seventy-two men—and a population of only about eight thousand. The city is known as the great gambling resort of the wealthy of the world.

We spent a few hours in the magnificent palace devoted to the God of Chance, and witnessed the gain and loss of many thousands. Most of the gambling is done by women, who, we were told, are regular habitues of the place; many spend half of their time at the tables, leaving only for meals and sleep.

"The Young Voyager," against my wishes and advice, decided to try his luck, and came out a dollar winner. It happened in this way: He made up his mind to risk ten dollars. He lost nine, so upon the principle that a dollar saved is a dollar made, he claimed to have made a dollar. At one time he was nine dollars ahead of the game, but with that natural covetousness incident to the gambling spirit, he wanted more, and thus lost what he had previously gained.

Perley decided he would go a dollar on the "red line," and so anxious was he to get his gains that as soon as the wheel of fortune ceased to spin he reached over the table to grab his winnings, whereupon the croupier rapped him over the knuckles with his rake and bade him keep quiet until he was waited on in regular order. This was one time Perley was not lost.

One of our lady friends from New York came out five dollars winner in the same way "The Young Voyager" did. Her father gave her twenty dollars to bank on. After she emerged from the fray we asked her how she stood on the game. "Oh," said she, "I made five dollars." "Where is the money," asked *pater familias?* "Well, here is five," naively replied Miss E. "Did you not say I could spend twenty? I have five left; surely I made five!" This incident struck me as a complete exemplification of the old saying, "A fool and his money are soon parted." Still a *fair fool* is better than a dullard.

A lamp post is conveniently arranged for those who lose their all, so that they may hang themselves on it. Frequently, alas, it is used for this purpose. Further on is a cliff over which many, in their despair, have thrown themselves, after having tempted Dame Fortune to their undoing.

It is quite interesting to look at the faces of those engaged in this fascinating game. The regular gambler plies his vocation with *"sang froid,"* while the novice shows his inexperience by nervousness and anxiety, which he in vain strives to conceal, or to disguise under an air of assumed indifference. The women we saw sustained the ordeal better than I supposed they could, and took their losses and winnings in a more quiet and orderly manner than one would have imagined; but their flushed faces, sparkling eyes and the intense watch they kept upon the wheel as it revolved, showed their deep interest and concern in the game. If they would only follow the poet's injunction—

"If yet thou love game at so dear a rate,
  Learn this, that hath old gamesters dearly cost;
Dost lose? Rise up; Dost win? Rise in that state,
  Who strive to sit out losing hands are lost."

We saw this illustrated in several instances, and yet no warning, no advice, no caution is heeded.

This gambling place is a magnificent marble palace with a series of parlors, marble floors, massive doors opening into one another, walls decorated with mirrors and paintings, ceiling ornamented with beautiful frescoes, and rooms radiant with light, while music from a distance lends its charm to steal away the senses and intoxicate the brain.

As we left the palace to take the cars for Lyons, we saw an omnibus bearing the name "Richmond." All three of us took off our hats in salutation and greeting, to the great surprise of the jehu, who thought we were honoring him.

At Nice we entered a restaurant and called for a bottle of beer. The waiter was a long time bringing it, and on investigation, we found he was actually drawing it from the keg and bottling it for our special accommodation, instead of saying he had it on draught. All over Europe and in the Orient, on land or water, when you buy a drink, it is poured out for you—about a thimble full. At Pompeii one of our party went into a restaurant, and to his surprise, the decanter containing whiskey was set on the table before him. He remarked: "Boys, this is the first time I have had the privilege of measuring my own drink since I left America, so I think I will take a good one," which he proceeded to do, but when the proprietor came around and took a look at the decanter, he made our friend pay double price.

Our next stopping place was Lyons, France. Here we purchased some lace handkerchiefs for our lady friends. We hired an automobile at four dollars an hour and "took in" the town, but when we came to pay the chaffeur, he displayed not only a bill for a two-hours' drive, but for the number of miles traveled. Sooner than have a fuss we paid it.

Mayence-on-the-Rhine was our next haulting ground. This is a quaint old town with narrow, crooked streets. It has many monuments and attractive buildings. In the Middle Ages the city, on account of its activity and wealth, was called "The Golden," a name it still bears. It is famous for its fine wines.

We took a drive through the city and visited the cathedral, museum and other public buildings. We were at Mayence on a Sunday and were impressed by the crowds going to and returning from church. It was quite a relief to be in a town where we were not annoyed by beggars.

Our trip up the Rhine as far as Cologne was delightful. The hills upon which are grown the grapes from which the famous Rhine wines are made are so steep it hardly looks possible to cultivate them. We were told that in some places, after a hard rain, the soil is washed from the rocks, and that the owner has to carry it back again. Terraces and retaining walls are used in many sections.

As we passed Bingen, with vine-clad hills in the background, and the lovely Rhine flowing at its feet, I could but recalls the last words of the soldier of the Legion, "who lay dying in Algiers." In the vision before his death—

"He saw the blue Rhine sweep along; he heard or seemed to hear,
The German songs he used to sing in chorus sweet and clear;
And down the pleasant river, and up the slanting hill,
The echoing chorus sounded through the evening calm and still."

As I recited this beautiful poem, I was joined by a lady originally from New York, but now residing in Paris, and we repeated it together. The love and attachment the German has for the Fatherland is not surprising; it is a beautiful country.

We passed many celebrated castles and places of interest—the Rock of Ehrenbreitstein, one of the largest fortresses in Europe, and also the famous Mouse Tower. Many legends are attached to these old castles on the Rhine; among others is one connected with Bishop Hatto. The legend goes that in a time of great distress, when he saw the people oppressed with famine, he assembled a large company of them in his barn, under the pretense of relieving their necessities, and after getting the barn full he closed the doors and set fire to the building, thus destroying the whole assembly of men, women and children.

The excuse the prelate gave for his cruel act was that he thought the famine would end sooner if there were fewer to feed. He said that these poor folks were like mice—they were good for nothing but to devour corn.

But God Almighty, to avenge the death of his victims, and to punish the Bishop, mustered an army of mice, which afflicted him day and night, and would not suffer him to rest in peace. Whereupon the Bishop, thinking he would be secure from the little rodents, moved into his castle and tower near Bingen-on-the-Rhine, or, as it is called in German, the "Mouse Turn," where he was pursued and destroyed by the mice. Southey, in his ballad, "God's Judgment on a Bishop," has immortalized the legend. He thus describes the advent of the army of mice, or rats:

> "And in at the windows and in at the door,
> And through the walls by thousands they pour,
> And down from the ceiling and up through the floor,
> From the right and left, from behind and before,
> From within and without, from above and below,
> And all at once to the Bishop they go.
> They have whetted their teeth against the stones,
> And now they pick the Bishop's bones;
> They gnaw'd the flesh from every limb,
> For they were sent to do judgment on him."

We went past Heidelberg, famous for its university, its schloss or castle, and its duelling grounds. When the hills bordering the Rhine are covered with vines and purple with grapes, they must present a beautiful sight. In the early part of April, when we took our trip, the lands were bare, but castles crowned every hilltop like sentinels. As we glided along up the noble Rhine, there were borne to our listening ears by the evening air, the voices of the German students singing their national air, which, in English, reads partly as follows:

> "While yet one drop of life-blood flows,
> The sword shall never know repose;
> While yet one arm the shot can pour,
> The foe shall never reach thy shore.
> Rest, Fatherland, for sons of thine
> Shall steadfast keep the Wacht am Rhein."

Coleridge has written of Cologne—

> "The river Rhine, it is well known,
> Doth wash your city of Cologne;
> But tell me, nymphs, what power divine,
> Shall henceforth wash the river Rhine?"

The writer, therefore, was pleasantly disappointed to find the River Rhine clear and beautiful at Cologne, and he regards Coleridge's lines as a travesty and an injustice to the city and the noble river.

We visited the Church of St. Ursula, where are arranged in wall cases the skulls and bones of eleven thousand virgins, who, with the saint and martyr, for whom the church is named, were put to death by an army of Huns. It is quite a gruesome sight.

Here also we were shown an alabaster vase, wherein it is alleged that our Saviour turned the water into wine at the marriage at Cana. Inasmuch as the Gospel says, "there were six waterpots of *stone*" that were filled with water that was made wine, we were somewhat at a loss to understand where the alabaster vase came in.

The cathedral is one of the greatest buildings in the world. Its towers and spires are so huge as to dwarf the immense structure. Some of the spires are over five hundred feet high and are occupied by a large concourse of daws, that fly in and out undisturbed by the noise in the streets. The cathedral is 468 feet long and it covers an area of 91,464 square feet. The interior is very impressive. It is notable for its splendid glass windows.

The horses in Cologne, apparently, are as huge as elephants, always excepting Jumbo, and move as slowly; in fact, they seem never to go out of a walk. There are several public squares or parks for the school children, with donkeys for them to ride, swings and other amusement features. The little ones who misbehave or fail in their recitations are allowed to look on, but are not permitted to participate in the games. This, we were told, is the only punishment inflicted.

As soon as the railroad going from France to Germany touches German territory the conductors and all the railroad employees are changed. There is another curious custom on the railroads in Germany; you pay for a ticket, but that does not entitle you to a seat. Every hour or so the conductor comes around and collects twenty-five cents for the use of a seat—a singular performance, we thought.

Our next stop was at Amsterdam, the capital of the Netherlands, built on marshy grounds and traversed by canals connected by many bridges. This famous city also has connection with the North Sea by canals. If Coleride had written his rhymes about the canals that traverse Amsterdam instead of about the Rhine and Cologne, they would apply perfectly. The waters in the canals are not only dark, but foul and offensive, as they receive all the garbage and sewage of the city.

In Germany and in Holland one is required to show a coupon after he gets off the cars before he is permitted to leave the depot or go to his hotel. When we debarked at Amsterdam, this writer could not find his coupon. He thought he had lost it and was detained by the guard. The unhappy Richmonder could not understand what the guard said, nor could the guard understand the Richmonder. Had the New York gentleman of the "Sunday School Class" been along, his knowledge of German would have relieved the situation. But finally, after the captive had searched his pockets again and again, the missing piece of paper was brought to light; otherwise, it is to be supposed that he would have been placed under arrest and would then have had to appeal to the American Consul.

There seems to be an immense business done in this

city. The people of Amsterdam do not entertain a very good opinion of their neighbors in Rotterdam. When we spoke of leaving and going there, we were advised not to do so; in fact, we were told that city was, as its name implied, a-dam-rotten town. What the Dutch of Rotterdam had done to offend the Dutch of Amsterdam we were not informed, but there seemed to be no good feeling between the people of the two municipalities.

We noticed scores of the houses all built on piles, many a foot and some two or three feet out of plomb, as though about to topple into the streets.

The King's Palace and the Museum were visited by us, and there we saw the characteristic costumes of men, women and children in effigy, showing the dress of centuries past, as well as the mode of dress of to-day in the different towns and villages. No two figures were habited alike.

In Holland—we presume to prevent adulteration—the hotels have pepper boxes in which the grain pepper is put and by turning the top you grind your own pepper and have it fresh and genuine. We commend this plan to the advocates and votaries of the pure-food law.

Here we took an automobile ride of about seventy-five miles, going for a great distance on the dykes of the Zuyder Zee, through villages of fishermen and farmers, and those engaged in milling, and other occupations. We visited one town composed almost entirely of wind-mills, and as they whirled their long arms round and round we thought of the adventures of Don Quixote, with what, in his infatuation, he called giants. It must have been just such a scene as this that excited him to action, and which resulted so disastrously to him and his gallant steed.

Our chaffeur carried us with such speed that some-
e we could hardly see, and we passed through narrow

streets and lanes like a streak of lightning. As soon as our honk, honk, was heard, women would rush out of doors and snatch up their children from the impending danger; the ducks would squawk and the geese would gabble and fly and waddle off in consternation. We ran quite through a flock of hens; one of the fowls, in an effort to escape, flew over our heads. The cattle along the roadsides beholding our rapid transit, would raise their tails in the air and run for life, and the horses and sheep sped away as fast as they could go; in fact, we cut a wide swathe as we went, and produced such a sensation among those quiet burghers as they never before had experienced. Everything cleared the path before us; the men driving cows hurried them down the banks, and those in carts and wagons went into ditches to enable us to pass.

"And still as fast as we drew near, 'twas wonderful to view,
How in a trice the turnpike men their gates wide open threw."

Several times we came so near having an accident and went so fast that the only comfort and consolation I had was in the knowledge of the fact that I carried a good accident policy.

We stopped for refreshments in one village, where the men with their wide breeches, the children with their wooden shoes or clogs and the women with their queer lace caps and jewels on their noses cut quite an interesting picture. It seemed that every man, woman and child came out to examine our machine, and when we mounted to leave and gave a warning honk, such a scattering and scampering was never before seen. The people fairly ran over one another to get out of the way, but we were followed as far as they could keep up, by every boy of the town, their clogs making an awful clatter in our rear. One of these chaps, boy like, and unknown to us, climbed up behind. After we had gotten up a pretty good speed we happened to turn and look back and down the urchin dropped. The last we saw of him he was spinning around like a top, but he made no stop, and for aught we know may still be spinning.

Outside of the towns the roads were fine and we hummed along at a terrific speed; so fast, that "The Young Voyager" had some of his mustache swept away, while the rest of us lost a few hairs from our scanty locks.

The land is cultivated by irrigation, water being conducted from the canals by a system of dykes and ditches. The farm houses are large and comfortable looking—just such houses as one would imagine a Dutchman would build. The crops are in a good state of cultivation; indeed, everything indicates thrift and prosperity.

The Hollanders are a very polite and courteous people. When we met them in places outside of the city they would almost invariably stop on the roadside, come to military attention and give the soldier's salute.

In the towns they use dogs hitched to carts to carry the milk to market. We noticed canal boats drawn by men instead of donkeys or horses; yet the hauling looked like pretty hard work.

The houses have no alleys, and coal and wood—in fact all heavy articles—are raised to the upper stories by ropes. The children, when they go into the house, take off their clogs, and it is no uncommon sight to see several pairs outside the street doors. In one or two of the villages which we passed through, the banks were lined with fishing nets, indicating that the whole community lived by this industry.

In other villages were immense flocks of contentedly-quacking ducks and joyously-cackling hens, who plainly indicated that there were fresh eggs for sale. We saw many women with their little push-carts carrying poultry, eggs and vegetables to the nearest markets. Peat was also carried around in wagons and sold for daily use for fires and cooking purposes. Everything in Holland, as I have said, indicates thrift—no beggars.

We left Amsterdam for The Hague, and while on the way, passed thousands of acres of tulip beds, laid off as symmetrically as a mosaic floor, and with variegated colors, looking like a carpet of beautiful tapestry. It was the most unique and lovely panoramic display of growing flowers we ever beheld. These blossoms are shipped all over Europe. The cultivation of tulips is an industry—and a very profitable one, we were told—peculiar to these people.

The Hague is the capital of South Holland, as Amsterdam is of North Holland. It is a quiet, rural town, but has some fine public buildings and lovely, well-wooded parks. These contain many deer, which are quite tame. The Hague is a popular summer resort, and has a great many saloons. We asked one of the citizens what was the chief industry of the town, and his ready reply was, "Making drinks for visitors."

From The Hague we took the train for Antwerp. This route reminded us very much of old Virginia, the familiar pine being much in evidence, as were also large fields of wheat. We found the railroad officials exceptionally polite—thanking us when we tendered our tickets, and requiring nothing extra for a seat, as they do in Germany.

Antwerp was the most quiet city we saw in our travels—a sort of Rip Van Winkle town. The streets appeared almost deserted and the people seemed to go to bed early and get up late. Perley was always "impressed," to a greater or less extent, with every city he visited, but generally one impression wore off as soon as we got to the next city. The last town almost invariably impressed him more than the one he had just left, but he announced that he was not pleased with Antwerp. It was the only town in which he did not get lost.

This city does an immense shipping business, but seems to have very little local trade. Its people use very large draft horses and huge trucks, which carry immense loads.

On our way from Antwerp to Brussels our eyes were gladdened by apple, peach and pear trees in full bloom, and our faces were fanned by delightful spring breezes. The country is densely populated.

Brussels is a fine, live city, the people chiefly French, and it reminds one very much of la belle Paris. The streets are clean and crowded day and night—quite a contrast with Antwerp. We took a carriage and visited all the places of interest, after which we left for Ghent.

This city is noted for its linen, cotton and lace, and has many fine buildings. Judging from the street display, its inhabitants live chiefly on eggs and onions. Every square has its own market, but only a certain class of goods are permitted to be sold at each; so the housewife has to make the rounds of the town in order to supply her larder. The women, by the way, do all the trading, both selling and buying. We presume, therefore, that a day's marketing means and all-day business. In Holland they hitch one and two dogs to a cart, in Brussels three.

From Ghent we went to London, arriving two days before Easter. Of course, we saw all the places of interest in this capital of the world. We attended St. Paul's Easter Sunday morning, and services at Westminster Abbey Sunday evening. Both buildings were so crowded that we could not get seats.

Standing in front of our hotel, the Cecil, Perley noticed

that the constantly-passing 'busses bore the signs, "Ludgate Circus," "Fleet-Street Circus," etc., so he decided he would go to see "the show." After riding several miles, the 'bus stopped and he asked the driver where was the circus. "Circus" in London means a circular space where different streets meet or cross one another. The driver pointed to the empty circle. "But where are the elephants, camels, and tents?" asked Perley. The driver looked at Perley as though he thought he was crazy. "Well," replied Perley, "if that don't beat thunder; put up signs to the circus, and set a man down in the street!" He thought he had been badly used. We had a good laugh on him, and Perley became indignant. He immediately went and lost himself, as usual.

From London we took the cars to Liverpool. As the day of our departure was a holiday we found them very much crowded. In our compartment were two English boys, residents of Liverpool, who entertained us with jokes and songs.

From Liverpool we went to Dublin. We found the weather quite cold. We rode over the city in the novel Irish jaunting cart, and realizing we had but a short time to catch the train for Cork, we offered the driver an extra fee if he would make the station in time. Off he started and down the street we went at a furious rate, sitting sidewise, as one has to do in these peculiar vehicles. We held on with great difficulty, expecting every moment that our Irish pony would go down on the slick stones. Paddy did not spare his beast, and we made the train in the nick of time.

The road from Dublin to Cork traverses a beautiful country. At the season of our visit the hedges of Irish furze were in full blossom, and their rich, yellow bloom gilded the landscape and crowned the hills with gold.

The greensward of intense verdure, which gives this country its name—the Emerald Isle—was dappled with primroses and buttercups, while peeping up to be kissed by the rays of the morning sun we saw—

> "O, the shamrock, the green, immortal shamrock!
>   Chosen leaf
>   Of bard and chief,
> Old Erin's native shamrock.
> O, the shamrock."

Ireland is one of the richest countries in the world, and yet it has the poorest people. Governed, as it is, by absentee landlords, who neither know nor care for their tenants, its inhabitants have no incentive or encouragement to take pride in their country, and consequently, all the best of the population emigrate and leave only the poorest and those physically disqualified for work.

The land, instead of growing cereals, is used almost exclusively for the pasturing of sheep and cattle. We saw some of the finest tillable soil in Great Britain as we journeyed along. When we reached a station called Mallow, we heard a great hubbub and commotion, and looked out to see what was the matter. There was Paddy in every conceivable form—men, women and children, the gray-haired mother, the toil-worn father, the buxom lassie, the young and the middle aged, as well as the babies. All were in a state of great excitement, for the crowd had assembled to bid farewell and good luck to a large party of emigrants bound for America on our train. It was a regular Donybrook Fair—some were crying and others were laughing; mothers clasped their sons and daughters in parting embrace, while wives held their bairns to the car windows to receive a last kiss from their fathers. Some were drunk; indeed, we beheld persons, respectively, representing all three stages—the jocose, the lachrymose and the bellicose. Such a scene I never before witnessed; it had both its pathetic and its humorous phases, but the pathetic side far outweighed the ridiculous, for if these people were encouraged to stay at home why should they leave?

A gentleman adorned by a silk hat and Prince Albert coat got into our compartment at the station, and as he seated himself near me, I asked him to explain the scene before us. He replied: "I presume from your speech you are an American; well, these people are bound for your land. Paddy will not work at home," added he, "and the country is being drained of its best and most useful population."

My fellow-traveler talked intelligently on the Irish question. Ireland's past, present and future were discussed but as to the latter, he was not very hopeful. The stranger proved to be the Lord Bishop of Limerick, and when he left the train at the next station he expressed pleasure at having met me.

We drove over Cork and found it quite a pleasant city. It has a population of about 75,000. Here and at Dublin we found the richest golden-colored butter we had seen since we left old Virginia. It offered such a contrast to the miserable, rancid stuff we had had on the ship and in the Orient, that we heartily enjoyed the change.

At Dublin "The Young Voyager," while in our hotel, started to go from the parlor to another room, but walked into a magnificent mirror, reaching from floor to ceiling. Seeing his own image in the glass, he did not recognize himself, owing to the wonderful change wrought in his physiognomy by his mustache. He made a profound apology to his reflection, and it was only after several bows and "after you, my dear Alphonso's," that he discovered his mistake and passed on.

It being uncomfortably cold in Cork, we ordered a fire, and "The Young Voyager," to hasten the combustion of the fuel, temporarily converted himself into a human bellows. We saw many idle people, and encountered many juvenile beggars. Our party "took in the city" in an Irish jaunting car, and notwithstanding the cold, greatly enjoyed the drive by the River Lee and over the hills to the suburbs. As we listened to the glorious peals of Shandon, we could but repeat the beautiful lines of Father Prout:

>"With deep affection
>And recollection
>I often think of
>Those Shandon bells,
>Whose sounds so mild would,
>In the days of childhood,
>Fling round my cradle
>Their magic spell."

After listening to their musical rhythm and silvery sound, we were not surprised that Father Prout should have added:

>"On this I ponder
>Where'er I wander,
>And thus grow fonder,
>Sweet Cork, of thee—
>With thy bells of Shandon,
>That sound so grand on
>The pleasant waters
>Of the River Lee."

From Cork we took train to Blarney Castle, the road running along the banks of a lovely mountain stream, whose limpid waters were sparkling in the sun as they rippled through the verdant valley. Here, as elsewhere, the landscape was beautified and adorned by the Irish furze.

At the Great Southern Hotel we had for breakfast the first hot bread we had eaten for many a day, and with it the most delicious of Irish butter. Here, too, for the first time since leaving America, "The Young Voyager" got his eggs to suit him. He had had trouble along this line on the boat, in every city of the Orient, on the Continent and in London, for he was very finicky about his "hen fruit." He generally preferred the eggs fried, and always gave the order, "fried on both sides," but he could never get them to suit him; they would almost invariably be brought in friend on one side only and about half done. At Killarney—blessed day!—they were done to a turn.

As we went down to breakfast, the bell for early mass was ringing, and Harry asked me of what was I reminded.

"Why! of old St. John's!" I replied. Had I not known where I was, I would have been certain it was our old bell ringing for service—dear old St. John's, within whose shadow I was born; within whose hallowed precincts for more than a quarter of a century I have worshipped, and from whose sacred portals ere many years I shall be borne to rest by the noble James, there to sleep the sleep that knows no waking until the resurrection morn. Of old St. John's bell, I can truthfully say—

> "I've heard bells chiming
> Full many a clime in,
> Tolling sublime in
> Cathedral shrine,
> While at the glib rate
> Brass tongues would vibrate
> But all their music
> Spoke naught like thine.
>
> "I've heard bells tolling
> 'Old Adrian's Mole' in,
> Their thunder rolling
> From the Vatican;
> And cymbals glorious,
> Swinging uproarious,

>   In the gorgeous turrets
>   Of Notre Dame;
>   But thy sounds are sweeter
>   Than the dome of Peter
>   Flings o'er the Tiber,
>   Pealing solemnly."

Perley seemed charmed with the Irish girls—he had received a fresh "impression"—but he could not get them to believe he was an American. One of them told him she knew he was a German from his talk—that no American talked as he did. To produce a good impression in parting, he remarked, "You had better go with me to America." She naively replied, "I will if you will furnish the ticket." It was "up to" Perley, but he did not rise to the occasion; on the contrary, he beat an inglorious retreat amidst the laughter of those present. As might have been expected, he was lost for a reply.

The Great Southern Hotel at Killarney is a fine building, but during our visit it was cold and raw, and had no fires; yet the guests, chiefly English, who do not, according to American ideas, know what comfort is, seemed to enjoy the draft of cold air passing through the parlors like a young hurricane. All the windows were kept raised and the doors open. The English are born and live in a damp, cold climate, and hence their blood becomes like that of a frog, and they dislike warmth and comfort. The hotel had all the modern improvements, except lights; only tallow candles were in use.

The drive around the lakes was delightful, as the trees and rocks were covered with verdant moss, while the leaves were just beginning to put forth, and the scenery of hill, dale, valley and sparkling waters was most enjoyable. Of course, we visited Blarney Castle with its famous stone, about which runs this tradition:

"There is a stone whoever kisses,
Oh! he never misses to grow eloquent,
'Tis he may clamber to a lady's chamber
Or become a mimber of sweet parliament;
A clever spouter he'll sure turn out, or
An out-and-outer to be let alone,
Don't hope to hinder him, or to bewilder him,
Sure he's a pilgrim from the Blarney stone."

We climbed up the winding turret stairs until we felt like a corkscrew. After viewing the stone, and reflecting on the difficulty of getting to it, we preferred kissing by proxy, so we touched the stone with our hands and then kissed them. "The Young Voyager" remarked that he thought they should keep within reach some pretty Irish girls, so that they could be used as proxies. He said he would prefer kissing a Mavourneen any time to a dirty stone.

From Blarney we went to Queenstown. Here we struck up with an Irish wit and story-teller in the shape of a junketing car driver, whom we employed to show us the town. As we were driving down a narrow street the horse shied at an empty barrel. "The Young Voyager" remarked to the jehu: "Your horse can't be Irish, or he would not be afraid of a barrel." Pat replied: "An' faith, he knows there's no beer in it."

As we drove around, Pat said: "You see that fine church over there? Well," added he, "that is what we call a High Church, and there is only one poor man in the church; he delivers the papers to the other members, who take care of him. On Christmas they make up an extra purse of four or five pounds for him. Well, on last Christmas they gave William, the paper carrier, the usual donation, so he went off on a spree for a week or ten days, and the church members missed their papers, and went after William. Ascertaining the trouble, they sent the

Cenon after the sinner. The good man asked William if he would take the pledge. William replied that he was already under the pledge, and had been for years, but had violated more pledges than were contained in a pawnbroker's shop.

"The Canon became indignant, and stamping his foot, demanded to know if he was not afraid to take a pledge and violate it. William replied, 'Of course, your Riverance, I am afraid at the mouth of a *cannon!*'" Pat gave us a good many tales and witty sayings, which added to our pleasure.

We left Queenstown April 21st on the splendid steamer Cedric for home. We had only about 240 first-class passengers on board, but we had about 2,000 emigrants. A good many of the first-class pasengers were English, and were not as sociable as the crowd we had on the Arabic.

While the weather was not as cold as when we went over, the "blasted English" would insist on having all the windows and doors open in the library, smoking and dining-room "to get a bit of fresh air," as they termed it, so we suffered considerable discomfort. A party of Americans would go into the smoker and close the windows for comfort; in would come a party of Britishers and request the steward to open the windows; thus there was a constant opening and closing.

On one occasion Lord Somebody wished to know who closed the windows. An American replied that he had, and said: "If you find it too warm in here, I would suggest that you go out and sit on deck, where you can get all the wind you want." His Lordship had no more to say.

When we got near New York and found the weather warm and balmy, these Englishmen kept all the windows closed, I suppose to bottle up the cold air for their comfort and pleasure. Verily, they are a queer set.

There was a good deal of betting on the log of the ship. Pools were formed daily on the run the vessel would make, and about $300 to $400 would exchange hands on the results. "The Young Voyager" took a bet at $20 to $2— pretty big odds. The next morning, just about the time the run of the previous day was to be announced, in came the party with whom "The Young Voyager" had his bet. The former held up a $20 bill and remarked, "Well, I guess this is yours." "The Young Voyager" rose with the flush of triumph on his cheek and the glint of victory in his eye, and started to reach for the $20, but on finding it was only a joke, and that he had lost his $2 instead of winning the $20, he assumed a lugubrious air, his cheeks paled with disappointment, and he quietly resumed his seat, a sadder if not a wiser man.

In the early portion of this narrative, mention was made of "the unconscious and amiable liar" on the Arabic. It was our fortune to strike up on the Cedric with the artistic liar, the Baron Munchausen of the entire trip— the Prince of Liars (the word is not used in an offensive sense). This gentleman was an American and said he resided in the State of Wyoming and had a sheep ranch. He declared that in the summer time it was so hot out there that he had to hire 1,000 boys, who used 8,000 fans, to keep his sheep cool by fanning them; moreover, in the lambing season, he used 10,000 nursing bottles for his lambs. This wondrous prevaricator further said that in winter he used from 8,000 to 10,000 blankets made expressly for the purpose, to keep his sheep warm, and that instead of dogs he had 400 trained coyotes to assist in corralling his flocks. To cap it all, he swore that he kept a sheep dentist to look after and keep his wooll-producers' teeth in order. Our redoubtable Munchausen would spin out these yarns to an admitting group without batting an eye or cracking a smile.

We also had a quiet gentleman who listened with interest to these wonderful tales. On one occasion, the "Prince" said that the mountains on which his sheep grazed were so steep that he had to have every one of them shod with iron tips. "Why," said the quiet gentleman, "I don't understand that; I have noticed sheep and they are so nervous that if a fly touches their legs they kick. I don't see how you could keep them quiet long enough to have them shod." But the "Prince" insisted that he was adhering strictly to the truth. He also stated that his house was built near a mountain stream, and that it was no uncommon thing for him to catch from his back porch two hundred pounds of trout before breakfast. Ah! as a liar, that man was a daisy!

We had quite a squall one day on our return voyage; the wind blew violently, and lashed the sea into a perfect mælstrom of foam. Great sheets of water came on deck, and the spray enveloped the ship. I enjoyed the sight very much.

We give an astract of the log of the Cedric, Liverpool to New York:

1906. April.	Miles.
21	19
22	384
23	410
24	402
25	397
26	405
27	367
28	404
	101 to Sandy Hook light vessel.
	2,889 Passage, 7 days, 11 hours, 33 minutes.

Our trip, as a whole, was a very delightful one, involving extremes in everything—cold and heat, snow-capped mountains in some places and balmy zephyrs and blossoming flowers in others. We saw the miserable mud hovels, indicative of abject poverty, and the palatial residences of those wallowing in wealth; we beheld the poverty-stricken toiling for a few cents a day, and others squandering their riches with the utmost prodigality. We visited the most fertile regions and the most barren. We saw some countries clothed in verdure and carpeted with Nature's choicest garlands; others the most arid and sterile in the world, with not a tuft of green or a blade of grass to gladden the eye and relieve the desolate waste. We experienced the most strenuous exertion and enjoyed the most comfortable repose—lovely calms and tempestous storms.

We were confronted sometimes by extreme rudeness and at others enjoyed chivalrous courtesy. The most indifferent hotel accommodations and the most enticing menus were our varying lots. We traveled by land and water, on ships, lighters and rowboats; on swift-moving trains and on the slowest cars on earth; on donkeys, camels and ox sleds; on the backs of Arabs and in automobiles. We breathed the bracing air of the ocean and also inhaled nameless odors.

We viewed with delight the picturesque islands of Madeira and Malta, and listened to the soft, dreamy melodies of their native guitara. We traversed beautiful Andalusia under the shadow of the Sierra Nevadas, and listened to the music of the rippling waves of the smiling Guadalquiver on its journey to the ocean.

We beheld with wonder the gorgeous magnificence of the Alhambra, and sorrowed over the death of a nation that could create such a structure. We stood upon the Rock of Gibraltar and enjoyed one of the grandest views in the world, looking out, as we did, on two continents and two different seas. We saw Algiers, a picture never to be forgotten, with its terraces of dazzling white, its emerald hills, its purple haze and azure sea.

After traversing the great Mediterranean, we sailed the blue Ægean. We trod the classic ground of Athens and marveled at the ruins of the Acropolis. We walked the streets of Constantinople after sailing through the Dardanelles, the Golden Horn and the Sea of Marmora.

We traversed the Holy Land, hallowed by so many sacred associations, and sailed up the mysterious Nile. We stood in reverence on the shores of the Jordan, and in silent awe by the dark waters of the Dead Sea. We looked upon pyramids and the inscrutable Sphinx.

In short, we have breathed the air of nearly every clime and enjoyed the most beautiful scenery; we have inhaled the redolence of the flowers of the Orient in all their beauty and exuberance; we have contrasted the past with the present; we have seen people from every tribe and nationality, and yet—we blush not to say it—we returned home with the full and settled conviction that—

> "The roses nowhere bloom so white,
>   As down in Virginia;
> The sunshine nowhere shines so bright,
>   As in Virginia.
> The birds nowhere sing so sweet,
> And nowhere hearts so lightly beat,
> For heaven and earth seem both to meet
>   Down in Virginia.

> "There is nowhere a land so fair,
>   As in Virginia;
> So full of song and free of care,
>   As in Virginia.
> And I believe that happy land
> The Lord prepared for mortal man,
> Is built exactly on the plan
>   Of old Virginia.

"The days are nowhere quite so long,
　　As in Virginia;
Nor quite so filled with happy song,
　　As in Virginia.
So when my time has come to die,
Just take me back and let me lie
Where the noble James goes rolling by,
　　Down in Virginia."

"FINIS."

INDEX.

A

Arabic S. S.	11-33, 41, 221
Agriculture	50-57, 95, 183
Aleazer at Seville	56
Alhambra	60
Arnda	63
Apes' Hill, Gilbraltar	64
Algiers	66
Arab Quarter, Algiers	67
Acropolis of Athens	75
Athena, Statue of	76
Athens	80
American Missionary School in Turkey	91
American School for Girls at Scutari	92
American Machinery	98
Arabs	166, 189
Abydos	187
Alexandria	175
Abukir Bay	175
Antiquity of Egypt	217
Amsterdam	231
Automobile—Wild Ride	231
Antwerp	234

B

"Backsheesh"	18, 126, 152, 188, , 210, 215
Bullock Sleds	46
Beggars at Madeira	47
Bull Ring at Cadiz	53
Buccaneers of Algiers	66

INDEX.

Bosphorus Shores	81
Bartle, Rev. S. D., 41; Description of Galilee and Samaria	103, 205
Baskets with False Bottoms	135
Bethany	166
Birds in Egypt	187
Battle of the Saddles	188
"Book of the Dead"	192
Bottles	196
Bethlehem	170
Birthpace of Jesus	171
Boys in Jerusalem	174
Bay of Abukir	175
Bingen-on-the-Rhine	227
Brussels	235
Blarney Castle	239, 241
Betting on Shipboard	244
Baron Munchausen	244
Bazaars of Constantinople, 88; of Smyrna, 94; of Algiers, 67; of Cairo	214

C

Consequential Lady	37
"Caros"	46
Church of Our Lady	46
Church of Los Capuchinos	52
Church of St. John, Malta, 70; at Ephesus	96
Church of the Monks	71
Church of the Holy Sepulchre	141
Church of the Nativity	171
Church of St. Ursula	229
Children of Madeira	47
Columbus	49-56
Cadiz	51
Chapel of San Carlo	70
Costumes in Malta, 71; in Greece, 74; in Turkey, 88; in Egypt, 182; in Granada	59

INDEX.

Curio Sellers	200
Cathedral Church of St. Paul	72
Cathedral at Granada, 61; at Cologne	229
Commodore Decatur	66
Carnival at Malta	71
Caryatids Porch of	76
Constantinople	81
Cave of Seven Sleepers, Cyprus	100
Carmel	100
Chapel of the Crucifixion	143
Cavalry	152
Crocodiles	195
Cauliflower	160
Camels	184, 202
Caravans	184, 191
Cairo	202-209
Copt, Egyptian Mason	211
Cologne	229
Cork	239
Cedric S. S.	245
"Circus" in London	236

D

Dominoes	16
Donkeys	17, 54, 90, 97, 160, 189
Demosthenes	77
Dogs of Constantinople	82-84
Diana's Temple	97
Dead Sea	147, 165
Doorsy, John	157
Dispensary in Egypt	187
Dublin	236

E

English Walnuts	51
Erechteum at Athens	76
Ephesus, City of	95

INDEX.

Esdraelon, Plain of................................ 101, 111
Enganim 118
Elisha's Cave and Fountain........................ 162
Egyptian People.......................... 183, 194, 202
Eagles 187
Egypt 176, 181, 217
English on Shipboard............................. 243

F

Funchal 46
Funeral at Madeira............................... 51
Flowers at Madeira............................... 51
Flies in Egypt................................... 179
Fakirs 180

G

Geraniums at Madeira............................ 51
Granada 57
Gibraltar 63-65
Garden of St. Sebastian.......................... 72
Grecian Waters................................... 73
Galilee, City of, 103; Sea of..................... 107
Gilboa 117
Gideon's Fountain................................ 118
Garden of Gethsemane............................. 153
Goliah's Shirt................................... 161
Grotto of Milk................................... 173
Gambling at Monte Carlo.......................... 224

H

"Hummingbird" Lady............................... 37
Husband Hunters.................................. 39
Henry, Patrick, Speech of........................ 40
Hill of Mars..................................... 77
Hill of Pnyx..................................... 77
Hero and Leander................................. 81
Hagia, Sophia.................................... 87
Holy Land.. 136

Hill of Samaria	120
Heliopolis	215
Heidelberg	228
Holland	231
Hague	234
Hotels in Jerusalem, 169; in Killarney	241

I

"Interrogation-Point" Woman	39
Irrigation at Madeira, 50; in Egypt, 179; in Holland	233
Island of Rhodes	100
Island of Roda	185
Ireland	237
Irish Girls	241

J

Judge and Donkey	17
Jordan, John D	41, 54, 78
Jezreel	117
Jenin	118
Joseph's Pit	119
Jacob's Well	121
Jaffa	128
Joseph a Monopolist	135
Jerusalem	137, 144
Jews	154
Jericho	160-162
Jordan, the River	165

K

Kansas, Traveler from	19
Knights of Malta	68
Kaaba at Mecca	186
Karnack, City of Temples	196
Khedive	209

L

Lincoln, Abraham, Honored at Sea	36
Larder of S. S. Arabic	42

Licorice Monopoly	95
Lydda, Town of	136
Luxor	186-196
Lotus Flowers	187
"Little Jorge"	158
Lyons Automobile Bill	226
London	235

M

Moore, Harry T.	11, 48
Mecca	187
Masonic Enthusiasts	30-34
Massachusetts Ladies	36
Masonic Association on Ship	41, 83, 157, 210
Murillo	52
Moorish Works in Spain	60-61
Malta	68
Mountain of the Bees	73
Marathon	74
Mars Hill	77
Maid of Athens	79
Madeira	44-49
Mosque of Sancta Sophia	86
Mount Carmel	100-111
Missionary Society at Nazareth	105
Mount Tabor	111, 116
Mount Gerizim	121
Mount of Olives	145
Mosque of Omar	149
Mohammed	151, 186, 193, 196
Mohammedan Wedding	218
Mummies	193, 200, 200, 214-215
Mount of Temptation	167
Monte Carlo	22, 222
Mayence-on-the-Rhine	226
Mouse Tower	227
McAtee, J. Q.	41

INDEX. vii

N

New York Boaster	20
New Jersey Pilgrim	23
Napoleon at Madeira, 50; at Malta	71
Nelson, Admiral	64
Nazareth	104, 123
Noah and his Ark	129
Nile River, 183; Boats seen on it, 184; Nilometer, 185; Fertility, 177; Seasons Observed	182
Nubians	188
Naples	219
Nice	221-225

O

Old Dominion Physician	23
Ohio Voyager	26
Old Maids	36-38
Olive Trees	54
Oriental Civilization	134
Ostrich Farm	215
Obelisks	216

P

Personnel of Party	11
Perley, J. Vincent.	11, 14 16, 30, 34, 41, 62, 68, 168, 166, 190, 235, 241
Passengers on Arabic	14
"Patriarch of Jerusalem"	34
Pyramids of Salt in Spain	53
Pontius Pilate, House at Seville	56, 156
Parthenon	75
Pigeons	78, 195
Power, Dr. F. D., Description of Plain of Esdraelon, 102; Ride to Nazareth	123
Polygamy	119, 210
Pool of Siloam	156
Pyramids	199, 204, 216
Pompey's Pillar	176
Pompeii	220

R

"Rattler, The"	16
"Rip Van Winkle"	26
Romans	55, 63
Rock of Gibraltar	64
Robert College, Turkey	91
Religion of Turks	92
Rugs made at Smyrna	95
Rhodes	100
Ravens	161
River Jordan	165
Riviera	222
Rock of Ehrenbreitstein	227
Railroads in Spain, 54-58, 63; in Germany, 230; Rotterdam	231

S

Sea Experiences	12, 244
"Sunday School Class"	15, 27
St. Louis Traveler	19
Steamboat Steward	12
Southerner's Sadness	25
Superstitious Crank	29
Snobs	36
Spinsters	36-38
Ship's Larder	42
Sleds Drawn by Bullocks	46
Salt Pyramids	53
Seville	54
Southern Confederacy Discussed	40
St. Paul's Bay	72
Salamis	73
Stadium, The	78
Shriner in Constantinople	83
Stamboul	86
Sancta Sophia Mosque	88
Sarcophagi	88

INDEX.

Sultan's Wives	90
Smyrna	93
St. Paul at Ephesus	97
Samaria	103
Sanders, Col. C. C.	112
Sea of Galilee	113
Shunem Village	117
Samaria, Hill of, 120; the People	121
Shiloh, Ruins of	122
Samson	136
Solomon's Quarry	157
Sphinx	198, 207
Sunsets in Jerusalem	168
Scarabs	201, 181
St. John's Church, Richmond	217, 240
Shandon Bells	239

T

"Tipping" System	12, 18, 126, 152, 188, 210, 215
Theseum, The	75
Tabnith Sarcophagus	88
"Turkish Delight"	89
Turkish Ladies	89
Temple of Diana	97
Troy, Ancient Site	99
Turkish Government	106, 115
Transfiguration, Mount	111
Tiberias	113
Temple of Solomon	148
Temple of Rameses	192
Thebes	197
Tombs of Egyptian Kings	198
Tomb of Seti	199
Theatre in Cairo	212
The Hague	234

U

Undertaker's Jokes	21

V

Virginia Physician	23
Valetta	70
Valley of Esdraelon	116
Via Dolorosa	156
Virgin Tree	215
Villefranche	222
Virginia	247

W

Warning to Travelers	1
Washington, George	50
Walnuts	51
Wines of Madeira	49
"Wingless Victory"	77
Women of Turkey	89
Water, Impure in Orient	108, 110
Wall of Wailing	154
Women of Egypt	182
Wedding, of Mohammedans	218

Y

"Young Voyager"..11, 16, 32, 71, 97, 159, 190, 201, 213, 224, 240, 242	244

Z

Zorah, Birthplace of Samson	136